FROM THE VAULT

The Windsor Star

FROM THE VAULT

Volume II: 1950 to 1980

A Photo-History of Windsor
FROM THE COLLECTION OF *THE WINDSOR STAR*

SHARON HANNA
CRAIG PEARSON

With foreword by former *Windsor Star*
photographer and photo editor Bill Bishop

BIBLIOASIS
WINDSOR, ONTARIO

FIRST EDITION

Library and Archives Canada Cataloguing in Publication

Pearson, Craig, 1962-, author
        From the vault / Craig Pearson, Daniel Wells ; with a foreword by The
Windsor Star, editor-in-chief Marty Beneteau.

Volume II written by Sharon Hanna and Craig Pearson ; with a foreword by
former The Windsor Star photo editor Bill Bishop
Includes bibliographical references and index.
Contents: Volume II. A photo-history of Windsor, 1950 to 1980.
Issued in print and electronic formats.
ISBN 978-1-77196-118-9 (v. 2 : bound).--ISBN 978-1-77196-117-2 (v. 2 : ebook)

        1. Windsor Star. 2. Windsor (Ont.)--History. 3. Windsor (Ont.)--History--
Pictorial works. I. Wells, Daniel J. (Daniel John), 1972-, author II. Title.
III. Title: From the vault : a photo-history of Windsor.

PN4919.W563W56 2015   071'.1332   C2013-906567-9
                                                        C2013-906568-7

Readied for the press by Daniel Wells
Copy-edited by Allana Amlin
Typeset and designed by Chris Andrechek

PRINTED AND BOUND IN CANADA

PHOTO CREDITS:
Andrew Foot: 433; Joe Bonasso: 83; Lynn Gelinas: 435; Metropolitan School of Nursing Archive: 34; Museum Windsor: 241; Museum Windsor, Bill Mechanic Collection: 145; Museum Windsor, Bill Tepperman Collection: 146; Museum Windsor, King Lee Collection 93; Museum Windsor, Richard Merlo Collection: 87; Museum Windsor, Windsor Essex County Chinese Cultural Association Collection: 220; Museum Windsor, Windsor Jewish Community Centre Collection: 150; South Western Ontario Digital Archive: 82, 83, 84, 146, 147, 154, 155, 373; South Western Ontario Digital Archive, Tony Techko Collection: 240; Stephen Garrod: 382; Unifor Local 444: 117, 121, 169, 171; Windsor-Essex Economic Development Corporation: 130, 191; and Windsor Public Library, 83, 93, 350, 369, 383, 384, 417, 418. All other images courtesy of the archives at *The Windsor Star*.

Contents

FOREWORD

Though it would be an overstatement to say that I was born in the pressroom—and in *The Windsor Star*'s, at that—it often felt that way. My working life, without almost a single exception, has been given to *The Star*. The best years coincide with those covered by this volume. I started as a paperboy at age twelve in the mid-'40s, and moved from there to become a jumper and comic inserter during my high-school years, making as much as $25.00 a week, a fairly princely sum. After school ended in 1951, though a career with the RCMP beckoned, I fell into a job as a night copyboy, which meant babysitting the teletype machines, answering the newsroom phone, and keeping track of photographers out on location. And in 1953, when I thought I'd reached the end of the line at *The Star* and began to root around for other opportunities, another door opened. I was invited to become part of the photography department after Don Grant jumped over to television, landing both his job and his Speed Graphic in one swoop, despite having not a day's experience. But the others in the department—Cec Southward, Gladys Cada, and Walter Jackson—took me under their collective wing. Whereas reporters were in and out like a revolving door, looking for bigger and brighter opportunities, *The Star* photographers were a tight-knit group, some having been there before World War II. I learned everything from them. In those early years, you could often find me in the off-hours in the archives studying their photographs, learning about light and composition. Then I'd head out into the Windsor streets to try and achieve the same effects. The amount of film, flashbulbs, and photo paper I went through, well, I shudder to think of it. But I must have learned my lessons fairly well, because in 1972 I moved on again, to become photo editor, a position I held until my retirement in 1994.

It's a career trajectory you couldn't duplicate now, in this more corporate and cut-throat age. *The Star* of that time was a family-run operation, and the Graybiels and Mrs. W.F. Herman and the rest treated their employees like family: they expected a lot from you, and would let you know it whenever your work wasn't up to snuff, but they took care of their own. One example: when I was put on the city beat, I was in immediate need of a car. Editor Harold Vaughan called me into his office and told me to go and buy one, and *The Star* would front me the money;

I could make small interest free payments from my weekly cheques until it was paid off. How many employers today would offer a relatively new employee as much?

To be a *Star* photographer at this time was a demanding job. We covered Windsor as if it was a small town, despite the fact that it was actually a growing metropolis. We were always hustling, and expected to do so. Even after the introduction of television, we acted as if we were the only game in town. We covered everything and everyone: weddings and funerals and engagements and car crashes; sod turnings and academic competitions and sporting events; city council and special events, and just about everything else you can imagine. We called it the rubber chicken circuit: the monthly round of Rotary and Kinsmen and Lions Club meetings. We were always so rushed, moving from one thing to the next, and then to the next; getting our assignments and running to complete and file them by the end of our shift, but always ready to drop everything if a big story rolled in. It all began again the next day. And we always, always printed wet.

Looking back, it was this unceasing work which has made *The Star*'s archive such an important resource. We may not have thought much of posterity as the shutter clicked; most often, we were thinking about how we could get to our next job in time. But as I went through the archives all these years later, I realized that what we'd done was capture a time and a place which, if only we could have slowed down for a second, we would have realized was changing before our very eyes. The fact that it is now gathered here for all of us is a very fine thing indeed. It's a way to give back a little to *The Star* and the city, and to acknowledge the long-standing commitment the paper and its employees have made to this community. For me, it goes a little further. This book is an homage to the photographers—the ones who trained and mentored me, allowing me to become one of their own. It's our work documented here and Windsor was ever the worthy subject. I'm thankful to have been part of it all.

Bill Bishop
Former *Windsor Star* Photographer
and Photo Editor

INTRODUCTION

Welcome to Windsor's heyday. The post-war economic boom that boosted much of the world also buoyed the Rose City, which enjoyed a renaissance for a few decades. The auto industry soared at times, especially as the second half of the 20th century began, and thus so did Canada's Motor City. The 1950s, 1960s, and 1970s saw progress in Windsor and the surrounding area—partly with population, but especially with buildings. With improved fortunes, city leaders sensed an opportunity for rebirth and capitalized on it. The skyline, the riverfront, and the suburbs—the city's physical look—all transformed in the three decades after World War II.

Yet Windsor's makeover, its conversion, tells a tale of more than just dynamic urban planning. It recounts a community's changing tastes—outlined in the words and pictures in these pages. While *From the Vault Volume I* surveys the history of Windsor up to 1950 based on *Windsor Star* photos, the most comprehensive pictorial archive in the region, *From the Vault Volume II* explores the period between 1950 and 1980. Those three decades

marked heady times, when society as a whole went through rapid changes: the conservatism of the Cold War 1950s, the counterculture of the rock 'n' roll 1960s, and the economic upheavals of the disco 1970s. But surprisingly for such rich history, in researching *From the Vault Volume II* it quickly became obvious that few books focus on Windsor's post-war period. Some touch on various events in the '50s through the '70s, but typically only as part of a larger narrative, rather than as the main focus. Even many organizations' own histories have little to say about those days. This book helps fill that gap in the historical record of Windsor and Essex County. Post-war Windsor evolved like the cars it built and deserves recognition on its own.

One difference between the first volume of *From the Vault* and the second, besides the era, is the photography. Journalism evolved over time, of course. In the late '60s and '70s, newspaper reportage on certain issues began delving deeper, with feature stories offering more creative use of the language. Likewise, many of the early

snaps from the first book show comparatively static photography. The later photos of this book provide a more inventive approach to visual storytelling. But all the pictures together tell the story of a developing city that serves at once as the automotive capital of Canada and the gateway to the country.

Between 1950 and 1980, downtown served as transformation Ground Zero. A number of prominent hotels, the Norton-Palmer and the Prince Edward among them, fell, while the Viscount and other buildings sprouted. Even more dramatic, however, was the riverfront. That amazing, storied strip of land finally took shape. The Cleary Auditorium was built in 1960. Under Mayor Michael J. Patrick, the waterfront began shedding industry while growing parkland and gardens in a striking transformation that helped give Windsor its modern personality. As the city's look changed, naturally, so did its demographics.

Windsor's population rose rapidly in the early part of the 20th century. The increase slowed in post-war years, coming in fits and starts, though the Windsor area still grew, thanks in part to the baby boom and to waves of immigration. According to census figures, Windsor's population was 120,049 in 1951, a 15 percent increase from a decade previous. In 1941, Windsor was Canada's 8th largest city, though it slipped to 10th by 1951—and continued to fall in size rankings as the decades wore on. In 1961, the city's population fell 4.7 percent to 114,367. In 1971, the population had rebounded again a remarkable 83 percent to 209,300—though much of that

increase came courtesy of the city's controversial 1966 annexation of Ojibway, Riverside, and parts of the county. Despite the protests of traditionalists, the annexation made the city significantly larger in one fell swoop. But by 1981, Windsor's population slid again, this time 8.2 percent to 192,083. Still, change continued.

"I considered it a town that had physically outgrown its mentality," Lloyd Brown-John, a political science professor emeritus, said about his initial perception of the city when he began teaching at the University of Windsor in 1968. "It was sprawling all over the place and gobbling up other towns, but it didn't really know where it was going."

But Brown-John feels the city's physical transformation in the '60s and '70s and its boom times—stemming in part from the 1965 Auto Pact—helped Windsor flourish. "Windsor at some point began to understand that it was becoming a city," Brown-John said in 2016. "One of the best examples of what was happening was on the waterfront. There were profound changes for Windsor during this period—and that's when its modernization began. The city decided to improve the waterfront and tear down buildings and build anew and it made a major difference. The psychology of the city changed."

The Cleary Auditorium opened in 1960 as the crown jewel of the city's Riverside Drive assets. But the real gem? The riverfront itself. It went from crowded industrial chaos to coveted manicured parkland in a matter of three decades—all with a million-dollar view thanks to the Detroit skyline. Yet, the banks of the Detroit River hardly represented the only area transformation during this era. Highway 401, E.C. Row Expressway, and the Jackson Park overpass were all born during this unprecedented period of development. New neighbourhoods formed. New roads appeared. In a few notable cases, old streets assumed new names.

After a year-long debate, in 1955 Sandwich Street was renamed Riverside Drive, except in Sandwich Town, where the original name remained in the hopes of retaining its history. London Street was renamed University Avenue in 1957 in honour of Assumption College's 100th birthday, an homage to the city's roots. A little street's noteworthy name—chosen by the Windsor Utilities Commission, which decided those things—came in 1980 when Cartier Place, beside the Armouries, was renamed Freedom Way in honour of Andrei Sakharov, the Soviet physicist and dissident who won the Nobel Peace Prize.

Buildings went up, buildings came down, as Windsor busied itself with altering its look wholesale. A stylish new City Hall opened in 1958, while a number of downtown blocks were razed to make way for new developments. The city started spreading out, with stores and plazas—and in 1970, a major shopping centre, Devonshire Mall, emerging farther and farther from the city core. Adding to the trend: growing hospitals, churches, and schools.

It was an era of big change, yes, but also of big names, such as: mayors Art Reaume and Michael Patrick, or Members of Parliament Paul Martin Sr. and Herb Gray,

and many others. And an era of big stories. To name just a few, in the '50s, there were missiles on Belle Isle and the Jackson Park Grandstand fire. In the '60s, there were the Dickerson Children and the Metropolitan store explosion. In the '70s, there was the Ambassador Bridge nuclear test protest and the Windsor Curling Club disaster. And so much more.

Everyday life revved in this automotive town. With the fortunes of Canada's Motor City tied inextricably to the auto industry, any moves the carmakers made rippled across the region. Ford's decision to move its headquarters out of Windsor in 1953 was particularly hurtful for the city, a longtime Ford town. But the 1965 Auto Pact helped boost business for the Big Three, as well as a host of local parts manufacturers. Plus, Ford, Chrysler, and General Motors occasionally pumped sizeable investment into Windsor. The results proved almost instant, lifting the community's spirits and economy.

Emboldened by the Ford Strike in 1945, unions also grew in strength from 1950 to 1980. For a time it seemed as though at least one union or another was on a strike at any given time in Windsor, though the determined attitude—some would say strident—paid off for workers, at least back then. Collective bargaining achieved numerous gains in wages and benefits in the post-war years. In turn, Windsor workers gave freely to local charities, such as the United Way's Red Feather Campaign that started in 1949.

Generous Windsor workers made more than cars, of course. They produced booze and chemicals and pharmaceuticals and so much more. A couple of the region's big industries came courtesy of Mother Nature. Essex County's unending flatness, which produced great farmland, stems from 15,000 years ago when the region sat at the bottom of a glacial lake. And the generous deposits of underground salt, still heavily mined in the area, are the byproducts of a shallow warm sea covering the region some 400 million years ago. In other words, the area was born to work. The other types of industry Windsor and Essex County residents built with initiative. But it all required sweat.

And a sales pitch. Enter various shops and hotspots that lured customers from across the area, as well as from across the river. Windsorites who grew up in this golden era for shopping know stores such as Gray's, Brotherhood, Tepperman's and Freeds. They know local haunts like Smith's, S.S. Kresge, and Woolco. They know nightclubs the likes of the Metropole Lounge, the Top Hat, and the flashiest of them all, the Elmwood Casino—which drew American name acts and customers for decades, putting Windsor on the map and feeding the robust tourism industry. And they remember parades and celebrations: Mary Day, Emancipation Day, Windsor's 1954 centennial, the Freedom Festival, and more. And don't forget the royal visits in 1951 and 1959: eager royal-watchers appeared by the street-full. Windsor, after all, liked to celebrate. People came out in droves, lining the streets and adding enthusiasm for assorted public parties.

Throughout Windsor's evolution one thing remained constant: merry-making. All thanks to a single river. The concept of the water border did not change over the decades, as Americans and Canadians continued to cross for business, adventure, and entertainment. As historian Patrick Brode wrote in *Unholy City: Vice in Windsor Ontario, 1950*: "Windsor's location on a kilometre wide strait across from the American metropolis of Detroit insured that while its laws might have been Anglo-Canadian, its culture was heavily influenced by modern America." Windsor was long known as a sort of Sin City North, with an American clientele to help boost business. However, as a border city, it also attracted more than its share of people from around the world.

In the second half of the 20th century, Windsor embraced multiculturalism, en route to becoming the fourth most ethnically diverse city in Canada. It was a more diverse city in 1980 than it was after World War II, shaped by changing immigration laws and by virtue of its reputation as a multicultural hub with vibrant ethnic communities. According to Brode, "This remarkable state of affairs existed in a Canadian city that was not typical of its times. In addition to its industrialized workforce, Windsor had a more cosmopolitan flavour than the rest of the country."

Windsor continued to advance, to transform. As the world evolved in the '50s, '60s and '70s, so did Windsor. Its auto industry grew into a powerhouse, its boundaries expanded into the suburbs, and its look turned more metropolitan. Windsor came of age.

BUILDING BOOM

For Windsor, the post-war period was a time to think big—and act big, too. City officials embraced the modernization craze that took over North America, pushing for a "forward look" through contemporary architecture. The real action revolved around the major projects, the city-defining affairs. In the late 1950s, the city embarked on a massive redevelopment scheme, aimed primarily at revitalizing the core, that saw extensive demolition and ambitious building projects transform the cityscape.

One of the first large-scale projects city leaders worked on after World War II, when aviation proved a particularly important factor, was Windsor Airport. Opened in 1928 as Walker Airport with only the second airport charter in Canada, councillors wanted to modernize. A grand 1950 proposal for a Detroit-Windsor International Airport on the southwest side of the city never materialized. But, in 1957, a $1.25-million new airport terminal opened at the facility's existing southeast location, complete with customs, immigration, and health officers. Plus, the next year Windsor connected properly to the new 401 MacDonald-Cartier Freeway

by adding cloverleaf entrance ramps. The city was opening up.

Councillors had other lofty goals, too. Enter a forward-thinking group called the Windsor Tomorrow Committee under Mayor Michael Patrick. Influenced by Detroit's plans for a civic auditorium (Cobo Hall), this group envisioned a civic centre on the riverfront and a new city hall. At one point, they even suggested combining both to overlook the scenic Detroit River. The two concepts ultimately turned into their own projects, however, leading the charge for progress in Windsor's architecture.

On June 28, 1955, a special present arrived for Windsor: a bequest from late lawyer E.A. "Bill" Cleary for $500,000-plus. The gift ensured the civic centre project moved into overdrive—and gave it a name: the Cleary Auditorium. So clearing the riverfront continued apace, molding what many believed would become a city gem, if only it could rid itself of commercial and industrial interests.

Meanwhile, City Hall cried out for renewal, given that since 1904 it had operated in the former Central Public School (built in 1871 on the site that three decades earlier began housing British soldiers and became known as Barracks Square). The changes in City Hall Square began with the opening of a brand-new Municipal Courts Building in 1955. In 1958, at the cost of $2.1 million, thanks to a contemporary building with smooth lime-stone, and distinct royal-blue porcelain-enamelled metal plates, Windsor welcomed its stylish new City Hall. Upon its dedication, *The Windsor Star* declared City Hall the "mark of a modern community on the march."

City council had momentum—and some unfinished business first championed by Mayor Michael Patrick: reimagining the waterfront. After years of discussion and construction, the Cleary Auditorium opened on May 28, 1960, at a cost of $2.6 million. The auditorium was an instant success, since a growing city such as Windsor needed a civic centre, a place to congregate for shows and conventions. However, one of its greatest features lay outside the building itself in Dieppe Gardens, which transformed the Windsor-Detroit Ferry docks into a carefully manicured riverfront park.

The city's unabashed building campaign sparked some controversy, however. In 1958, City Council declared war on urban blight, proposing a "Redevelopment Area" that would raze over twenty blocks east of City Hall Square. Truth is, the so-called "slum clearage" displaced a number of low-income families, many of them African-Canadian. This neighbourhood, known as the McDougall Corridor, was the traditional heart of Windsor's Black community. Yet the city pushed ahead anyway, expropriating land and demolishing old buildings in the name of progress. A significant result was the Glengarry Courts Apartments housing project, designed for young families, in 1969.

The second phase of this redevelopment project focused on the downtown core around Ouellette Avenue, launching big-budget affairs including Dominion and Steinberg's. Downtown high-rises began to sprout, such as Le Goyeau Apartments in 1967 and the 14-storey office tower that became known as the CIBC Building in 1971. This development again came with a cost to the community. Windsor's original Chinatown—on Riverside Drive East between Windsor Avenue and Goyeau Street—was demolished to make way for this project.

The riverfront also continued to transform. In 1965, an imposing project was proposed: a Holiday Inn complex with twin towers rising nine and 20 storeys apiece, flanking a futuristic octagonal office building. In 1967, the $4 million Holiday Inn materialized, though at just three storeys and with a decidedly plainer look. It came amid notable opposition. Some members of City Council argued against developing land north of Riverside Drive that could provide spectacular green space with a million-dollar view of Detroit. But the hotel that became known as the "Plywood Palace" burned down in 1999 in a case of suspected arson.

In 1970, another major building endeavour came to Windsor—this time far away from the city's core. Devonshire Mall opened on Howard Avenue on the site of the former Devonshire Raceway horse track. Thousands of Windsorites lined up outside the shopping centre on its opening day, August 12, 1970. Some felt that the mall killed downtown shopping, but Devonshire Mall was there to stay.

As the city aged and its population increased, driving around grew trickier. That would not do, not in Canada's car capital. First, the city had to deal with increased traffic heading downtown. On February 1, 1963, another defining feature of Windsor was born: the Jackson Park Overpass that let cars zip over the still largely undeveloped green space. Around the same time, the Windsor Area Transportation Study was released, fuelling a long-term idea to build some sort of east-west freeway. In 1967, plans were unveiled for a $67-million expressway. Obtaining the money and the land proved thorny, though, so not until 1970 did construction begin along E.C. Row Avenue, named after the former head of Chrysler Canada. The first 1.2-mile stretch of the E.C. Row Expressway finally opened on July 14, 1973.

Progress on the expressway continued to inch along, though not without a political storm. Many people were displaced in the process. Some citizens fought the highway that physically sliced the city in two, restricting access to such neighbourhoods as Remington Park and Walker Homesites. As well, a proposed exit near Huron Church Road ran beside an ancient Native burial ground, where a 1935 archeological dig uncovered 27 human skeletons. While the City promised to leave the confirmed gravesite undisturbed, the First Nations community argued that the adjacent construction site contained skeletal remains. In the fall of 1978, First Nations people from around the country came to protest as the City of Windsor conducted an archeological survey of the contested area. While most just kept vigil, police physically removed one Native protester who planted himself in the way of work trucks. In the end, no human remains were found on the construction site. City leaders pushed the project slowly along and by 1980, E.C. Row extended east to Walker Road. By 1982, the four-lane expressway ran from Huron Church Road in the west to Lauzon Parkway in the east, largely thanks to provincial money. As Marty Gervais wrote in *The Windsor Star*, "this expressway had been mired in controversy and major construction delays." But 15 kilometres happened. Eventually.

Windsor, like most cities, experienced some growing pains. The city responded with some ambitious concepts, though. The 1950–80 period provided nirvana when it came to local development—sparking much progress. The building boom mentality highlighted a fascination with the "new" and a willingness to tear down on a massive scale to build up their idea of a modern utopia.

In 1950, American investors expressed interest in building a Detroit-Windsor International Airport in Sandwich West Township. The artist's conception, pictured at left, shows a "closed access road" to the Ambassador Bridge—plus, the land would be considered American soil to free cross-border travellers of customs and immigration. At top right is the proposed site on Malden Road, showing homes that would be expropriated. While the Canadian authorities were initially interested, the airport plans were terminated, due in part to citizen complaints.

May 26, 1950: Mayor Arthur J. Reaume broke the first sod for the new City Hall annex, with K.E. Shaw, city building inspector; L. McGill Allan, contractor; and Ray J. Desmarais, city engineer, from left to right. At right is an aerial view from 1952 of the old City Hall with the newly completed Annex behind it. An entirely new City Hall would be built in 1958 and the Annex was moved to Assumption University.

October 10, 1953: Mayor Albert E. Cobo of Detroit strikes the first demolition blow during the opening ceremonies for the construction of Windsor's civic auditorium and riverfront park. Mayor Arthur J. Reaume, Harry Rosenthal, and Donald McGregor, from left to right, look on. Pictured at right are the original plans for the centre, the Cleary Auditorium, which featured a large hotel complex that was never built.

The car entrance of the Windsor-Detroit Ferry Company docks, 1953. As the site of Windsor's new civic centre, the city expropriated the docks—and the buildings behind it, including Windsor Tent and Awning—for demolition.

These three storefronts on Sandwich Street East (Riverside Drive) were the site of Windsor's first post office and the place where the village council first met. Most recently occupied by fortune tellers, the buildings were sold to Bartlet, MacDonald & Gow department store with plans to be razed for a parking lot.

Windsor embarked on a massive building campaign in the 1950s, a move praised by Ivan Russel Johnson's political cartoon in *The Star* on June 28, 1955.

Hundreds Impressed With New Windsor Municipal Courts Building

The new Municipal Courts Building in City Hall Square, pictured at left, had its grand opening on June 27, 1955. During the open house, Evelyn Annis, Caroline Millar, and Dorenda Annis, from left to right, tested the prisoner detention cells while other Windsorites explored the facilities and got their fingerprints taken.

October 9, 1954: Controller Lawrence A. Deziel, at left, hands the keys to the condemned buildings behind him to A.J. Maheu, president of Cumming Wrecking Company. These buildings on the south side of Sandwich Street (Riverside Drive), many dating as far back as the 1830s, were torn down to make room for what would become the Cleary Auditorium.

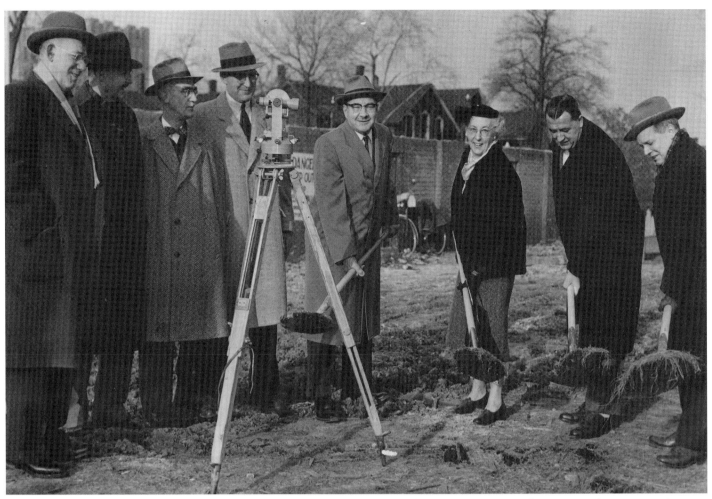

In what *The Windsor Star* called a "historic moment," the sod was turned for the new City Hall on December 12, 1956. From left to right are R.J. Desmarais, commissioner of works; George Y. Masson and Hugh P. Sheppard, architects; Louis L. Odette, president of Eastern Construction Company; Controller W. Ernest Atkinson; Controller Mrs. Cameron H. Montrose; Mayor Michael J. Patrick; and Controller Thomas R. Brophey.

June 22, 1957: Stonemasons Gilbert Gyori and Denys Mortimer work to install an outside wall during the construction of City Hall.

C.S. McWhinnie, S.E. Dinsmore, and D.C. Johnson, from left to right, were the architects and contractor for the Cleary Auditorium. Johnson & McWhinnie Architects were a top local firm, responsible for many of Windsor's modern buildings from the 1950s and 1960s.

The wrecking of old Windsor-Detroit Ferry Company docks between Station Street and the Government Dock began in 1954. A new retaining wall was built by the Canadian Dredge and Dock Company of Toronto as the first step to create Dieppe Gardens riverfront park.

June 3, 1957: Citizens gathered downtown to witness the groundbreaking ceremony for the Cleary Auditorium. From left to right: Mayor Michael J. Patrick and his daughter Lynn, Mrs. H.L. Boynton, acting as a stand-in for Norah Cleary, and A.F. Fuerth, turn the sod. Pictured at right, Boynton gives an honorary shovel to Norah Cleary. Norah's brother, Windsor lawyer E.A. "Bill" Cleary QC, died in 1955 and bequeathed $500,000 for a civic auditorium, plus additional funds for a guest house, to the city in his will.

June 10, 1957: John Whiteside and W.J. Carter show their relief at making the deadline to begin building the Cleary Auditorium under the terms of Edmund A. Cleary's will (or risk losing the endowment). *The Windsor Star*'s addition, Baum & Brody Furniture, and the François Baby House are located behind the excavation-in-progress by Dinsmore Construction, from left to right.

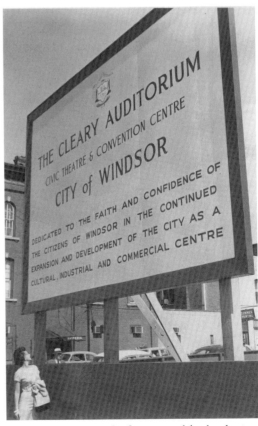

An aerial view of downtown Windsor, at left, shows results of the demolition work with the removal of two city blocks during the construction of Cleary Auditorium. Tourists couldn't miss the sign on Ferry Street, pictured at right, calling attention to the building project.

Windsor's brand new air terminal was opened in October 1957. It would be ten years before Windsor joined the ranks of other Canadian airports by becoming Windsor International Airport.

January 27, 1958: Les Girard and Vic Driscoll, employees of the Canadian Bridge Company, climbed down from their perch on the new Cleary Auditorium building site to get a ground view of their work (and pose for a quick photograph).

February 8, 1958: Johnny Marcon, at left, and George Bower, two van company workers, haul a desk into the new City Hall.

Windsor's new City Hall opened its doors in 1958. Designed by Sheppard and Masson, the architects described the building as one of the first structures of modern design that didn't have to rely on vast glass walls. *The Windsor Star* called it an "imposing piece of architecture in the 20th century motif, befitting this great Canadian industrial metropolis."

June 9, 1958: Fred M. Cass, Minister of Highways for Ontario, cuts the ribbon to open the Windsor entrances to the Highway 401. Pictured with him, from left to right, are Lieutenant-Colonel William Griesinger, MPP for Windsor Sandwich; Harry Lassaline, Windsor Chamber of Commerce; G.V. Howell, engineer; W.J. Fulton, deputy Minister of Highways; and William Murdoch, MPP for Essex South.

23-Block Area in Proposal for Redevelopment

In 1958, the City of Windsor proposed a massive "Redevelopment Program" to remove urban blight. The 23-block area bordered by Goyeau Street, Wyandotte Street East, Glengarry Avenue, and Riverside Drive would see nearly every building torn down and replaced with high-rise apartment buildings, prestige office buildings, and commercial ventures. Referred to as "Windsor's worst slum" by *The Star*, much of this area (particularly the McDougall Street corridor) were traditionally African-Canadian neighbourhoods. These "dilapidated homes" east of City Hall, pictured at left, and on Glengarry Avenue, pictured at right, were both areas that would be expropriated by the city.

"Wrecker's First Target": This 50-year-old house at 478 McDougall Street was the first to meet the wrecking ball as demolition started on October 21, 1959, in the Redevelopment Area One east of City Hall. Representatives of the city and Central Housing Corporation, which was to build new apartments in the area, were on hand.

The Cleary Auditorium and Memorial Convention Hall was officially opened by Honourable J. Keiller Mackay, Lieutenant Governor of Ontario, on May 28, 1960. According to *The Star*, the modern facilities would make Windsor "Convention City." Pictured here at night, the Cleary was a bright addition to Windsor's skyline, overlooking Dieppe Gardens.

'Music' of Construction Keynotes Windsor Potential

An aerial view of Windsor's "Redevelopment Area One" shows the demolition-in-progress plus the addition of row housing behind Windsor Arena. Other area landmarks include City Hall Square with All Saints Church to the far left, with the City Market behind it, slightly to the right.

May 2, 1961: Norman Spencer, MP for Essex West, snips the ribbon into the first housing unit of Windsor's multi-million "Redevelopment Area One" for Mr. and Mrs. George McGuire and their children Ronald, Richard, and Nancy, from left to right.

January 24, 1962: The Walker House Hotel, an old hostel built in 1883, disappears as wreckers demolish it and many other old structures in the area. The Walker House was owned and operated by African-Canadian family the Smiths, and the tavern served as a community gathering place for more than eight decades.

Mayor Michael J. Patrick opened the new Jackson Park overpass on February 1st, 1963. The new traffic artery divided the park into two, connecting Ouellette Avenue and Dougall Avenue directly.

Only trees remain in "Redevelopment Area One," where "ramshackle buildings" once stood in the words of *The Star* on November 29, 1963. The blocks pictured here are bound by Wyandotte Street and University Avenue to the north and south, and Glengarry Avenue and Mercer Street to the east and west.

Windsor's "Redevelopment Area Two" saw old commercial buildings in the downtown core, including Lee's Curio Shop, Victor's Upholstery, and Jolim Restaurant, from left to right, torn down in 1964. This became the site of Le Goyeau Apartments in 1967.

Two ambitious proposals for the future Holiday Inn site on Riverside Drive were revealed to the public in 1965. At left, an artist's conception by Argosy Construction Limited of Toronto features twin towers, with an octagonal office building in the middle. A competing bid, shown at right, is explained by John Partyka of Allied Innkeepers Ltd. to L.R. Keddy, the city's Director of Planning and Urban Renewal, at left. A scaled-down version of Argosy Construction's proposal turned into the Holiday Inn.

The official start on excavation work for a $4 million Steinburg department store began on August 18, 1965. Hats are off by company officials, from left to right: William Sherman, Nathan Steinberg, Oscar Plotnik, and Mel Dobrin. The site, pictured at right, was part of the city's "Redevelopment Area Two," at Goyeau Street and Chatham Street. In a quick reversal of fortunes, the store was closed in 1975 and the building sat vacant until demolition in 1992.

The Holiday Inn under construction in 1967. The land for the hotel site was formerly a government dock and the Jamieson Building, which another crew is busy demolishing in the background. The Holiday Inn was called the "jewel of Windsor's waterfront" by *The Star* in its year-end round-up of construction projects, but is better remembered by many Windsorites for its nickname "The Plywood Palace."

Row-mer
CLOUDY, WARMER
6 a.m. 21, 9 a.m. 21, 2 p.m. 41
Low tonight 30, high Thursday 47
(Complete weather page 6)

The Windsor Star

FINAL
★ ★ ★ ★

VOL. 99, NO. 57   64 Pages   WINDSOR ONTARIO WEDNESDAY NOVEMBER 8 1967   TEN CENTS

WINDSOR'S EXPRESSWAY PLAN

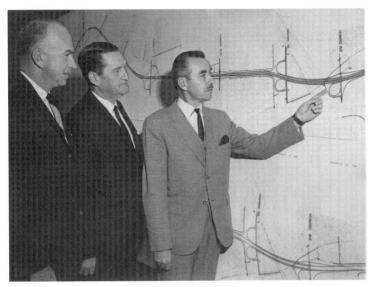

Plans for the construction of a multi-million dollar expressway through Windsor were announced on November 8, 1967. At top left, district engineer F.C. Brown, at far right, explains the blueprints to Mayor John Wheelton (at left) and Ontario Highways Minister George E. Gomme. The project was slated to begin construction in 1970, with the provincial government paying 75 percent of the estimated $67,500,000 cost. Pictured above are some of the planned intersections, including Dominion Boulevard (top right), and Howard Avenue (bottom).

An aerial view of "Redevelopment Area One" in 1967, with the completed Glengarry Court public housing development including row housing and an apartment building. A *Star* feature questioned whether Windsor's new system of public housing was a form of social segregation.

The future site of the Devonshire Shopping Centre was announced in 1968. This 65-acre tract of land was formerly the Devonshire Racing Track.

The bare-bones interior of Devonshire Mall, mid-construction on April 7, 1970. The shopping centre would feature two major department stores on either end: Sears-Simpson and Steinburg's Miracle Mart.

Opening day crowds at Devonshire Shopping Centre on August 12, 1970.

The first phase of the E.C. Row Expressway was opened on July 17, 1973. Here, cyclists enjoy the stretch from Dougall Avenue to Howard Avenue where they were allowed to freely ride in the month leading up to opening day, while builders waited for final parts.

In October, 1978, construction stalled on E.C. Row Expressway to investigate claims that the site for a cloverleaf exit to Huron Church Road was a First Nations burial ground. Archeologist Peter Reid and a team of anthropology students conducted a survey of the area. At left, student Kirk Walsedt uncovers the skeleton of a horse, observed by a First Nations vigil who kept watch at the site. When the excavation failed to produce human skeletal remains after a month of digging, city administrator Hilary Payne announced that construction would resume.

HOSPITALS & HEALTHCARE

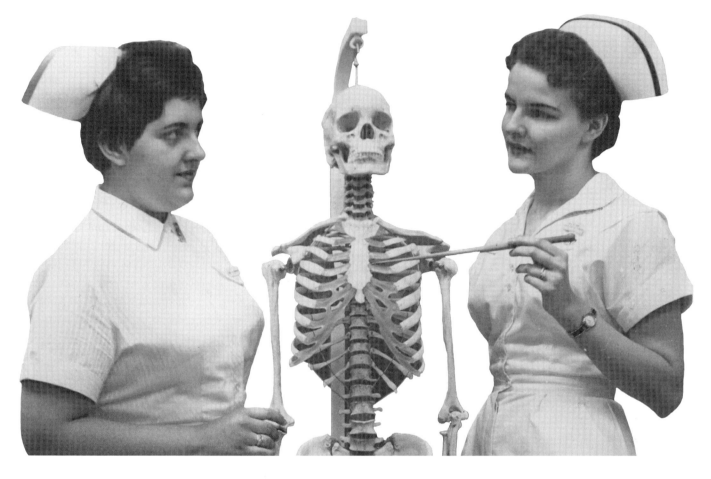

A healthy community starts with good healthcare and, in Windsor's case, a bit of gumption. A continual struggle for proper facilities locally began almost with the idea of launching public healthcare itself, especially as the local population grew. The baby boom affected Windsor as it did much of North America, so the local community found itself in a constant battle, seeking more funds and better medical care as the population increased.

Hôtel-Dieu was the first such facility opened locally, founded in 1888 by five indomitable Montreal nuns from the Religious Hospitallers of St. Joseph. They stepped off a train with a few supplies and an idea, met by St. Alphonsus Church pastor Father Dean James Theodore Wagner. Their determination was contagious: a building opened in near record speed in 1890. Others soon pitched in to care for the community, as well. Two other major hospitals—Grace and Metropolitan—were soon created, forming Windsor's own 'Big Three' of healthcare. In 1917, the Salvation Army's Grace Hospital

opened in the Ellis House and quickly expanded, adding new wings in 1922, 1942, and 1945 to meet the growing demand for beds. Meanwhile, Metropolitan General Hospital, which opened in 1928, was busy pursuing the latest technologies and innovations, including a cancer clinic in 1935 and an experimental, independent nursing school in 1947.

Smaller hospitals also helped to shore up support for Windsor's sick and elderly. What would become IODE Memorial Hospital, named after the Imperial Order Daughters of the Empire, opened in a home as a tuberculosis sanatorium in 1913 at Union-on-the-Lake between Kingsville and Leamington on Lake Erie. After a devastating fire, IODE moved to Prince Road in 1923, where it grew steadily until the decline of tuberculosis as a major public threat saw the facility converted into IODE Memorial Hospital in 1959. Ford City Public School, erected on Riverside Drive East in 1917, transformed into Riverview Hospital in 1942—giving East Windsor its own healthcare facility in an era when getting around wasn't as easy. In 1972 the hospital became a branch of Windsor Western Hospital, providing long-term continuing care, until it closed in 1995, and was partly renovated into apartments.

From Spanish Flu to much more, Windsor's healthcare system tackled it all. In the '30s, '40s, and '50s, hospitals in Windsor fought a scourge that threatened much of the world: polio. Of note, future Prime Minister and local boy Paul Martin Jr. was stricken with polio in 1946 at age six, though he went on to succeed at the highest levels, mirroring his father who also contracted the disease as a small child. Still, the epidemics of the 1950s and general misinformation about the disease led to widespread public anxiety. Local doctors embraced all cutting-edge treatments for polio, from the iron lung to the first vaccines, introduced in 1955 and again in 1962. Whether it be an outbreak of polio or a local tragedy—from the 1946 tornado to the 1960 Metropolitan store explosion—Windsor's hospitals were well-versed in disaster and quickly stepped up to the plate to care for its city's people.

By the 1950s, the building boom and modern ideas that had taken Windsor and the rest of North America by storm boosted the city's hospitals. Metropolitan led the charge, adding a new west wing in 1953 and a counterpart east wing in 1956. Over the decades, the grand old Hôtel-Dieu building had aged and grown cramped, leading to milestones like the opening of a new eight-storey tower in 1962 and the demolition of the original hospital building in 1963. When the Ellis House was destroyed by fire in 1960, officials at Grace Hospital capitalized on the opportunity to build a brand-new addition which opened in 1966.

The 1970s were heady times for Windsor hospitals. The IODE Hospital welcomed a new tower, built in 1972, around the time the facility became known as Windsor Western Hospital. Meanwhile, Metropolitan General Hospital also enjoyed a towering expansion around that time, courtesy of a $17-million, eight-storey wing added in 1974 to accommodate 500 beds.

"At the time, the expansions were dramatic," Windsor Regional Hospital CEO David Musyj said in 2016. "The 1970s represented the largest physical expansion IODE and Met had ever gone through up to then. It was impressive. But the style then was still very institutional. I can remember it was all white walls. Colour did not get added until later. But the towers were state of the art when they were built."

Area health-care facilities would see increasing amalgamation over the years, though to a lesser degree with Leamington Memorial District Hospital, since it was the main emergency room in the county. Hôtel-Dieu and Grace merged in 1994, while Western and Metropolitan became Windsor Regional Hospital in 1995, all moving towards one acute-care hospital in Windsor. But in the mid to late part of the 20th century, Windsor hospitals were still largely going it alone. The best example of this phenomenon is the in-hospital nursing schools—Hôtel-Dieu, Grace, and Metropolitan hospitals ran competing nursing schools until they were all amalgamated into one program at St. Clair College in 1973.

Yet the never-ending march towards improved health-care continued in Windsor, serving a growing population in the post-war years—and keeping the community healthy in the process.

February 21, 1951: The VON uniforms and little black bags were a familiar sight to Windsorites in need of home healthcare. Pictured here are the staff of the Windsor headquarters ready to start a long day of work.

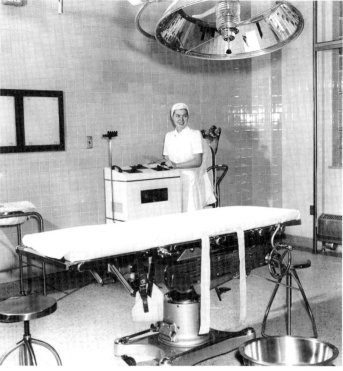

February 23, 1950: Muriel Morgan, a public health nurse with the Victorian Order of Nurses, on a home visit to the Windibanks, the new parents of twins. Morgan, at centre, prepares one of the twins, Cort, for a bath, while the other, Cory, is held by his mother. At back, Lorne Windiback holds his 13-month-old son, Kirk Allen. Established in 1897, the VON provides home care and other social services to this day.

February 25, 1950: The interior of a new operating room at Grace Hospital.

In 1952, East Windsor Hospital was the centre of a Royal Commission by the provincial government into their financial affairs and medical practices. Commissioner Gordon Fraser QC spoke favourably of the hospital's facilities, but condemned the monopoly of power held by superintendent Dr. P.J. Morgan. He further concluded that the hospital acted more as an "old folks home" and lacked proper diagnostics and medical treatment. The hospital, later known as Riverview, remained open under a new board of directors and was ultimately closed in 1995. The building was partly converted into apartments, which still stand at the corner of Belleview Avenue and Riverside Drive.

Salvation Army Grace Hospital, circa 1952. Ellis House, the original home of Grace Hospital in 1918, is located in the centre. The Ellis House was destroyed by fire in 1960 and demolished to make way for a new wing in 1966.

The third graduating class from the Metropolitan Demonstration School of Nursing in 1952. In the front row, from left to right, are Irma Besler, Audrey Beck, Ina Grain, Jean Anderson, Amie Sato, Gertie Gesser, Joan Irwin, Shirley Best, Lucina Stewart, Susie Martens, and Margaret Walwin. In the back row are: Elsa Lundgren, Patricia Shannon, Joyce Fast, Katherine McCallum, Betty Verwey, Jocelyn James, Marcia Knox, Lillian Farrier, Barbara Ward, and Dorothy Upper. The Metropolitan Demonstration School of Nursing, from 1947 to 1952, was an experimental two-year program for an independent school run directly by nurses.

Metropolitan General Hospital, circa 1954. A massive addition in 1973, including the construction of a central tower to replace this front entrance, transformed this structure into the hospital that stands today.

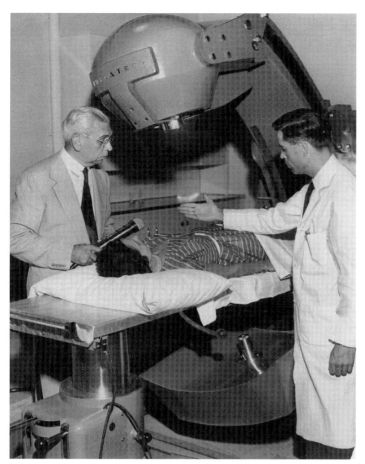

July 21, 1954: Dr. McCormick, at left, demonstrates how the cobalt bomb works with two of his staff members, the "patient" Janet Millard and radiotherapist John Maus. A Canadian invention, the use of cobalt 60 radiation and concentrated dosage revolutionized cancer treatment.

May 13, 1955: Members of the Hôtel-Dieu ladies auxiliary took a tour of the hospital's facilities. Here, Mrs. A.F. Fuerth, Mrs. N.A. Alewick, Mrs. F.P. Scarfone, student nurse Pauline Guillbeault, and Mrs. John McCabe, from left to right, carefully examine the operating room.

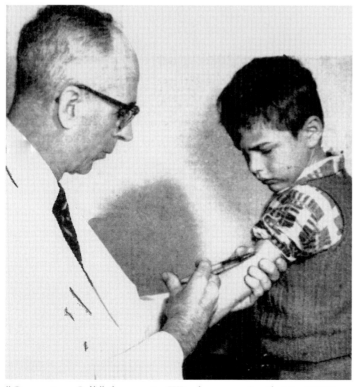

"Operation Salk" began in Windsor on April 18, 1955 as 928 children lined up for their shots of the revolutionary new polio vaccine. First to be inoculated was seven-year-old Donald Higginbottom, pictured here with Dr. John Howie.

"Wading Doctor": Dr. E.B. Butt wades barefoot in water up to his ankles as he leaves the diet kitchen at Grace Hospital after a record flood on July 8, 1957. Six inches of torrential rainfall caused flooding and other damage across the city.

July 26, 1958: Despite the provincial government's refusal to license ambulance attendants under supervised first aid course, both Windsor and ABC Ambulance companies went ahead and trained their men. Robert Ballantyne, Tom Thomas, Richard Ecksteen, and Gregory Ballantyne, from left to right, go over the equipment. Paramedics and their pre-hospital care were unregulated until the Ontario Ambulance Act in 1966.

The new Windsor Medical Services building, at 1427 Ouellette Avenue, officially opened on March 21, 1959. Windsor Medical Services, established in 1939 under a grant from the Rockefeller Center, offered voluntary health insurance plans targeted at automotive workers.

Members of staff at Riverview Hospital in 1958. Largely a chronic care facility, Riverview merged with IODE Memorial Hospital to form Windsor Western Hospital Centre in 1972.

The main wing of Hôtel-Dieu, Windsor's first hospital, in 1960. Constructed in 1888, the original building was condemned as a fire hazard and slated for demolition. It faced the wrecking ball in 1963.

The Ellis House, the original structure of Grace Hospital, went up in flames on June 5, 1960. At left, firefighters use an aerial ladder to reach the fire's source, while at right, the extent of damage to the third floor is shown during an inspection by fire chief Ovila Bezaire (centre). Fire doors prevented the blaze from reaching the newer wings, and swift emergency protocols prevented any life-threatening injuries. The Ellis House was mostly an administrative building, but was so fire-damaged that the Salvation Army opted to replace it with a six-storey addition with 134 new beds.

Windsor gained a new general hospital in 1959, IODE Memorial Hospital, after the Alice Casgrain building (pictured above) of the Essex County Sanatorium on Prince Road was turned into an active-treatment centre. After a merger with Riverview Hospital in 1972, it became Windsor Western Hospital Centre and eventually the western campus of Windsor Regional Hospital in 1992.

January 11, 1961: Sister Marie de la Ferre, at left, and Sister Lafond, superior, watch as a subcontractor from Fuller Construction Company begins the excavation for Hôtel-Dieu's new main wing at the hospital's south end. The new addition, here in 1962, at eight storeys and 350 beds, almost doubled the hospital's capacity and served as the replacement for the original building.

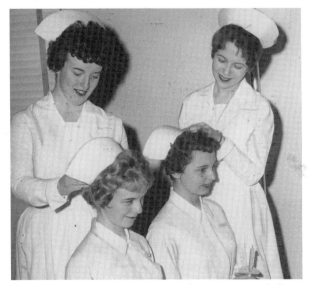
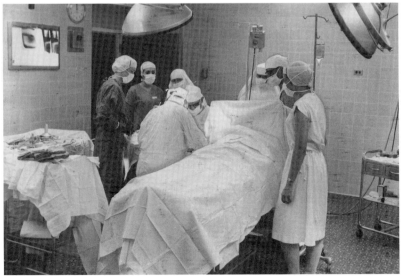

"Capping Ceremony": 59 graduating nurses from Hôtel-Dieu received their caps on February 13, 1962. From left, kneeling, are Mary Anne Breen and Coral Anne Lindquist, while Jill Joungson and Carol Simpson do the honours.

"First Operation": When Carson Edwards fell off his ladder and fractured his elbow on August 25, 1962, his doctors opened the new wing of Hôtel-Dieu a few days early to accommodate his emergency. The christening surgery was done by surgeon Glenn Sproule with Harvey Tonken assisting and Jules Winemaker as the anesthetist.

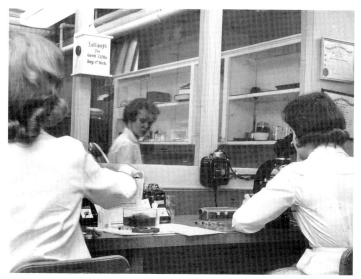

March 30, 1963: Lab technicians Jo-Anne Colautti, Esther Briand, and Sally Murray run tests at Grace Hospital. The majority of tests had to be performed by hand.

October 29, 1964: Barbara Duke, a member of the local VON branch, is shown leaving the office for her busy schedule of calls.

A class of third-year students at Hôtel-Dieu Nursing School in 1965. From humble beginnings in the basement of the hospital in 1907, the nursing school moved into the Jeanne Mance nurses' residence in 1946. The school could accommodate 157 students, but attendance was down due to competition from Metropolitan Hospital's own nursing school.

June 7, 1965: Betty Scott receives the Maternal Child Care award from school director Kathleen Moderwell, at left. After the Demonstration School was closed in 1952, the hospital opened an in-house nursing school in 1954 which was run by Moderwell from 1960 to 1973.

Dr. Henri Breault demonstrates how to use his invention, child-proof protective caps for solid and liquid drugs, on June 21, 1965. A pediatrician, Breault developed the product out of his work as the head of the Poison Control Centre at Hôtel-Dieu Hospital. After the "Palm N Turn" was adopted in Windsor in 1967, the incidence of child poisonings dropped by 91 percent. The caps were made mandatory in Ontario in 1974, and the rest of North America followed soon after.

Local 439, the lathers union, went out on strike to fight for higher wages on June 8, 1965. Here, a one-man picket patrols in front of Grace Hospital, one of several major construction sites around the city where all work was halted as other unions refused to cross the Local 439's picket line. After four days, the picket line was lifted to allow other unions to return to work, while the lathers union reached an agreement over wages on June 15.

Nursing assistants from the IODE Memorial training centre celebrated their graduation on June 25, 1966. The award winners, from left to right, are J. Marie Sibley, Catherina Kok, Tallulah Jenkins, Alice Pula, and Beverley Girard.

Several hundred people attended the opening of the six storey addition to Grace Hospital on September 10, 1966. The crowd was addressed by Mayor John Wheelton, Reeve Fred Cada of St. Clair Beach, who is pictured above at the microphone, and W.B. Lewis of the Ontario Hospital Services Commission. The new wing replaced the Ellis House, which was destroyed by fire in 1960.

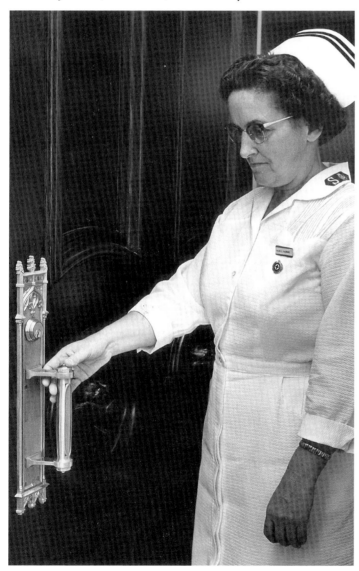

September 9, 1966: Major Gladys McGregor, administrator of Grace Hospital, shows off the century-old door to the Ellis House, which was refinished and placed as a memorial in the new front lobby. The door is currently on display at Windsor Regional Hospital, Ouellette Campus, as one of the last remnants of Grace Hospital, which was demolished in 2013.

Grace Hospital nurses parade down University Avenue to the Salvation Army Citadel for their graduation service on September 11, 1966.

Dorothy Booth, a lab technician at Grace Hospital, uses a new automatic chemical analyzer on March 9, 1968. Time-saving automation introduced at the new laboratory helped Grace Hospital to nearly double its number of lab tests.

August 3, 1968: Michael Stockwell of Suburban Ambulances wheels out the first ambulance in Essex County built to Ontario Department of Health specifications. The 1966 Ambulance Act standardized care and safety standards for paramedics and emergency services, which had been unregulated.

"Popular Man": Laurie Stockwell, the first male graduate of the Hôtel-Dieu Hospital School of Medical Laboratory Technology, greets five of his fellow graduates on May 5, 1968. The female line-up, from left to right, are: Beverley Ann Sitarz, Jeannine Gagno, Sandra Lynn Langlois, Peggy Dufor, and Evelyn Barrette. A *Star* reporter surmised: "being the only man in a class of girls has its advantages."

Line-ups were forming at the Windsor Medical counter, as the insurance program joined the government's new healthcare initiative OHSIP (Ontario Health Services Insurance Plan) in October 1969. Ontario's first health plan, OMSIP (Ontario Medical Services Insurance Plan), was introduced in 1966, but was quickly replaced by OHSIP, the provincially administered national medicare plan that is known today simply as OHIP.

September 4, 1968: Student nurses at Metropolitan General Hospital rid themselves of "granny shoes" after graduating from their second year of school. As was the custom, students had special permission to toss their mandatory black Oxfords off the Ambassador Bridge. Third-year students got to wear the traditional white nursing shoes and stockings for their hospital placement.

"We've Graduated!": Hilda Pitters dances and cheers with excitement as she leads the graduates from the nursing school at Grace Hospital to Cleary Auditorium for their convocation ceremony on June 12, 1971. Forty-one students received their diplomas.

September 7, 1977: Over 75 nurses blocked the driveway to Windsor Western Hospital Centre, IODE Unit, protesting the announcement that Riverview Hospital would be closed. In the end, the hospital remained open until 1995.

Award-winning nurse Linda Baerg laughs with Sister Evert Haynes and Senator Paul Martin following the 63rd and final full Hôtel-Dieu School of Nursing Graduation at Cleary Auditorium on June 9, 1973. For the 1973–74 academic year, all of Windsor's in-hospital nursing schools were transferred to St. Clair College.

The last graduating class from Grace Hospital's nursing school celebrated in fine fashion on June 14, 1973. Student uniforms were tossed out of windows, and a streamer of pantyhose hung across the roof of the nurses' residence. Later, it was a cancan dance on University Avenue and a parade with the class dummy, Ms. Chase, RN.

Dr. Godfrey Bacheyie and Dr. Joseph Galiwango are surrounded by some of the 200 premature or acutely ill babies they helped deliver in 1982. They headed up Grace Hospital's neonatal intensive care unit that opened in May.

PLACES OF WORSHIP

If ever something showed the power of religion locally, it was the Mary Day Parade. Born unapologetically as a counter to communism, the Soviet Union, and atheism, the Mary Day Parade—held on May 1—was instead proudly religious. The Mary Day Parade was a show of strength and devotion, proudly asserting that Windsor was Catholic before anything else.

But the Mary Day Parade was no little vanity project attracting a few religious devotees. In the mid-1950s, Windsor's Mary Day Parade was a force, a divinely inspired display that attracted enthusiasts from abroad for communal worship and showed the area's deep Catholic roots—which, of course, extend back to the very beginnings of the community. The original settlers created Assumption Parish in the mid-1700s, and the Windsor area formed around it. The Mary Day Parade debuted in 1949, thanks to the Catholic Lay Guild of Windsor, and gained steam from there.

In 1954, the three-hour Mary Day Parade featured a dozen bands, 24 floats, and 60-plus marching groups from Windsor and Detroit. It was presided over by Cardinal and Archbishop of Toronto, James Charles McGuigan. TV and film star Danny Thomas even added celebrity power when he dropped by and kissed the ring of His Eminence riding past mid-parade. About 50,000 people attended. The event continued well into the '60s and developed a reputation, even outside the area, as a particularly noteworthy Catholic celebration. As one Canadian Press report from 1958 said simply, "May Day is Mary Day in Windsor." The Mary Day Parade ended after 1966, however, when priests noted declining attendance.

It was an era of religious modernization. Assumption Church remained a hub of activity, hosting services and events as diverse as Assumption University graduation ceremonies and traditional First Nations displays by Walpole Island residents, plus in 1975 launching a choral group that would become known as the Windsor Community Choir. As a commemorative edition of *The Windsor Star* said in 1992, "Before Windsor, before Essex County, before Ontario, there was Assumption Parish." A parish that instrumental to the area was not about to just remain in the past.

New churches sprouted all over the place in the '50s and '60s—with a distinctly different architectural style. Gone were the stately stone structures of old, replaced by a trend of modern design, often with long thin stained-glass windows, as if to show religion could adapt with the times. St. James United Church went one step further, holding a Windsor 'first' on July 11, 1965—by hosting a drive-in church service. Whereas churches declined in number at the beginning of the 21st century, in the mid-20th century they were increasing, as was dedication to them.

"Religion may be as old as humankind, but it is certainly neither static nor simple," reads a report by Gallup Poll, which says in modern times religious adherence peaked in the US in 1955, with 70 percent of respondents saying they were either Catholic, Protestant, or Jewish. "Over the last 50 years in Canada," Statistics Canada reported in 2000, "the percentage of the adult population attending religious services has declined dramatically. In 1946, a Gallup poll reported that 67 percent of adults attended religious services during a typical week; in 1998, only 22 percent did." Religious observance was alive and well in Windsor in the '50s, perhaps best evidenced by the sheer number of churches built during the post-war decades.

Some of the new churches and upgrades included: St. Luke in the Fields Anglican Church opened in Remington Park in 1950; the Missionary Alliance Tabernacle Church at Goyeau and Tuscarora was dedicated in 1951; St. Barnabas Anglican Church was built in white concrete with a slender square steeple on Tecumseh Road East in 1955; St. George's Church, built in 1921, had a contrasting modern extension with a bell tower added in 1955; St. George's Romanian Orthodox Cathedral with a unique tower rose up in 1955; the uniquely stylish, steep-roofed Paulin Memorial Presbyterian Church was built in 1955, but greatly expanded in 1964; Glenwood United Church opened at Hall and Grand Marais in 1956; the Trinity United Church was built in 1956; Knox Presbyterian Church was dedicated in 1957; St. John's Anglican Church, first built in 1805, enjoyed extensive renovations in 1957; the Emmanuel Baptist Church at Foster and Woodward Avenues with a modern "floating roof" style appeared in 1960; the Tanner African Methodist Episcopal Church at Tuscarora and McDougall streets was constructed in 1963; the British Methodist Episcopal Church, built in 1856, was replaced with a new one on University Avenue in 1963; the Riverside Evangel Tabernacle Church welcomed its flock in 1965; St. Alphonsus Roman Catholic Church enjoyed extensive renovations in 1965; the Church of God in Christ opened at Mercer and Cataraqui in 1968; Our Lady of Mount Carmel Church burned in 1976, though a new church was built in 1977; and Most Precious Blood Catholic Church also burned down to a shell in 1978, but was rebuilt the next year. Still, it all added up to a lot of religious rebirth, and not just Christian.

In the 1950s and 1960s, churches were the dominant force in religiosity in Canada and the United States. Windsor was no exception. But other religions, and lack of religion, have grown in popularity since. The first Jewish settler in Windsor, David Moses, came from Detroit in 1797. The community continued to grow for more than a century. The Shaar Hashomayim Synagogue was built on Giles Boulevard in 1929 and Congregation Beth EL, affiliated with the Reform Jewish movement, opened in 1960 on Ouelette Avenue, diversifying the local Jewish community.

Muslims began moving to Windsor in the early 20th century. By the 1940s, 16 Muslim families lived in the area. The first Windsor mosque opened in a house on Wellington Road in 1960. The mosque at Dominion and Northwood, which became the area's largest, opened in 1969. The Muslim community continued to grow, reaching 20,000 strong by 2016.

Faith played an important role in the Windsor area in the mid-20th century, to which many places of worship attest. Though Catholicism took root in the area in the 1700s thanks to French settlers, as Windsor became an increasingly diverse place in the post-war years, faith also blossomed in variety and contribution to the community.

Central United Church on Ouellette Avenue, circa 1950. Built in 1906, Central United still holds service today.

October 4, 1949: Students of Assumption and Holy Names College fill the pews at Assumption Church for a commencement mass to begin a new school year.

October 21, 1950: A group kneels in front of the altar at the shrine to Our Mother of Perpetual Help at Sacred Heart Church. Five novena services were held every Tuesday, drawing upwards of 5,000 people each week. *The Star* estimated that 3.5 million had visited the shrine in the 18 years since it had opened in 1932.

June 16, 1950: The 55-foot spire is raised into position onto St. Peter's Anglican Church at Ellrose Avenue and Tecumseh Road.

January 20, 1951: Fred "Tip" Beacom repairs the spire of All Saints' Anglican Church.

A packed service at All Saints' Anglican Church in City Hall Square in this undated photograph.

St. Alphonsus Church on Park Street East in the 1950s. The church celebrated its centennial in 1965 and still holds service today.

Alliance Tabernacle, a Christian and Missionary Alliance church, at 706 Goyeau Street, in its final stages of construction on October 6, 1951. Designed by Windsor architect D.J. Cameron, the structure now houses Linh Son Buddhist Temple.

The interior of St. John's Church in Sandwich on the occasion of its 150th anniversary in 1952. The church still holds regular service today, and is the oldest organized Anglican parish west of Niagara-on-the-Lake. More than 50 veterans and well-known Windsorites like J.L. Forster and Howard Watkins are buried in the church's cemetery.

January 18, 1953: Members of Giles Boulevard United Church burn the mortgage on the church and parsonage in front of the congregation. From left to right are William Greaves, T.A. Larmour, Mrs. Theodore Ouellette, J.W. Schooley, Thomas Duncan Sr., and Mrs. Dan Burgess.

September 30, 1954: Most Reverend John C. Cody, Bishop of the Diocese of London, lays the cornerstone of the new Christ the King Church at the corner of Dominion Avenue and Grand Marais Boulevard. From left to right are Henry Damien, contractor; Reverend Hebert Roy; Reverend John McCormik; and Bishop Cody. The Grand Marais Urgent Care Clinic, built in 2015, now sits in this location.

The Holy Name of Mary Church on McEwan Avenue was originally called Our Lady of Prompt Succour. Father J.A. Rooney requested the name change in 1943 because the children of the parish were being called "Prompt Suckers." At right, Bishop John C. Cody was back in Windsor on October 25, 1954, to bless the church's three new church bells. The church was closed in 2012, but was reopened two years later.

May 1, 1954: The 6th annual Mary Day Parade passes by the Windsor Centennial birthday cake reviewing stand where dignitaries watched the annual religious demonstration, staged by the Catholic Lay Guild. The parade consisted of 24 floats, 60 marching groups, and over a dozen bands. The parade was a response to the rise of Communism and state-sponsored atheism in the Soviet Union.

June 28, 1954: Members of a Sunday School (that was held at Central School in South Windsor) got to turn the sod for a new Presbyterian church hall. The children are Charlene Groombridge, Joyce Neilson, Betty Jane Smith, Ian MacDonald, and Carol Hollenshead, from left to right. Behind them are Ian Troup, Reverend Scarth Macdonnell, and T.U. Neilson. The hall—and sanctuary that would be built ten years later—were named after Dr. H.M. Paulin, former minister of St. Andrew's Presbyterian Church.

The new Most Precious Blood Roman Catholic Church on Tecumseh Road, July 1955. The church burned to the ground in 1978 and was rebuilt the following year at Meldrum Road.

An aerial view of the Mary Day parade in 1955 as it travelled down Ouellette Avenue. According to *The Star*, it was the largest and most successful parade yet, taking two hours to pass any given point on the three-mile route.

September 17, 1955: An overflow crowd packed into St. George's Anglican Church for dedication services for the new structure. Conducting the ceremonies, at the altar, is Right Reverend George Luxton, Bishop of Huron. The church's rector was Reverend M.C. Davies, who also served as Windsor-Walkerville's MPP from 1945 to 1959.

April 23, 1956: The ceremony of "knocking on the door" opened the first service at the new Glenwood United Church in Sandwich West Township. From left to right are Austin Craig, Reverend H.A. Bunt, Reverend E.G. Turnbull, and Donald H. Sirett, chairman in charge of dedication services. The congregation would build a new church building only six years later.

The construction of St. Barnabas Anglican Church on Tecumseh Road was nearing completion in 1956. With its use of concrete and modernist style, *The Star* called the church a part of Windsor's "future look." The city's heritage committee denied a demolition request in 2015, calling it one of Windsor's best examples of 1950s architecture.

"All Together Now": Trinity United Church on Tourangeau Road used a unique method of sod-turning for their new church on October 28, 1956. Over 100 representatives of the congregation—including choir members and Scouts and Cubs—pulled on the ropes attached to a plow as their pastor Reverend C.L. Lewis cut a furrow, aided by Larry Ryan, at left, and Andy Iannicello, at right.

September 14, 1956: Jerry Glanz, president of the congregation; Rabbi Samuel S. Stollman; Cantor Saul Shenker; and Elder Michael Noble, from left to right, prepare to lead the ceremony for Yom Kippur at Shaar Hashomayim Synagogue.

May 1, 1957: Dozens of young Catholic girls, in their First Communion white, pass by Wyandotte Street, joining thousands of other participants in the annual Mary Day parade. The demonstration was witnessed by 25,000 people who jammed the sidewalks of Ouellette Avenue.

Knox Presbyterian Church at 2320 Wyandotte Street W. was dedicated on June 23, 1957. In 2001, the church became University Community Church, and currently hosts Green Bean Café in its basement.

July 11, 1959: 100 cars form "pews" for the first drive-in church service by St. James United in Remington Park. The church's slogan for the services was: "Come in Your Car. Come as You Are."

September 1, 1960: Windsor's first Liberal Jewish congregation, Temple Beth El, opened their temple at 1172 Ouellette Avenue in the home of the late Simon Meretsky (who owned Palace Cinemas). Rabbi Sherwin T. Wine, with the help of Arthur B. Weingarden, at right, places the Torah in the Ark during the formal dedication of the sanctuary on November 19.

November 6, 1960: The first service at Emmanuel Baptist Church at Foster Avenue and Woodward Boulevard began with a march of the congregation to the new building from their old church at 3249 Turner Road, led by the Salvation Army band. The new building featured a modern style: a "floating roof."

Pictured here in 1960, the Gracanica Serbian Orthodox Church on Tecumseh Road was the largest church of its kind in Canada when it was built in 1952. The Byzantine-style church is a replica of the Gračanica monastery in Kosovo.

After a Sunday service at St. Joseph's Church in River Canard, circa 1960. At the time, the church was the third largest in the Diocese of London.

June 3, 1961: Sister Antonia looks over her handiwork, a mosaic of the crucifixion behind the main altar of St. Michael's German Roman Catholic Church, with Reverend C. Moullion.

November 14, 1960: St. Michael's Slovak Greek Catholic Church on Byng Road celebrated its Saint Day with special services, including a processional pictured here.

January 6, 1962: The boys' choir of All Saints' Anglican Church practise with their music director Graham Steed. Three members of the choir were selected to sing with the national choir in 1963.

Paulin Memorial Presbyterian Church was built in 1964, and features a non-conventional, modern design by local architectural firm Johnson & McWhinnie. Located at 3200 Woodland Avenue at Norfolk Street, the church still holds service today.

The boy's choir at St. Mary's Anglican Church in Walkerville, 1962.

"Vanguard of 50,000": Crucifix bearers and altar boys lead the Mary Day parade on Ouellette Avenue in 1963. *The Star* estimated that 50,000 people took part in the annual march.

September 30, 1963: Over 75 men and women staged a protest at Gracanica Serbian Orthodox Church against what they called "communist infiltration" of the church, claiming that the newly appointed Bishop Stephen Lastavica was a puppet of the Tito regime in Yugoslavia. A fistfight broke out between the demonstrators and other members of the church, who accused the protesters of being instigated by the John Birch Society, an extremist right-wing political group from the United States.

The interior of St. Luke in the Fields Anglican Church in Remington Park, which opened in 1950. Pictured here in 1962, likely during a harvest celebration service.

According to *The Star*, Windsor's Muslim community had grown to 100 members by 1965, though they had to attend special services at mosques in Detroit. Walking outside of the Islamic Centre of Detroit with its Imam Mohammad Jawa Chirri, at left, are local Muslims Audrey Edwards and Nafi Jasey.

A breakaway congregation from Bethel Pentecostal Church, the new Riverside Evangel Tabernacle opened in 1965. This church would become Calvary Community Church and relocate, while this building, located at St. Rose Avenue and Wyandotte Street East, is now the Foot Care Institute.

Over 300 nuns from Essex County met at St. Mary's Academy to study their religious life on November 1, 1965.

June 8, 1966: Reverend A.M. Mallory inspects posters advertising a tent crusade featuring evangelist Jack West, held in the "tent cathedral" beside Riverside Evangel Tabernacle.

A 20th-century folk mass, sometimes referred to as the "jazz mass," was presented for the first time at St. Barnabas Anglican Church on February 26, 1966. Traditional hymns were presented with a lively "hip-beat," courtesy of the church's York Club and teenage choir. The band, from left to right, are moderator Ken Copeman, guitarist David Light, cantor Ronald Wilson, and Reverend Derwyn D. Jones with Denis Mahoney on the drums.

The white church building at 1604 Dougall Avenue changed hands in January 1966, from the "evangelical fundamentalism" of Faith Tabernacle to a "liberal religion," the Windsor Unitarian Fellowship, in the words of *The Star*. Now painted blue, the building houses Rose City Community Church.

March 28, 1966: Reverend James Ko, assistant minister at St. Andrew's Presbyterian Church, baptized seven members of Windsor's Chinese community: Joe Gain, Mrs. Quo Ying Gain, Mrs. Fun Yung Lim Jean, Mrs. Wai Jing Wong Ng, Mrs. Wai Mai Geu, Wayne Chuck Gan, and Mrs. Joanne May Gan. These were the first Chinese residents to join the church.

The focal point of the Mary Day parade in 1966 was a large wooden cross weighing 700 pounds, to be erected in Jackson Park. Teams of men took turns carrying the 28-foot cross along the parade route. This was the last year a Mary Day parade was held in Windsor due to declining support and attendance.

October 15, 1967: Walpole Island residents gathered at Assumption Church to help mark the 200th anniversary of the parish by simulating the first Catholic mission to the Huron. Performing a traditional dance, from left to right, are Charles Altiman, Lioness Sands, and Leroy Altiman, as Joseph Tooshkenig, chief of the Chippewas, Clarice Nahdee, and Nelson Shognosh look on.

Said Zafar, the imam of Windsor's first mosque, stands at the head of the prayer room. By 1966, Windsor's Muslim community had grown to almost 300 persons.

January 3, 1967: A special Centennial service was held at St. George's Romanian Orthodox Cathedral with all Orthodox clergy in the city participating. From left to right are Reverend Vladimir Milinkovic of the Gracanica Serbian Orthodox Church; Reverend Lukian Steciuk of St. John the Divine Russian Orthodox Church; Archdeacon Valeriu Anania of the Romanian Orthodox Missionary Episcopates; His Grace Bishop Victorin of the Romanian Orthodox Missionary Episcopate; Very Reverend George Nan of The Descent of the Holy Ghost Romanian Orthodox Church; and Very Reverend Nestorian Cicala of St. George's Church.

December 11, 1969: Imam Said Zafar leads prayers during the celebration of Eid-al-Fitr or Eid Ramadan at the newly built mosque at the corner of Dominion Boulevard and Northwood Avenue. An addition to the building was made in 1993, and the mosque is currently Windsor's largest.

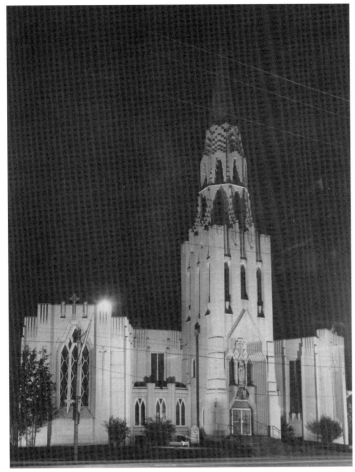

St. Clare of Assisi Roman Catholic Church, circa 1968. Completed in 1931 and designed by local architect Albert H. Lothian, it is believed to be the only Art Deco church of its kind in Canada. The church was slated for demolition in the late 1990s, but was saved by the purchase of St. Peter's Maronite Catholic Church.

"Mass Walkout": About 90 of the 110 parishioners walked out of mass at Sts. Cyril and Methodius Church on November 5, 1973, as part of a month-long campaign to have fired priest, Reverend George Kadlec, reinstated to the parish. A petition, calling for the retirement of the church's senior priest, Reverend Frank Kurta (age 73), drew 87 signatures. Kadlec was fired for refusing to take a post in a London parish.

Right Reverend Charles Carrigan and his housekeeper Alice Ouellette narrowly escaped from a fire that destroyed Our Lady of Mount Carmel Church on March 20, 1976. A passerby noticed the blaze, and with the help of another priest, smashed down the back door of the rectory to rescue Carrigan and Ouellette. The church was rebuilt the following year.

Once considered a "prime example of modern church architecture," St. Philip's Anglican Church opened as the House of Sophrosyne, an addictions recovery centre for women, in 1978.

THE BORDER

People north and south of the Detroit River have long crossed the waterway—before an official border even existed—first by canoe, then boat, ferry (late 1800s), rail tunnel (1910), bridge (1929), and car tunnel (1930). By the 1950s, the border was more than an international boundary; it was a bond between two nations and their Motor Cities.

The joke around Windsor was that "Canada stops at London." Windsorites work, shop, and play across the border; however, in the '50s and '60s, the process was more reciprocal than it seems today. The novelty of Canada was in high demand, and American tourists flooded into Essex County. Records—and *Windsor Star* photos—prove a steady river of cars poured over the bridge and through the tunnel both ways pretty much since their creation.

Certainly by the 1950s, crossing the border was as popular as ever—to which the oft-long lines of cars

using the bridge and tunnel would attest. International bars, restaurants, shopping, outdoor activity: it all beckoned from just a river's width away. As *The Windsor Daily Star* said in 1952 of the popular July 4 American holiday, when an aerial shot showed vehicles stretching from the American side to the Canadian side across the Ambassador Bridge: "Windsor was the largest US city in Canada today as American tourists swarmed across the international border in the vanguard of what travel industry leaders said would be the busiest July 4 weekend in history." *Star* archives also note that the heavy traffic started the previous evening and that "All available Windsor police traffic officers were on duty to cope with the rush." That was hardly the only time cross-border traffic overwhelmed authorities, of course.

Both sides of the border capitalized on millions of annual tourists, mostly visiting just for day trips, to eat, drink, shop, or take in a show. Having a major American city a mere mile across the Detroit River represented such a pot of gold, that Windsor stores and restaurants began marketing specifically to Americans, even before Prohibition. In 1963, Windsor officials took it one step further, erecting a massive lighted sign atop the tunnel's brick ventilation building on the Canadian side, blasting a welcoming message: "Canada: Shop. Stay. Save. Play. 5 mins away!" The same thinking kept a lighted Hiram Walker sign for years atop the waterfront Windsor distillery, until it became too costly to maintain. Even *The Windsor Star* pointed its rooftop lighted sign towards Detroit for decades.

The long-standing good friendship between Canada and the United States, naturally, bubbled over through more than just large signs and hectic border traffic. The international neighbours wanted a lasting symbol of their friendship. So in 1959, the two cities created the International Freedom Festival, a joint event held in Windsor and Detroit to celebrate their cross-border camaraderie. The highlight of the festivities was a fireworks show over the Detroit River, sponsored by J.L. Hudson, the retail department store chain based in Detroit. More than a million people lined both banks to watch the first annual Freedom Festival fireworks, which became an enduring tradition as the largest annually held international fireworks display in the world. A parade, a beauty pageant, a flag raising, an air show, an international Freedom Beacon, and runners crossing the Ambassador Bridge with a flame for a lighting ceremony highlighted just some of the events the Freedom Festival hosted in its grand display of international rapport. A midway coinciding with the festivities eventually popped up to bolster the fun on the Canadian side, as did other activities, such as tugs-of-war between competitors in the two countries.

A particularly memorable event happened on June 27, 1980, when the Ambassador Bridge closed for the first time in its half-century history. Why? So 1,862 Scouts and Guides from Canada and the United States could join hands across the span, once again illustrating the close relationship between the two countries. The International Freedom Festival persisted until 2007 when Detroit and Windsor held separate affairs: Riverdays and Summer Fest, respectively. But the yearly fireworks show continued with a bang.

The border between Windsor and Detroit is more than a physical demarcation, but a potent symbol of international friendship. As a result, when violence erupted in Detroit in July 1967, Windsor was not removed from the action—or the consequences. For two days, the border was closed to non-essential traffic. Windsor firefighters went to the aid of the Detroit department, sending crews of men in rotating shifts. Many citizens feared the violence and racial tensions could spread across the border, prompting City Council to cancel events that attracted Detroiters, like the annual Emancipation Day celebrations. During the five days of rioting, Windsorites gazed across the river as their long-time neighbour burned, with a *Star* reporter distilling their feelings of concern into one remark: "This is the Detroit that we thought we knew."

Windsor and Detroit have a storied relationship that was both celebrated and tested in the post-war decades. And yet, in some ways, Windsor's identity mirrors Detroit more closely than it does the rest of Canada, whether through industry, cultural traditions, or simply close community. Why? More than people and goods crossed the border—so did a shared history.

Vehicle inspection at the Detroit-Windsor Tunnel, July 4, 1953.

March 24, 1949: Maureen Sunstrum, at left, has her purse inspected by customs officer Isabelle DeSalliers. Female agents were a rarity until 1947, when the federal government imposed more rigorous personal searches, as pictured here.

George Trevor, customs appraiser, holds up a hat at a customs auction sale held in the Federal Building in 1949. The items sold were all contraband seized from smugglers and American visitors. The monthly sale, which lasted for several hours, was so wildly popular that customs employees were on hand to prevent eager bidders from stampeding.

July 15, 1949: Freighters began to outnumber the number of passenger boats in the Detroit River after the ferry service between Windsor and Detroit ended in 1938. Pictured here are the remaining regulars: the Bob-Lo ferry *Ste. Claire*, at left, and the *City of Cleveland*, at right, with the *City of Detroit III* in between them.

July 5, 1950: Extra police were on hand to corral American tourists returning home after enjoying their Independence Day holiday weekend in Windsor. Over 5 million people crossed the border into Windsor the year previous.

The Ambassador Bridge, April 1950, one year after the bridge's 20th anniversary. Until the late 1990s, the bridge was painted gloss black.

Canada Customs at the Detroit-Windsor Tunnel Plaza in an undated photograph.

A view of the Detroit skyline, titled "Detroit, Our Friendly Neighbour" by *The Windsor Daily Star*, on June 12, 1951. The tallest building in the skyline is the Fisher Building, while a notable missing feature is the Cobo Center, which opened in 1960.

Memorial Day traffic, May 30, 1951. A sign welcomes American visitors to Essex County, the "Sun Parlor of Canada," while a billboard advertisement for Gray's department store, at far left, beckons potential shoppers. Storefronts along Ouellette Avenue are also visible, including Ritz Millinery, Brown's Silk Shoppes, and Lewis Flowers.

July 4, 1952: American tourists swarmed the Ambassador Bridge in what industry leaders called the "busiest July 4th" weekend in history.

August 21, 1952: The biggest job in Windsor's frequency conversion program, which saw the city change over from 25-cycle power to 60-cycle, was the Detroit-Windsor Tunnel. Here, conversion engineers install the last two transformer units in the tunnel ventilator on London Street East (University Avenue).

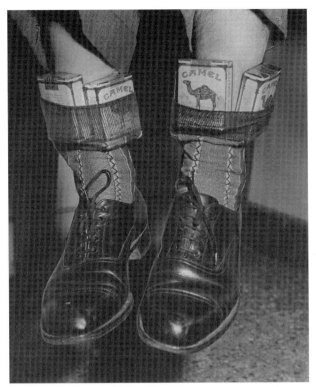

October 18, 1952: A pair of anonymous legs demonstrate a popular method of bringing cigarettes into Canada illegally. While *The Star* insisted the border lacked "big operators," Windsor was fighting a reputation as a 'wide-open' town for smugglers.

An aerial view of Windsor, looking north towards the Detroit skyline, circa 1954.

Bumper-to-bumper traffic emerges from the Detroit-Windsor Tunnel onto the Canadian side, 1954.

June 4, 1955: The Detroit tug *Sachem*, at far left, roars over the finish line in the International Tugboat Race on the Detroit River, while the *Atomic of Amherstburg*, at extreme right, and the *Superior of Detroit*, second from right, battle for second place. The annual tugboat races were a major attraction in the 1950s, and were revived after a long hiatus by the International Freedom Festival in 1977.

This political cartoon from July 2, 1954, shows that cross-border camaraderie as Windsor and Detroit feted each-other on their respective birthdays.

May 5, 1959: Freighters from Europe jockey for dock space in the Detroit River, with the American shoreline in the background. The opening of the St. Lawrence Seaway in 1959 led to increased traffic leaving both Windsor and Detroit scrambling to expand their shipping facilities.

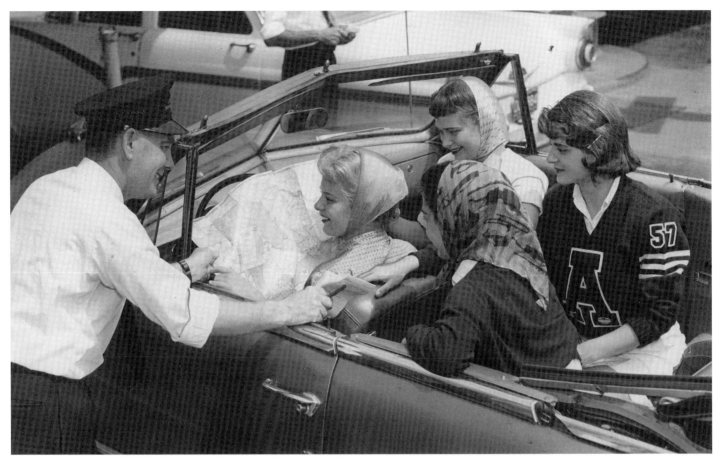

May 30, 1957: Frank Murphy of Canadian Customs gives directions to Susan Grieger and her three companions as they head off for a day of fun in Essex County.

Crowds gathered on both sides of the Detroit River for the International Tugboat Race on May 17, 1958. Here, the *G.F. Becker* tug crosses the finish line in front of the Veterans' Memorial building in Detroit.

July 3, 1959: Thousands of people flocked to the riverfront for the first annual fireworks display sponsored by the J.L. Hudson Company. The show attracted over a million spectators, capping off the first International Freedom Festival, a joint Windsor-Detroit celebration.

"Tunnel Tim" was the newest addition to the Detroit-Windsor Tunnel on September 19, 1959. A mechanical "cop," Tim directed motorists to make a sharp right-hand turn towards customs. Tunnel Tim was axed on November 4, 1959.

July 4, 1961: Windsor's finest hotel waiters practise for the first-ever champagne foot race against Detroit for the Freedom Festival. The team, from left to right, are Ivan Fenkanyn (Norton Palmer), Emil Bertoia (Elmwood), Eric Langlois (Killarney), Vic Fowkes (Elmwood), Jerry St. Denis (Killarney), Joe Wayne (Elmwood), and Lloyd Kelly (Prince Edward). Pictured at right, Vic Fowkes topples a glass while Pius Caruanza of Detroit, in white, moves to pass him. The Detroit squad claimed the champagne trophy, winning out in both order of finish and bubbly left in the glasses.

January 19, 1963: A new sign atop the tunnel ventilating building beckoned Americans to shop in Windsor. Cross-border shopping weighed heavily in favour of American merchants, as Windsorites flocked over the border for larger selection and lower prices.

18-year-old Lorraine Pope was Miss Windsor International Freedom Festival in 1964. Both Windsor and Detroit chose queens who went on to compete in their nation's respective pageants: Miss Dominion Day of Canada or Miss USA.

All available customs and immigration officials were put to work on July 4, 1963, as overwhelming traffic passed over the Ambassador Bridge and through the Detroit-Windsor Tunnel into Windsor. At left, an officer conducts an interview in the car line-up, while at right, traffic piles up at the tunnel. The billboard welcomes visitors to Windsor, "Canada's Biggest City South of the USA."

"We Want You!" Committee chairmen Paul Van der Meer of Detroit and Alderman Frank Wansbrough of Windsor urge residents of both cities to attend the annual Freedom Festival. Wansbrough went on to be mayor of Windsor from 1970 to 1974.

June 30, 1966: Windsor Mayor John Wheelton, at front left, passes the Canadian torch to David Loaring, while Detroit Mayor Jerome Cavanagh hands off the United States' torch to James Maganas. Starting at the international boundary on the Ambassador Bridge, relay runners delivered their torch to their neighbouring country's Freedom Beacon.

This giant scale model of the Ambassador Bridge won first prize for best float in the Dominion Day parade on July 1, 1966.

The International Freedom Festival flag-raising ceremony on the grounds of CKLW television station on July 2, 1966.

Drivers and navigators gather for final instructions before setting out on a 12-hour cross-border Windsor-Sarnia-Detroit race as part of the 1966 International Freedom Festival.

The Tunnel Bus crosses the international boundary between Canada and the United States, circa 1966. The Detroit-Windsor Tunnel is the only international underwater automobile border crossing in the world.

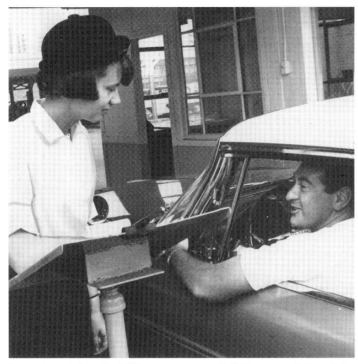

June 21, 1967: Gail Hancox quizzes Bill Somers of Ferndale, Michigan, at the tunnel about his birth, destination, and length of visit. By the early 1980s, nearly 40 percent of customs agents were women.

"A Swing and...": Huntley Farrow pitches to Alderman Frank Wansbrough to launch the Freedom Festival's Sun Parlor International Fastball Tournament on June 27, 1969. Batter Wansbrough's audience, the Hiram Walker and Border Cities baseball teams, faced off following the first pitch.

Fires burn across the border during the Detroit Riots in July 1967. Windsorites flocked to the riverfront to watch the sky, which "glowed red above Detroit's west side by more than 70 fires blazing in the riot-torn area," according to *The Star*. The border crossing was heavily restricted for the first two days, while Americans came across the river on recreational boats to dock at Windsor's marinas. Windsor's Fire Department sent over 20 men and two pumpers in rotating shifts to assist the Detroit Fire Department.

Mayor John Wheelton lights the Freedom Beacon on July 1, 1969. In the background is the Cleary Guest House, packed with sightseers for that night's fireworks display.

Comedian Gordie Tapp accepts a gold medallion, a festival "first" on July 2, 1971. Tapp was the host of the CBC show "The Performers" and appeared on the CBS show "Hee Haw."

A Republic P64, with a smoke generator marking its path, comes in low over a crowd of 25,000 at Windsor Airport on July 1, 1973, for the Second World War air show, part of the International Freedom Festival.

July 1, 1975: Early-bird spectators claim their spot for the J.L. Hudson fireworks later that night. Here, they are entertained by showboats as they wait. 500,000 people packed onto both sides of the border to watch the popular fireworks display.

"Festival Femmes" Narlyn McLean, Chris Bates, and Patti Millar, from left to right, help festival chairman Huntley Farrow (far left) light the International Freedom Festival torch on June 27, 1976. The 20-foot torch in Dieppe Park was "a symbol of unity" between Windsor and Detroit according to *The Star*.

Astronaut Colonel James Irwin was the main attraction at the Freedom Festival parade in 1978. Pictured here riding on a replica lunar buggy, Irwin walked on the moon as part of NASA's Apollo 15 mission.

Festival organizers staged a confrontation between cops and gangsters from Windsor's prohibition era during the Freedom Festival parade on July 1, 1978.

The first annual Detroit Free Press International Marathon took off in 1978. Here, the last runner enters the tunnel.

1862 Guides and Scouts from Canada and the US joined hands along the Ambassador Bridge as part of the "Salute to Friendship" ceremony on June 27, 1980. The bridge was closed for the first time in its 50-year history to kick off the 22nd annual Freedom Festival.

LOCAL HAUNTS

Windsor always knew how to party. Perhaps it was the city's legacy of rum-running and speakeasies during Prohibition. Or maybe it was the influence of a large US neighbour, given that Americans long streamed across for recreation and entertainment on the Canadian side of the Detroit River. Whatever the reason, the generation that came of age in the '60s and '70s frequented a regular circuit of local haunts—whether it be the neighbourhood tavern, a glamorous nightclub, or anything in between, Windsor offered it all.

"Three decades ago, Windsor truly was where the stars came out at night," *Windsor Star* entertainment writer John Laycock wrote in 1998. "So did an international crowd wanting to see the name acts." The glitzy king of late-night entertainment was the Elmwood Casino, which actually offered no gambling. Billed as "Canada's largest and gayest supper club," it opened with an accompanying hotel in 1946 on Dougall Avenue

and closed in 1974 (in a twist of fate, it became the Brentwood Recovery Home in 1983) when showrooms fell out of popularity in the rock 'n' roll era outside of Las Vegas. But it was a heck of a ride along the way in Windsor.

Al Siegel, who also ran jukebox and vending machine operations, launched the Elmwood. Plus, he went on to open the $7-million Windsor Raceway in 1965, adding horse betting to the list of entertainment the city offered. But at the Elmwood, the sometimes prickly, business-minded Siegel—as Laycock wrote, "he counted the olives on the canapé tray"—offered a dance chorus, a house band, vaudeville-style acts, and name stars. Sammy Davis Jr., Jimmy Durante, Sonny and Cher, Rudy Vallee, Victor Borge, Danny Kaye, Wayne Newton, Louis Armstrong, Patti Page, Bob Newhart, Mel Torme, Ray Charles, The Supremes, Tony Bennett, Peggy Lee, Eddie Fisher, Herman's Hermits, and many more visited the Elmwood Casino for gigs, sometimes for a week or more at a time. In June 1972, Tom Jones showed what's new, pussycat, when he sold out 22 shows in 11 days, charging a record $10.50 a ticket.

Since no equivalent venue existed in Detroit, Americans routinely crossed the border for the Elmwood party. "Windsor thought it was part of Detroit, in a way," Laycock said in 2016. "The Big 8 (CKLW, the Windsor station which dominated rock radio in the Detroit market in the mid-'60s) was us. There were a lot of live shows back then. Many of the bars had live bands. It was a fun time." Another spot that drew an American crowd for its shows was the downtown Top Hat Supper Club, owned by Mike Drakich. It attracted the likes of comic/impersonator Rich Little, Syd Caesar, Bette Midler (before she made it big), and Buddy Rich, and lasted into the '90s. Across town, Drakich's brother Nick owned the Metropole Tavern (later the Metropole Lounge) out on Walker Road, which also garnered big names in the '50s and '60s, such as Ricky Nelson. Both establishments offered fine dining, fancy cocktails and top-notch entertainment.

Other swinging downtown hotspots included the Norton Palmer Hotel, the Bamboo Garden, the Prince Edward Hotel, the Radio Tavern, the Lotus Garden Restaurant, and Mario's Tavern on Ouellette Avenue, offering its specialty, prime roast beef. But the party carried on outside the city core, as well. A notable public house on the west side for sheer longevity is the Dominion House, the oldest continually run bar in Windsor. It opened in its current location in 1883, and is going strong more than 100 years later. The famed and fashionable Edgewater Inn, owned by socialite Bertha Thomas, sold in 1964 and became Adam Martini's, featuring a groovy sign that hinted at its newly renovated interior. The Lido had the former Chappell House jumping. Other famed joints also kept the scene alive: the Tecumseh Tavern, the Rendezvous Tavern, The Riviera, The Embassy, the Drop-In Tavern, the Bellevue Hotel, Abars Island View Hotel (demolished in 2016), and the Canada Tavern, which advertised the largest dance floor in southwestern Ontario. The Intersection was a popular teen club before Ontario's drinking age lowered from 21 to 18 in 1971 (then up to 19 in 1978).

The days of rock 'n' roll took the Windsor party scene to another level—when the music was considered counter-culture. Under the influence of Detroit, John Laycock became one of the country's first rock writers in the late '60s, when he penned his lively reviews of the daring new scene for *The Star*. It was an era when local arenas held sock hops, presided over by deejays, sometimes sponsored by CKLW. Windsor Arena held rock festivals, with headliners such as Iggy Pop and the Stooges, attracting local hippies in the '60s and '70s. The Jackson Park band shell, the Griffin Hollow Amphitheatre, and the Jaycees Showmobile all provided popular outdoor venues. A slew of Detroit acts played Windsor high schools in the early days, such as Bob Seger, Mitch Ryder, and Ted Nugent. Shock rocker Alice Cooper caused a stir when he played Walkerville High School, at the height of his outrageous behaviour, when he offended the establishment by his name and look alone.

Local haunts also included various eateries, from diners to fancy fare. A students' favourite, Sam's Italian restaurant opened in 1946 on Wyandotte near Assumption College, while Volcano Pizzeria, one of Windsor's most famous spots, opened in 1957—both among the first pizza parlours in Canada. Volcano's pizza pies proved such a success that the eatery operated a fleet of delivery vehicles, including a number of Jeeps. Windsor pioneered the fast-food drive-in with Hi-Ho Drive-Ins, opened in 1937, with joints like A&W to follow. The United Grill on University Avenue West started in the late '40s, with a major renovation in 1982, offering home-style cooking throughout. Tunnel Bar-B-Q, opened in 1941, provided chickens and ribs for decades. Malic's Delicatessen opened in 1960 on Wyandotte Street East. Elias Deli started in the Bowlero in 1968, and moved to the downtown Norwich Block in 1983. And the champion of downtown meeting spots was S.S. Kresge, whose popular lunch counter even into the '70s provided a nice quick bite for perhaps $2 or $3, not to mention a great place to sit and chat. The Old Fish Market started in 1977 and the Coach and Horses began in 1980.

Plus, the Press Club of Windsor operated with scribes, stories, and suds for almost four decades in the downtown Norwich Block, starting in 1961. Fast Eddy's Arcade opened nearby on Riverside Drive West in 1974, followed the next year by Wheels Roller Rink on Dougall Avenue—both popular hangouts. Dari de Lite and Peerless Dairy in the city and Dairy Freez in the county also attracted throngs in the summer.

Hanging out in Windsor wasn't the problem. Choosing where to hang out was the issue. Depending on whether you were looking for food, drinks, rock 'n' roll, or Hollywood, Windsor, back in the day, had a spot for you.

The Radio Tavern, at 546 Ouellette Avenue, opened it doors on September 27, 1950. The advertisement, at left, boasts of the "Sky Room," air-conditioning, and their ultra-modern dining room. The tavern, with its signature sign, is pictured at right in 1969.

The YMCA building on 511 Pelissier Street, circa 1950. Opened in 1926, the building was a residence and had a gym for community fitness classes. The "Y" moved to Victoria Street in 1974 and this building now houses Chelsea Apartments.

The Talbot House Hotel and Stan's Snappy Snacks, on Wyandotte Street West, circa 1952.

Thanks Kids!

For Our Biggest

Opening Night in Years

- - It Was Grand to

See You Back Again

And Say - - -

Wasn't That 11-Piece Band

A Knockout With

Annette Bernard on the Vocals

Well what are you waiting for

they're back again tonight and

every Saturday at the Beautiful

Masonic Ballroom

BILL RICHARDSON AND HIS ORCHESTRA

It's Gay! It's Colorful! Oh, Well,
You Tell 'Em I'm Stuck For Words

ADMISSION 60c   **THE IONIC CLUB**

The Masonic Ballroom, with its big band led by Bill Richardson, held weekly dances throughout the '50s and '60s.

A fourth Hi-Ho drive-in opened on Walker Road on June 5, 1954. This local chain opened up in 1937—after receiving permission from Walt Disney to use the Seven Dwarfs and Hi-Ho name—and was the first drive-in fast food restaurant in Ontario. The Grumpy Burger was arguably their most popular fare.

Peerless Dairy, at the corner of Monmouth Road and Wyandotte Street East, circa 1950s. The popular dairy bar had several locations across Windsor.

Tunnel Bar-B-Q, at 58 Park Street East, 1957. Opened in 1941, the restaurant was a downtown staple—famous across Windsor and Detroit for their ribs. TBQ closed in 2014 and was demolished soon after to make way for the downtown campus of the University of Windsor.

An interior view of the Pig-N-Whistle Restaurant at 950 Wyandotte Street West, December 1954. Known for their light lunches, exterior signs advertised "Borden Ice Cream" and "Hotdogs & Hamburgs." The building is now part of Szechuan Gardens Restaurant.

Rumoured to be the birthplace of "Windsor Pizza," Volcano Pizzeria Restaurant opened in 1957 and quickly became one of the most popular spots in town. Located at Wyandotte Street and Victoria Avenue, the restaurant was closed in 1986 and is now the site of Jade Chinese Cuisine.

De Soto's Bar-B-Q, at Tecumseh Road East and Drouillard Road, circa 1957. A Windsor Family Credit Union now occupies this site.

Esquire Soda Bar, at Wyandotte Street East and Moy Avenue, 1960.

A *Star* advertisement for the Chicken Court from May 15, 1959. The restaurant remained a favourite date spot for many Windsorites until it closed in 1988.

A local dance hall, the Purple Cow Jazz Clu,b was located on the corner of Drouillard Road and Charles Street in 1961.

An A&W drive-in opened up on 3041 Dougall Avenue in 1960, offering its customers car hop or take home service. While their drive-ins closed in the '80s, a dine-in A&W restaurant eventually reopened on the same block on Dougall Avenue, across the street from the original location.

July 27, 1960: The Windsor Recreation Building, at 41 Pitt Street East, housed White's Tavern, featuring the Elbow Room. It also had two floors of bowling, a billiard parlour, and a cigar store.

February 19, 1960: The Press Club held a fundraising dinner at another local spot: Rendezvous Tavern. East coast lobster and papaya from Hawaii were flown in by Air Canada for the event.

Pictured here in 1964, Island View Tavern—better known as Abars—was an infamous Prohibition roadhouse, rumoured to be frequented by the likes of Al Capone and Babe Ruth. It remained a popular bar for local bands throughout the post-war decades. The bar was controversially denied designation as a heritage building and demolished in 2016.

May 13, 1961: Mayor Michael J. Patrick, at left, and Honourable Bryan Cathcart, Ontario minister of travel and publicity, cut their way into the new Press Club during its grand opening. The Windsor's Men's Press Club found new quarters in 83 Riverside Dr. West and remained there until the Norwich Block was demolished in 1999.

Uncle George's Ice Cream Shop, pictured here in 1962, was a favourite spot for kids in the summer months. To the left is the Sandwich Post Office, which was converted into a cafe in 2016.

Signs light up Ouellette Avenue, looking north from Wyandotte Street, in 1962. Some of Windsor's famous spots can be seen, including: the Norton Palmer Hotel, Bamboo Garden, Prince Edward Hotel, Radio Tavern, and Lotus Garden Restaurant.

Mario's Tavern was most famous for their roast beef, as advertised in *The Windsor Star* in 1962 (pictured at left). The location at 755 Ouellette Avenue, pictured at right in the early 1950s, was one of three locations—the other two located at 493 Ouellette and at the corner of Tecumseh Road and Ouellette Avenue.

The Dominion House, pictured here in 1963, is Windsor's oldest continuously run tavern, dating back to 1878. During Sid Walman's ownership from 1948 to 1986, the DH (as it is often called) became a hangout spot for students at the nearby University of Windsor. The DH is still open for business today.

Elmwood Casino was the leading nightclub in the Windsor-Detroit region in the late '50s to early '70s, regularly bringing in top entertainment acts to play a block of shows. Pictured at the top of the page is the exterior of the club in 1974, with the famed Ambassador Room below. Some of the acts that graced that stage are pictured on the opposite page, during their appearances at the Elmwood: Sammy Davis Jr. in his dressing room in 1961; Herman's Hermits relaxing poolside in 1969; Sonny and Cher during their nightclub tour in 1969; Tony Bennett in 1971; The Supremes (sans Diana Ross) in 1971; Ray Charles in 1972; and Tom Jones (a top-seller) in 1972. *The Star* rarely took pictures of artists during their performances, so many of these shots are staged press-ops or taken during rehearsal.

August 29, 1963: Proprietor Mike Drakich sits in his new Top Hat sidewalk cafe (a Windsor first). The Top Hat Supper Club, located at 75 University Avenue, drew big name acts including Syd Caesar, Bette Midler, Rich Little, and Buddy Rich. A Burger King now occupies this site.

The Bob Seger System played the Intersection, a teenager 'booze-free club' on January 11, 1968. The Intersection featured bands like The Woolies, The Blues Train, and Ted Nugent (who, legend has it, knocked a block out of the stage wall with his guitar).

The Star House, pictured here in 1972, at 792 Gladstone Avenue was owned and operated by the Buchok Family. This building now houses the Gladstone Grill.

The Tecumseh Tavern, 1970. The town's oldest tavern, located at Lesperance Road and Tecumseh Road, was still a popular "suds factory" 160 years later, according to *The Star*.

The Red Barn on Dougall Avenue, 1969. The second location in Windsor, the American fast-food franchise was most popular for their "Big Barney" burger.

July 14, 1973: "Attention salesmen for blue jeans, eye make-up, cigarettes, and bubble gum! They're off and rolling again at the arenas in Windsor, the roller skating capital of Canada." An average of 3,000 teenagers crowded into Riverside Arena (pictured here) or other local arenas every weekend for roller skating. Local sales of roller skates were the highest in Canada.

Bobby Brew's Dalhousie Street Stompers played at the Bali-Hi Motor Hotel on February 4, 1974. Bobby Brew was known as "Windsor's King of Swing" and his bands played the regular circuit of bars and nightclubs.

June 9, 1974: 11,000 people crowded into the Griffin Hollow Ampitheatre, the outdoor venue at St. Clair College, for a free two-day rock festival organized by CKLW Radio. Performers included Bachman-Turner Overdrive and Fantasy Hill. Later that year, the venue hosted a notable music festival—the Ann Arbor Blues and Jazz Festival, even though attendance was not nearly as large as the event pictured here.

July 27, 1974: Camping on Peche Island was a yearly tradition for many Windsorites. High-rise apartment buildings along Riverside Drive East can be seen in the background.

December 11, 1974: Fast Eddy's, the pinball arcade on Riverside Drive, was a popular gathering spot for teenagers. Fast Eddy's was demolished as part of the Norwich Block in 1999.

Lee's Imperial Tavern, located at Riverside Drive and Ferry Street, underwent a complete renovation in 1975. Pictured at left, the Lee brothers—Pete, Jimmy, and Ben, from left to right—raise their glasses while workmen start the construction. The tavern, post-renovations, is pictured at right. Lee's was a downtown staple since its opening in 1932 by their father King Lee (one of Windsor's first Chinese immigrants), and a particular haunt for *Star* staff.

United Grill, pictured here in 1975, is one of Windsor's most enduring downtown spots, dating back to the '30s. Now a luncheonette, the Grill is still open for business.

August 12, 1975: Hordes of customers flocked to Kresge's counter daily for a quick, inexpensive lunch. Most diners told *The Star* that they spent $2–$3 per meal at the downtown department store. S.S. Kresge closed in 1991 and a Royal Bank of Canada was built in its place.

Players pack the tables at Santa Anita Bingo Hall on Ouellette Avenue in the late 1970s. This building, known as the Knights of Columbus Auditorium, housed Coral Gable Ballroom in the '40s and '50s.

January 17, 1976: Belly dancer Naga performs at the El Morocco Tavern at 1190 Wyandotte Street West.

"Restaurant Row," 1978. Pictured here looking east are The Old Fish Market, which opened in 1977; Fiddler's Restaurant with DD's Disco; and L'Auberge de la Bastille which specialized in Acadian cuisine. By 2016, these buildings were all closed with their last tenants being the Loop Complex, the City Beer Market, and the Chatham Street Grill.

Canada's first Big Boy restaurant set up shop in Windsor in 1978. This location on Tecumseh Road eventually became a Golden Griddle and is now another breakfast joint: Rise 'n Shine Cuisine.

July 11, 1977: Pat Suttak leans against her bicycle in Ambassador Park, watching Cloud, a local rock band. Free concerts, sponsored by the Department of Parks and Recreation, were regularly held at the riverfront or at other parks around the city during the summer months.

Rendezvous Tavern, another of the former Prohibition road-houses, was still in operation in 1980. It was eventually torn down to make way for a housing development, Rendezvous Shores.

June 29, 1976: According to *The Star*, The Garrison Room's discotheque at the Richelieu Inn (formerly the Seaway Inn) is one of the "swingingest places in town."

September 25, 1979: Windsor's first pancake house opened on Tecumseh Road with an ambitious plan to be open 24/7. It would soon face competition from an IHOP, also located on Tecumseh Road, just east of Lauzon Road.

The Bavarian Tavern, formerly the Metropole Tavern, at Walker Road and Niagara Street, was closed in 1975 due to financial difficulties. The Metropole, owned by Nick Drakich, was famous for its Smörgåsbord dinners and big-name entertainment acts. The site has been occupied by many restaurants since, including: California's, Big Tony's Original Wood Fire Pizza Co. and now Walkerville Eatery.

The Ye Olde Steak House opened on Chatham Street West in 1966 and quickly became a Windsor institution. Pictured here in 1980, the spot was famous for its fine dining—and French onion soup. Ye Olde Steak House was closed in 2007.

The Coach and Horses opened in the basement of the Old Fish Market complex in 1980. An infamous Windsor haunt, countless local bands played at the Coach and Horses until it closed in 2015 when the Loop Complex was sold.

Mother's Pizza Parlour & Spaghetti House, a franchise out of Hamilton, Ontario, drew a devoted following for its 99 cent "Noodle Nights" and family-friendly atmosphere. In 1980, a second restaurant was opened at 6415 Tecumseh Road (pictured here), in addition to the popular location on Ouellette Avenue.

FORD

The Ford Motor Company's rebranding campaign "Go Further," which debuted in 2012, might as well have been Windsor's slogan in the 1950s. The company launched the automotive industry in Canada in 1904 with its Windsor plant, originally called Walkerville Wagon Works, on Riverside Drive East. The Ford Motor Company of Canada's popular products could, of course, literally take people far. And the company itself fared well, becoming Canada's biggest company in the 1970s. But from a Windsor perspective in the 1950s, "going further" had a more ominous meaning—the company's operations started shifting out of town. In 1953, the unthinkable happened: Ford Motor Company of Canada announced it was moving its Windsor assembly operations to Oakville. Moving out of Canada's Motor City? Windsorites were aghast.

The *Windsor Daily Star* reported the shocking news on October 31, 1951: "Oakville gets huge Ford plant." Just two years earlier, some 13,700 Ford employees toiled in Windsor. But one heart-wrenching decision from the company that many considered inextricably linked to Windsor would cost the city 3,800 jobs, or 40 percent of UAW Local 200, which represented local Ford workers. New Ford of Canada president Rhys M. Sale said in a statement that the Oakville plant would be "better than 200 miles nearer to our principal automotive markets," meaning the greater Toronto area. But Windsor watchers suspected something else. They couldn't help but

think the move was really in retaliation for the historic 99-day Ford strike of 1945, as well as other union moves that boosted worker strength. UAW Local 200 was not about to rest on its laurels, despite orchestrating what a union publication calls "the most significant event in Canadian labour history." The 1945 Ford strike, helmed by reserved-but-determined Local 200 president Roy England, was only the beginning of the battle, bringing union security, improved vacations, overtime premiums and more. The push continued under Jack Taylor, who took over as Local 200 president in 1951.

The company wasn't about to simply stand by and lose ground, however. It had its own plans, regardless of union wishes—including shifting operations to Oakville. Sending work out of town stung that much more given that Sale was a born-and-raised Windsorite. He started locally as a Ford clerk before being named president of the Canadian company on January 1, 1950. Regardless of what his personal feelings or motivations might have been, as a company man, Sale facilitated the whole controversial deal—and many in Windsor took it personally. Nevertheless, the tall, athletic Sale was at heart a determined businessman (who only retired in 1962 after 47 years as a Ford employee).

However, Ford had not abandoned Windsor completely. In fact, earlier in 1951, the company broke ground on a multi-million-dollar expansion of the Windsor power plant, originally designed in 1923 by famed American industrial architect Albert Kahn. Not finished yet, Ford also announced a major investment into a state-of-the-art engine plant. Still, some Windsor Ford workers felt betrayed, and for a number of years tensions—if not an all-out power struggle—seemed to percolate just below the surface between the company and the union. In 1951, two separate wildcat strikes erupted over the dismissal of workers. In 1952, Ford workers struck again, this time only for two days. Yet the company-union relationship was far from repaired. A strike in 1954 was at first postponed, thanks to the intervention of Mayor Arthur Reaume; however, 4,000 workers nevertheless walked off the job a week later. Though this strike didn't go down in history quite the way the infamous 1945 Ford strike did—perhaps because there was no car blockade at ground zero—it actually proved even longer. The work stoppage dragged on for a record 110 days. When the dust finally settled, however, workers had won hourly increases, hospitalization insurance, and vacation benefits. Plus, the healing began.

Perhaps as a symbol of improved relations, Henry Ford II himself visited Windsor on February 8, 1955, to tour what had been known as Plant 4, but was retrofitted to turn out a product that would prove particularly lucrative for Windsor: Ford engines. That said, Ford—renowned for having invented the assembly line—continued its trend of manufacturing efficiency, making the new plant particularly automated for the day. The high-tech facility prompted *The Windsor Daily Star* to predict that automation was bringing a "pushbutton plant steadily closer."

The push-pull relationship, however, remained part of the Ford-Windsor narrative—perhaps as a defining characteristic—for some time. Investment in Windsor seemed to coincide with Ford continuing to pull away from the city. In 1955, the company moved its head office to Toronto. Still, production continued apace in Canada's Motor City. In fact, a symbolic gold-painted product—the two millionth engine—rolled off the line at the Windsor plant on September 12, 1955. Ford added an afternoon shift in 1960, creating 400 jobs. But it closed its trade school in 1961, as the back-and-forth continued between the Canadian company and Ford City.

In 1966, thanks to the Auto Pact signed a year earlier, Ford considered its engine plant "single purpose." It followed the trend of most Canadian automotive companies, reducing the number of models but increasing the amount of production. So Windsor focused on the beefy V-8 engine for Canada and the United States. By the late '60s, Ford was roaring along, thanks in part to the quintessential muscle car: the Mustang. Yet in 1969, in another bitter pill for Windsor, the original Ford of Canada factory on Riverside Drive East, known as the Walkerville Plant or Plant 1—and the former site of the company HQ—came to an end. The plant where Model Ts once rolled off the line, but which had sat idle since the '50s, was torn down in favour of grassland.

Then on August 15, 1978, good news came: Windsor was selected for a $553-million engine plant in the east end, creating 2,600 jobs. Good times, they were a-rollin'. Prime Minister Pierre Trudeau even came to town to turn sod with a golden spade, alongside Ford of Canada president Ray Bennett and Minister of Intergovernmental Affairs Thomas Wells. The Essex Engine Plant opened in 1981 to pump out V-6 engines. Over the years, Ford built six plants in Windsor, though only two, the Windsor Engine Plant and Essex Aluminum Plant, would remain active past 2009.

Despite the changing relationship, Ford never completely abandoned the city, making significant investments into both its factories and the community. One thing about the auto industry, which Windsorites know well, fortunes fluctuate up and down. People must adapt. In that way, Windsor was built Ford Tough.

Ford Motor Company of Canada, circa 1950.

The last model of 1949 came off the line on August 16th, the eve of the company's 45th birthday. From left to right are: Cecil G. Sampson, George H. Bates, Horace H. Greenfield, and Robert S. Bridge, all company executives. In 1949, Ford Motor Company of Canada Ltd. employed 14,500 workers, 13,700 of which worked in plants and offices in Windsor.

March 27, 1950: Over 6,000 members of the Local 200 UAW-CIO packed into the second floor of the City Market to hear a report on the stalemated negotiations between the union and Ford of Canada. Roy England, Local 200 president, addresses the crowd at the microphone.

April 3, 1950: Local 200 officials give the thumbs up after Ford workers voted overwhelmingly in favour of a strike. From left to right are: Roy England, president; Jack Taylor, vice president; Jack Lawler, financial secretary; George Burt, Canadian director of the UAW; and Thomas MacLean, assistant director. In a dramatic turn, the strike was averted the night before it was scheduled to begin, as the membership accepted a last-minute contract offer.

September 22, 1950: Theodore J. Emmert, vice president for Ford of Canada, left, and Robert S. Bridge, vice-president of manufacturing, operate the digger to start excavation on a multi-million dollar addition to the power plant. At right is the Ford Powerhouse post-construction, with two new, shorter smokestacks. Designed by Albert Kahn, the Powerhouse was originally constructed in 1923 and still stands today on Riverside Drive East.

"In Demand": A backlog of more than 3,000 new cars were jammed into factory storage lots due to a shortage of box cars in 1951. Transports worked overtime to haul away cars, as manufacturers were producing a record 1,100 vehicles per day. Car-hungry dealerships from across Canada started shipping drivers into Windsor by car, plane, and train to drive back new cars.

October 2, 1951: Members of the Local 240, for Ford office workers, set up a impromptu picket line to protest the dismissal of a co-worker and the demotion of two others. After six days of strike, office workers voted almost unanimously to return to work.

The Windsor Daily Star

Windsorites received a massive shock on October 31, 1951, as Ford of Canada announced that all vehicle assembly operations would be transferred from Windsor to a new plant in Oakville. A statement by president Rhys M. Sale gave the reasoning that the plant would be closer "to our principal automotive markets," but many in Windsor believed the move was in response to Windsor's growing notoriety as a militant union town. Though Ford promised new investment in Windsor's engine plant, the immediate impact of the move was the loss of 3,800 jobs.

A vote on January 21, 1952, resulted in 93 percent in favour of strike action at Windsor's Ford plants. Negotiations were tense between Ford and the union, particularly after the Local 200's wildcat strike in December 1951 over the firing of 26 employees that the company considered instigators.

February 19, 1952: Ontario Labour Minister Charles Daley announces to the press that a new contract had been reached between Ford Motor Company and Local 200. The new contract meant the end of a two-day strike, dispelling anxiety for Windsorites who feared another drawn-out Ford strike.

August 19, 1952: The massive Ford of Canada water tower dominates the foreground with the chassis plant, the foundry, and the engine plant stretched out behind.

The Regal Building, used for the storage of maintenance supplies, caught fire on May 15, 1953. With flames and smoke reaching hundreds of feet in the air, it took ten units of the Windsor Fire Department, plus workers from the plants, to put the blaze out.

Ford of Canada officials made a full inspection of the new powerhouse expansion on February 25, 1953. From left to right are: Rhys M. Sale, Ford of Canada president, with his hand on the main control valve; Homer F. Bickhart, manager of power and utilities; and R.S. Bridge, vice-president of production. According to *The Star*, the Powerhouse was capable of generating sufficient power for a city the size of Windsor.

May 11, 1953: Rhys M. Sale, at left, and senior executive Mike Cochrane pose next to the first car off the line at the newly opened Oakville Assembly Plant. Born and raised in Windsor, Rhys M. Sale became president of Ford of Canada in 1950 and was in charge of moving the assembly plant and head offices from Windsor to Oakville. Windsorites, most of whom had a personal connection with "Ford's", felt betrayed by Sale as one of their own.

Labour Day, 1953. While the float laments the "20,000 jobs" lost to Oakville, it also warns that Windsor could become a "ghost town" if the city's industries didn't work together.

October 4, 1954: Local 200 president Charles McDonald addresses a meeting of Ford of Canada workers, where they agreed to postpone a strike at the Windsor plant. The vote was held at the behest of Mayor Arthur J. Reaume, who attempted to mediate last-minute talks to prevent a walkout.

Despite postponement and prolonged talks, 4,000 Ford of Canada workers walked off the job on October 10, 1954, after unanimously voting in favour of a strike—an escalation alluded to in that day's political cartoon in *The Windsor Daily Star*. George Burt, regional UAW director, declared that the "company is determined to break the union in this strike." Pictured here are Local 200 members William Hughes, George Lee, Al Liddell, and Hank Renaud, preparing signs for the picket line.

January 18, 1955: On day 101 of the strike, the wives of Local 200 members joined their husbands on the picket line.

Enough, Enough!
Mostly cloudy, -cold
6 a.m. 4; 2 p.m. 13
Low tonight 8, high tomorrow 13
Low yesterday 8, high 22
Sun sets 5:20, rises tomorrow 7:50

The Windsor Daily Star Extra

The Canadian Press—Associated Press—United Press—Reuters—Associated Press Wirephoto

Weather page 14, financial page 29
Theatres, amusements page 43

VOL. 73, NO. 124   50 PAGES   WINDSOR, ONTARIO, CANADA, THURSDAY, JANUARY 27, 1955   Authorized as Second Class Mail Post Office Department, Ottawa   FIVE CENTS

110-DAY-OLD FORD STRIKE ENDED

Relieved workers on the picket line celebrate as news of a settlement between Local 200 and Ford Motor Company of Canada reached them on January 27, 1955. At bottom left, the Ridleys, one of thousands of Ford families in Windsor, excitedly read the details in an extra edition of *The Star*. The strike, which lasted for a record 110 days, produced a contract that included hospitalization insurance and vacation benefits.

Henry Ford II, in the front middle, toured Windsor's engine plant on February 8, 1955. Formerly Plant 4, the new plant was completely refitted to turn out Ford of Canada engines. Walking on either side of Ford are R.S. Bridge, vice president of manufacturing, at left, and W.F. Tyson, plant manager, at right. In the back row are T.J. Emmert, vice president of Ford of Canada, and Rhys M. Sale, president, from left to right.

Clarence Payne performs checks in the engine testing section at Ford Plant 6 on February 12, 1955.

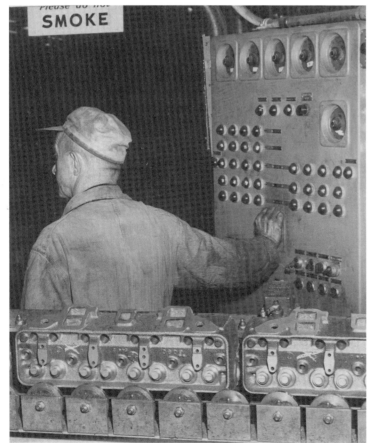

April 18, 1955: Automation was becoming commonplace in Windsor's busy auto plants, particularly in the refitted Ford engine plant. At left, a machine operator, with his hand readied on the control, determines if all is well in the plant based on the coloured light panel. At right, a worker examines an automatic balancing machine for testing motors.

Painted gold in celebration, the two-millionth V-8 engine produced by Ford of Canada came off the line at Windsor's engine plant on September 12, 1955. W.F. Tyson, plant manager, W.P. Park, manager of manufacturing, and Fred Gordey, from left to right, give the engine its final inspection.

This advertisement from June 25, 1955, features Ford's V-8 engines, made for the Canadian market at Windsor's engine plant.

Holding their textbooks, these three students, F.R. Lakeman, L.E. Smith, and G.A. Kudo, from left to right, were top of the class at the Ford Trade School in 1955. Here, they are congratulated by school superintendent C.B. Moncrieff, at far left, and Ford of Canada president Rhys M. Sale. The Ford Trade School closed its doors in 1961.

"Engine City": Ford of Canada added an afternoon shift at its engine plant in 1960, creating more than 400 jobs. The production hike meant that Windsor was churning out nearly 7,000 engines daily between Ford and Chrysler Canada.

"Thumbs Up at Ford": Company and union representatives at Ford of Canada were pleased with the results of their canvas for the United Fund's Red Feather campaign (United Way) in 1964. From left to right are J.G. McIntyre, general manager of Ford in Windsor; Reginald Rudling, Jack Taylor, and Al Liddell from Local 200; Sam Millinoff, campaign representative, and T.L. Wickett, company canvas chairman.

May 25, 1966: J.S. Stevens and Robert McCaig, Ford of Canada engineers, study the blueprints of the equipment that will replace the old cupola from the power plant.

"Single Purpose Plant": Ford's engine plant reopened in 1966 after undergoing a complete transformation. Instead of creating nine basic engines, the plant now produced a single series of V-8 engines that it supplied to Ford plants all over Canada and the United States. This V-8 engine would be affectionately nicknamed the 'Windsor.'

Wrecking hammer Ford plant's Joshua

"The Walls Tumble Down": The original Ford of Canada Plant 1 complex met the wrecking ball in December, 1969. This was where the Canadian automotive industry was born in 1904, and where thousands of Windsorites worked the assembly line, churning out Model Ts and other vehicles until the plant closed in the early 1950s. Pictured at bottom is the site post-demolition in March 1970, looking west towards Hiram Walker. The 17-acre riverfront property remains undeveloped.

13,000 Ford of Canada workers walked off the job on January 19, 1971, including 5,000 at Windsor's plants. The week-long strike resulted in wage increases and improved dental benefits.

This advertisement, from *The Windsor Star* on June 2, 1966, reflects the success that Ford Motor Company and its Canadian counterpart experienced in the late 1960s. Fuelled by popular models like the Mustang, production reached record levels by the end of the decade.

"P-P-P-Picketing": Sub-zero temperatures greeted the picket line on November 29, 1973. Ford of Canada workers endured the cold for two weeks, returning to their jobs after ratifying a new contract that featured voluntary overtime.

The Windsor Star

106 Pages   Tuesday, August 15, 1978   20 Cents

⋆ Final

Ford plant: It's official

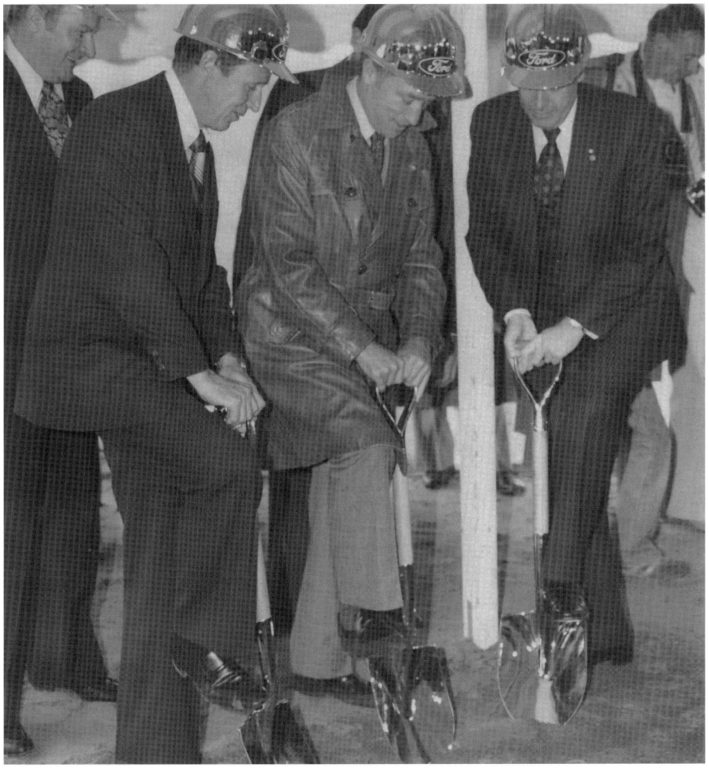

In 1978, Ford of Canada announced that Windsor was officially selected as the site for a $553 million engine plant. Located in the east end, the plant would add 2,600 jobs to Windsor's economy, plus thousands of jobs for supplier industries. Prime Minster Pierre Trudeau, centre, does the honours at the sod turning on October 6, 1978, with Roy Bennett, president of Ford of Canada, at left, and Thomas Wells, Minister of Intergovernmental Affairs. The Essex Engine plant was opened in 1981 and created V-6 engines.

April 12, 1980: Tradesmen from the Local 200 demonstrate for jobs at the new engine plant that was under construction. The union insisted that many of the jobs that were being done by outside tradesmen had historically been done by its members.

"Mothballed": Windsor's casting plant was closed, albeit temporarily, in 1980, putting 965 out of work. The foundry was revived in 1981, and stayed open until Ford's *The Way Forward* plan announced its closing in 2007.

CHRYSLER

Chrysler Canada's glory years were something to behold, especially from a Windsor perspective. Like most companies, Chrysler had its ups and downs, but at various points in the 1950s, 1960s, and 1970s, the company churned out cars like candy—making Windsor's fortunes particularly sweet.

The Chrysler Corporation of Canada began June 17, 1925—taking over the Maxwell-Chalmers Motor Company in Windsor—only 11 days after Walter P. Chrysler founded the Chrysler Corporation in Detroit. The Canadian branch expanded its factory at what was then the outskirts of Windsor in 1929 and added an engine plant next door in 1938, but a new era began in 1949 when it built the Chrysler Centre office building beside its factories and really focused on its Canadian operation. Ohio-born Edward Charles Row took over as Chrysler Canada president in 1951. A second shift was added at the assembly plant in 1954, creating 2,000 jobs, while construction of the iconic V-8 engine began at the expanded engine plant in 1955. In the late 1950s, Windsor produced a number of stylish Chrysler vehicles, often with the then-fashionable "Forward Look" design. E.C. Row made such a mark presiding over this period of post-war growth that the city named what would become its biggest road after him, the E.C. Row Expressway.

"When E.C. Row retired as head of Chrysler Canada in 1956, the industry was abuzz with rumours about his possible replacement," writes James Mays in *The Chrysler Canada Story*. "Who would run the Canadian subsidiary? Would head office finally appoint a Canadian?" Head office did indeed finally choose a Canadian to lead the increasingly successful Canadian division. Toronto-born Ron Todgham—who started in the company mailroom in Windsor and once worked as a chauffeur for Chrysler Canada's first president, John Mansfield—assumed operations north of the border.

Under Todgham in the early 1960s, Chrysler Canada production jumped 50 percent. In 1964, he doubled the production run to more than 100,000 cars a year. In 1965 the US-Canada Auto Pact came into effect and, as a result, in the following year, Chrysler Canada boosted its exports of Valiants and Darts to the US market—given that the international deal meant Canada would produce fewer models but more of each type. In fact, in 1966 Todgham predicted that Chrysler would double its production again by 1970. Windsor continued pumping out cars like they were going out of style. In some ways, the big cars *were* going out of style. By 1971, overproduction forced Chrysler to store excess vehicles at a Highway 3 drive-in theatre. Meanwhile, by 1974, largely due to the OPEC oil embargo the year before—when motorists endured long lines to buy gas—demand for smaller cars made some of Windsor's beefier products harder to sell. Still, Chrysler went ahead with a new $44-million Pillette Road Truck Assembly Plant, which operated until 2003.

Todgham had taken 15 years off from his career at Chrysler to run some successful dealerships, but when he grabbed the reins at Chrysler he once again shone as a company man—going on to become the longest-serving Chrysler Canada president, with 19 years at the helm before he retired September 30, 1975. C.O. Hurly became the next Canadian-born president until 1979, while Canadian Donald H. Lander took over until 1980 when fellow Canadian Moe Closs was tapped for the top job.

More than just the company and executives flourished in the post-war period, of course. So did employees. Windsor's Chrysler union began life in 1942, when workers voted to join United Auto Workers Local 195, an amalgamated union that represented most of Windsor's autoworkers at one time or another. In 1956, Chrysler workers decided—hesitantly—they needed to branch out on their own, so they formed UAW Local 444, which would go on to become the most powerful union local in Windsor. It didn't happen easily. Many workers opposed the idea, and mounted a determined campaign against a split union. But the fledgling local won out—as did a new era in Windsor unionism. The creation of Local 444 ushered in the most legendary local labour leader of all time, Charlie Brooks, who spearheaded a series of advances for workers over the years. In those days, Chrysler workers also established their big-hearted nature. In 1964, for instance, Chrysler Canada employees raised $113,000-plus, the largest amount of any employee group since the United Fund (which would become the United Way) began in 1947.

With Brooks at the helm and relative solidarity among members, over the next two decades Local 444 achieved gains in wages, cost-of-living allowances, improved working conditions, supplementary unemployment benefits, pensions, relief time, and much more. Local 444's gains were often replicated at other area union locals, though it took serious resolve. Between 1956 and 1977, Local 444 went on strike five times, the longest lasting 56 days (in 1962). After an almost six-week strike in 1965, the union secured a three-year contract featuring a 7.8 percent wage increase and improved working conditions, which the union boasted was "the largest single monetary package in the history of industrial unionism in Canada and the United States." In 1976 another milestone came about when 75 women joined the assembly line. And in 1977, the 500,000th Cordoba—Chrysler's answer to their big-car conundrum—rolled off the line.

But the heady days of 444 ended in tragedy on January 17, 1977: Brooks was shot dead by a disgruntled Chrysler worker. The union, and much of the city, was in mourning. Frank LaSorda took over as Local 444 president from 1977 to 1982, though he had to contend with a period of strife, when the company demanded concessions. In 1979, declining market share brought labour unrest, given that the union claimed Chrysler had created 3,500 fewer jobs than promised under the 1965 Auto Pact.

Chrysler needed help. And since the company was so important to the country, the federal government intervened. Gord Henderson wrote in the May 12, 1980 edition of *The Windsor Star*: "It took nine harrowing months but Windsor's battered economy has been given a billion-dollar reason for renewed faith in the future." Industry Minister and longtime Windsor MP Herb Gray helped secure a $200-million aid package that saved Chrysler from bankruptcy. The loan guarantees were to begin in 1982, and in return the company pledged to invest $1 billion back into Canada.

Unfortunately for Windsor, 1980 was also the year Chrysler closed the Windsor Engine Plant, which was demolished to make way for a Windsor Assembly Plant expansion. Times were tough. But Chrysler would rebound again. The city couldn't know it yet, but it would be only three years before famed American Chrysler president Lee Iacocca would visit Windsor to personally launch a front-wheel-drive revolution that would again boost the area's fortunes: the super-successful Dodge Caravan and Plymouth Voyager minivans. The ups and downs of Windsor mirrored the highs and lows of the auto industry—especially Chrysler, which for decades served as Windsor's largest employer. The health of Chrysler also stood as a symbol of the well-being of an entire area, which at times fared very well indeed.

Jobless auto workers line up in front of the Chrysler of Canada employment offices on November 22, 1954. An expansion at the corporation included the employment of a second shift, opening up 2,000 spots for these hopefuls.

July 5, 1955: Kenneth Crittenden, vice-president of manufacturing; William Eddie, operating manager; and Fred J. Cowell, plant manager; inspect the first Chrysler V-8 engine produced in Canada, made at the engine plant in Windsor.

Chrysler Corporation of Canada, circa 1955. Looking north, the building in the background is the assembly plant, with the power plant to the left, and engine plant in the foreground. The administrative buildings called the Chrysler Centre are located at the middle right.

October 27, 1955: E.C. Row, at far left, president and general manager of Chrysler Canada, shows off the new Canadian Dodge model, a four-door hardtop convertible, to Reeve Bernard Roy of Sandwich East, Controller Thomas R. Brophey of Windsor, and Joseph Morand, planning board chairman, from left to right. Edward Charles Row was president of Chrysler Canada from 1951 to 1956, and spearheaded a period of rapid expansion. The City of Windsor named their expressway in his honour.

December 15, 1956: This 45-foot Christmas tree, located on company property on Tecumseh Road East, was Chrysler of Canada's Christmas gift to Windsor. The silver-coloured spruce tree was decorated with over 300 lights and ornaments. Christmas music played daily until January 2.

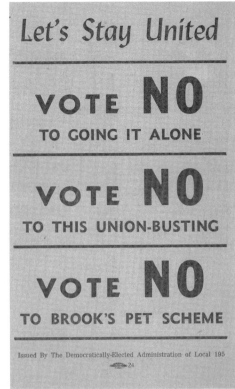

On June 13, 1956, a vote was held to determine whether the Chrysler unit of Local 195 would form a separate local. Pictured here are union members Albert Rutt, Frank Nantais, Gil Gervais, and Clifford Taylor, from left to right. Local 195 president Earl Watson was strongly opposed to the idea, as is seen in the strong language against Charles Brooks, leader of the new local movement, in the "Vote No" pamphlet, at right. The Local 444 for Chrysler workers received its charter on July 2, 1956, with Charles Brooks as its first president.

Chrysler of Canada and Local 444 UAW settled contract differences for a new collective agreement on December 17, 1956, the first negotiated with the new local. Union spokesmen estimated that the deal would yield 34 cents an hour, including wage hikes and fringe benefits, over the next two years. The union negotiating committee, in the front row are, from left to right, Thomas MacLean, George Burt, Canadian regional director; Charles Brooks, Local 444 president; and Ron Johnson, committee member. In the back row are, from left to right, John Eldon, UAW representative; Nels Dearing, Nick Radu, Arthur Taylor, Donald Knight, and John Costello.

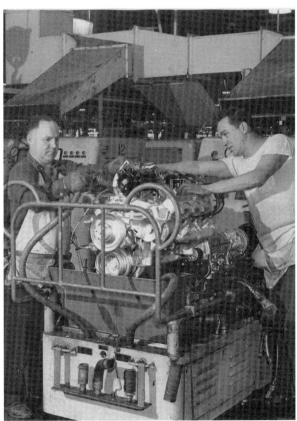

Russ Ducharme, at left, and Danny Bannon test new Chrysler engines at the Windsor plant on December 31, 1957. The engine plant underwent a multi-million dollar expansion in 1955 and was now equipped to produce 650 units per working shift.

August 4, 1960: Lorne Wheelter, electrician, at right, and Bill Ellwood, clean and adjust electrodes during the retooling process. That summer, Chrysler plants in Windsor were closed for three weeks for a "retooling shutdown," as the plants were reorganized for production on the next year's models.

The headquarters of Chrysler of Canada, circa 1960. *The Star* labelled it as "one of Windsor's most attractive structures." Designed in 1948 by William R. Souter & Associates of Hamilton, the building was demolished in 2003 and is now a parking lot. Chrysler's headquarters are now located at 1 Riverside Drive, commonly called the "Chrysler Building," erected in 2002.

Body finishing at Chrysler, 1961.

Chrysler advertisement with the famous slogan "What Chrysler Builds Builds Windsor," 1962.

August 27, 1962: For the first time in several years, Chrysler turned out a 'made-in-Canada' New Yorker. Previously imported from the United States, its return to Windsor signalled a policy shift of increased Canadian production. Standing by the car at the end of the main assembly line are: John J. Ricardo, vice-president and operations manager; Joseph Neal, vice-president of manufacturing; and Ron W. Todgham, corporation president, from left to right. Todgham was the first Canadian-born president of Chrysler Canada, and he helmed the company from 1956 to 1975.

"Chilly Chore": Strikers at the main gate of Chrysler reward themselves with coffee after braving a winter storm to maintain the picket line on February 19, 1962. After fifty-six days of strike, thousands of Windsor workers returned to their jobs, including Jack Robertson, Gordon Spink, and Gerald Drouillard, from left to right, who enter the main gate of Plant 3 for their 7:30 a.m. shift. The strike resulted in a new three-year collective agreement.

Workers crowd around a 1963 Dodge, the first convertible ever to be built by Chrysler of Canada, as it came down the production line on September 18, 1962. In the left foreground is Ray Smith, production manager. Increased production of different models made in Canada was part of the company's strategy to reduce imported vehicles from the United States.

"Economic Boom": By the end of 1963, production at Chrysler Canada was boosted 50 percent. The 1964 production run of 100,100 passenger cars was more than double the number of cars that the Windsor plant built in 1962.

Stock was rolling out of Windsor's Chrysler Canada Ltd. plants in the fall of 1964. Large trains moved out of the plant twice daily, with the train pictured above carrying 120 new Chrysler products, the equivalent of two hours' production at the plant.

Chrysler was thriving in the late 1960s, particularly in the eyes of company president Ron W. Todgham, who made this bold claim (which *The Star* borrowed for their headline) during a speech in Windsor on February 2, 1966. In 1965, retail sales of cars were up 18 percent and truck sales were up 25 percent from 1964.

November 14, 1964: Chrysler Canada Ltd. employees pledged the largest amount of any employee group since the United Fund (United Way) was founded in 1947. The total pledge of $113,132 was 31 percent more than the plant's quota. The fund workers holding up the banner, are Norm Wheeler, Shirley Irwin, J.C. Pike, Charles Brooks, A.F. Kennedy, general chairman; James Phillips, and Frank McKinnon, from left to right.

"Record-Setting Contract": Chrysler workers walked off the job on January 22, 1965, shutting down operations at the three plants and Walker Metal Products Ltd., a Chrysler subsidiary. After nearly six weeks of strike, Chrysler Canada Ltd. and Local 444 agreed on a new three-year contract, considered to be record-breaking by the union. A firm, three-way handshake between John H. McGivney, director of personnel; Charles Brooks, Local 444 president; and George Burt, Canadian Regional Director of UAW, from left to right, marked the conclusion of the marathon negotiations. The agreement featured a 7.8 percent wage increase over three years, the introduction of a more comprehensive Green Shield drug plan, and improved working conditions.

"That's a Big One!": Chrysler Canada Ltd. reached another milestone on June 15, 1966, as the 150,000th passenger car came off the Plant 3 assembly line, setting an all-time production record for a single model year. C. Ray Smith, left, and Sam Kain, production manager, stand by the 1966 Chrysler Windsor two-door hardtop.

Chrysler Canada Ltd.'s truck plant at the corner of Tecumseh Road and McDougall Street, circa 1966. Plant One, the original Maxwell-Chalmers factory, was converted in 1931 and remained in truck production until 1978. The factory primarily made Dodge and Fargo trucks. It served as the Imperial Quality Assurance Centre from 1980 to 1983 and is now a shopping centre.

A combination of fashion and automotive design for 1968 was previewed at the annual Chrysler Girls' Club fashion show, where Chrysler Canada Ltd.'s new car lines were unveiled on September 15, 1967. Here, Evelyn Lesperance, Alice Miller, and Eleanor Green, from left to right, model the latest fashions in a special sneak peek for *The Star*.

THIRD CHRYSLER MYSTERY FIRE

March 8, 1967: D'Arcy Cole, president of the Cedar Springs Hospital Auxiliary, receives the keys to a 1967 station wagon by the presidents of Chrysler Girls' Club, Bev Minnis and E.T. Huggard, from left to right. The Chrysler Girls' Club raised money for charities like their 1967 beneficiary, the Cedar Springs Hospital in Chatham-Kent.

March 18, 1968: Firemen survey damage from a third mystery fire in the cushion department of the Chrysler assembly plant. The same storage area was hit with fires on March 9th and 11th. While the first fire was chalked up to careless smoking, by the third incident Fire Chief Harold Coxon declared that there was "suspicious origin."

Chrysler workers in Windsor, Etobicoke, and Ajax went on strike on January 24, 1968, as company and UAW negotiators continued marathon discussions to try and reach a settlement. At left, workers at the truck assembly plant decided to express their feelings by walking out early. They were soon joined by workers at the engine plant, pictured at right, who formed a picket at the main gates near Chrysler Centre. A new three-year contract agreement was reached by February 1st, ending one of the shortest strikes for Chrysler in several years.

June 19, 1968: Ron W. Todgham, president of Chrysler Canada Ltd., is shown here with the record 200,000th car to come off the Windsor production line that model year. Chrysler officials estimated that 212,000 cars would be produced before the 1969 models started production at the end of July.

President Ron W. Todgham presents the keys of a 1970 Plymouth wagon to Junior Achievement president Paul Almost on May 8, 1970. Chrysler had a strong legacy of supporting students through organizations like Junior Achievement of Windsor or their own scholarship program, established in 1964.

The Local 444 executive was booed and pelted with empty beer bottles during a ratification meeting for Chrysler Canada workers in Windsor Arena on January 28, 1971. The incident started when nine men carrying placards paraded onto the ice to protest the contract negotiated by the union and Chrysler. As this contract covered all UAW Chrysler workers, many in Windsor felt that even though the agreement did not alleviate their in-plant conditions, they could not reject it because it was tied to the Americans. The contract was ratified by a narrow margin.

"Sneak Peek": *Star* photographer Jack Dalgleish found an opening just big enough for the lens of his camera to get a "preview" shot of the new 1971 Plymouth Satellite, a totally new model that Chrysler was attempting to hide from prying public eyes.

February 21, 1971: Chrysler Canada Ltd. had to get a little creative with its storage space, turning to the drive-in theatre on Highway 3 to temporarily store its 1971 models. The company claimed that it had not overproduced, but was building cars faster than they could be shipped.

The administration of Local 444 was re-elected on June 9, 1972, defeating the candidates from Workers Unity. Celebrating the victory are, from left to right: Glenn Watkins, second vice president; Charles Brooks, president; Nels Dearing, financial secretary-treasurer; and Ed Baillargeon, first vice president. Workers Unity was composed of young workers who were opposed to the union's international ties.

Local 444 members packed into Windsor Arena to vote on their latest contract on September 20, 1973. The vote would end a nine-day UAW strike across Canada and the United States that idled fifty plants and over 100,000 Chrysler workers.

July 20, 1972: J.B. Neal, Chrysler Canada's vice president of manufacturing, at left, and Windsor engine plant manager J.L. Woodard draw attention to a new record. This engine was the 500,000th passenger car engine built in Windsor during the 1972 model production run. The Windsor engine plant turned out over 2,000 engines a day, and was most famous for their V-8 engines.

Windsor Assembly, 1974. By the mid-1970s, Chrysler sales in the United States were starting to drop as the OPEC oil embargo saw demand increase for smaller, more efficient vehicles. Canadian sales held steady, but cars began to pile up in storage areas around Windsor plants. At right, the last model of 1974 rolls down the assembly line on July 29th.

Chrysler's new truck plant in December, 1975. The light-truck assembly plant was completed in 1974 and largely produced their popular B-vans. The plant remained in production until 2003, and was demolished shortly after.

The assembly line at the Pillette Road Truck Plant, circa 1979.

November 4, 1978: Engine plant workers block traffic as they march along Chrysler Centre to the company personnel office on Tecumseh Road. They were objecting to working conditions in their plant and the slow negotiations for a local contract.

Chrysler Canada's truck assembly plant welcomed its first female workers, as 75 women took their places on the assembly line on August 24, 1976. Wielding a torque wrench is Pat Tanguary, on the left, assisted by Betty-Anne Conliffe.

June 7, 1977: Charles Regal, owner of the 500,000th Cordoba produced at Windsor's Chrysler plant, gets a handshake from plant manager Don Leask as he wheels the car off the assembly line. The Cordoba was produced exclusively in Windsor, and its high-margin sales saved the Chrysler brand, whose specialty, 'full-size' vehicles, had fallen out of favour with the American market.

May 3, 1979: Local 444 leader Frank LaSorda stands to make a point during a meeting between union officials and area MPs and MPPs to discuss the planned layoffs and production cuts at Chrysler Canada Ltd. Seated at LaSorda's left is Buzz Hargrove, UAW Canadian regional administrative assistant, who declared that Chrysler Canada employed 3500 fewer workers than promised under the Auto Pact. By 1979, Chrysler was facing a market crisis, with declining shares and high inventories, prompting plant closures and mass layoffs across the United States and Canada.

"Demonstrate for Jobs": More than 200 UAW members marched in front of Chrysler Canada Ltd.'s administration building on their lunch hour on May 10, 1979, to protest the planned layoff of 550 workers at the company's engine plant. The UAW demanded that the layoffs be halted and that six-cylinder engine production be returned to Windsor. Far left is Local 444 president Frank LaSorda, who succeeded Charles Brooks, who was tragically murdered in 1977.

"Chrysler's Secret Saviours": The all-new Chrysler Cordoba, middle, and Dodge Mirada, far left and right, were the company's biggest hopes to turn their sales around in 1980.

Industry Minister Herb Gray was largely responsible for a $200 million dollar aid package that would save Chrysler and its Canadian offspring from inevitable bankruptcy. The loan guarantees, which would begin in 1982, were intended to prompt a renaissance for Windsor's biggest employer. In return, Chrysler promised to invest $1 billion back into Canada, meaning that Windsor stood to be the biggest beneficiary.

GENERAL MOTORS

General Motors of Canada's Windsor adventure took a lot of turns over the years. The biggest twist came in the 1960s, when it switched from engines to transmissions and interior accessories. And though GM was the first of the Big Three automakers to leave Windsor entirely, it also displayed a particularly impressive expansion in the city when business boomed.

General Motors made a gradual entry into Windsor, given that it took over a number of plants and companies before the GM name was actually used locally. The company officially started in Windsor in 1928, when plants were retooled to assemble truck chassis (and eventually GMC and Chevrolet trucks). Another facility started building engines. The peak of engine production came in 1953 when Windsor made 203,500 of them, churning out such powerful fare as Rocket V-8 engines. Things were speeding along, but GM had even bigger plans for the city down the road.

In 1955, General Motors even rolled in a little fun with a Windsor stop for its Parade of Progress, a four-day affair featuring a 44-vehicle caravan and 40-minute stage show seen by some five million people around the continent. The assemblage included a dozen "Futureliner"

vans camped out on the grounds of Kennedy Collegiate in a circus-like atmosphere with a show GM at the time said, "dramatizes the vital role of science in everyday life." It added some zip to what, for many workers, was mostly all business at the factory: punch in, work the line, punch out.

In 1963, however, something changed that defined Windsor GM—and had local employees shifting gears. The public, too. Engine production moved to St. Catharines, while Windsor became the only place in Canada making automatic transmissions. Besides the manual Synchromesh, Windsorites made the two-speed automatic Powerglide. The result was a sprawling 1.6-million-square-foot Windsor Transmission Plant that encompassed several buildings eventually connected by a landmark covered bridge over busy Walker Road. You couldn't drive down that part of Walker, squeezing between giant structures and under the bridge, without feeling the massive presence of GM. By 1980, the company grew again, tearing down its beautiful art deco administration building in the name of expansion, making room for Hydra-matic transmissions and boosting workers from 1,200 to 3,800.

Yet investment didn't stop on Walker Road. GM opened the Windsor Trim Plant in 1965 on Lauzon Road at the cost of $20 million, marking the largest project in GM Canada's history at the time. "This modern factory ushered in a new era of manufacturing with its tinted glass, light-coloured stone exterior and brightly lit airy factory floor," recalls *GM: 90 Years of Windsor History*, a commemorative union publication. The factory, which pumped out a variety of automotive interior components, also employed a significant number of women, another anomaly of the times. In 1977, the Lauzon Road facility added plastics injection moulding in order to up the ante in terms of products. The plant was sold in 1997 to Peregrine and then to Lear Corporation.

Of course, more than just the company made its mark in Windsor. So, too, did General Motors employees. Well-paid autoworkers developed a reputation of generosity and GM workers were no different, with Christmas funds, special events, and a host of charitable causes. In fact, in 1962 GM workers made history thanks to the highest participation rate of any company or group with 97 percent of employees contributing. GM workers joined forces on behalf of one another, as well—voting to join the UAW Local 195 in 1937. But the biggest GM union move in Windsor came in 1973. That's the year General Motors workers branched out on their own; naming their brand new local after the year it began, under first president Alix Sinkevitch who reigned until 1981.

Like most strong union movements, even before their individual UAW Local 1973 ever materialized, GM's workers didn't shy away from a fight. Much effort and strife was required. On September 18, 1955, for instance, some 17,000 GM workers across the country walked off the job, launching the longest automotive strike in Canadian history. It lasted a gruelling 148 days, though when the dust settled workers had secured better wages and working conditions. In March 1968, Windsor police arrested 13 people over two days, charging GM protesters with obstructing police who were ushering supervisors into the plant during another strike. Yet after two months on the picket line, the conflict paid dividends: Windsor workers achieved wage parity with their American counterparts. The workers struck again in 1970, though at just a few days, it was short-lived compared to the marathon work stoppages of the past. Long strikes became as outdated as car fins. Both the company and the union had perhaps learned how to work better as a team—at least for a while.

The city later would endure utter shock when GM shut down its Windsor operations completely. In 2010, the company shuttered its 46-acre transmission property and equipment such as the 1,000-ton presses—ending nine decades of history in Canada's Motor City. But along the way it helped create not only scores of distinctive cars, but generations of families raised on the work of General Motors.

General Motors of Canada building, early 1960s.

General Motor's "Train of Tomorrow" made a brief stop in Windsor on September 22, 1949, en route to London, where a new diesel locomotive factory was under construction.

The site for a new addition to the General Motors engine plant on Walker Road in 1950. In the 1950s, Windsor-made General Motors engines were being exported to ten countries around the world, including Peru and Pakistan.

The General Motors "Parade of Progress" road show visited Windsor in June 1955. The travelling science exhibition featured "modern wonders and curiosities," including mammoth diesel vehicles and a miniature hydrogen explosion. The show attracted 6,000 Windsorites.

Windsor's plant produced a variety of General Motors engines, including the "Rocket" V-8 engines found in the popular Oldsmobile line.

Plant workers Ray Rivait and John Kereks cast their ballots during a strike vote on September 12, 1955. GM locals across Ontario voted overwhelmingly in favour of coordinated strike action. The strike would last 148 days.

Headon!

September 18, 1955: 17,000 workers set up picket lines at five General Motors of plants across Canada, including Windsor's Local 195. At left, strikers in Windsor march outside the engine plant with placards advertising their demands, including guaranteed annual wages. As alluded to in the day's *Star* cartoon, this was the largest strike Canada's automotive industry had yet faced.

February 13, 1956: Local 195 picketers at General Motors received a morale boost when 100 members of Local 200, from Windsor's Ford plants, joined the picket lines for a joint demonstration. Leading the parade are Alix Sinkevitch, far left, chairman of the General Motors' plant unit, and Charles McDonald, at right, president of the Local 200, walking behind the pipers.

News that the 148-day strike was over reached the picket line in the early hours of February 14, 1956. Keeping the midnight watch, from left to right, are Lance Hodges, Del Coulsey, John Egeto, and Ted Brown. General Motors largely gave in to the union's demands, and workers walked away with wage increases, improved working conditions, and health plan coverage.

Windsor's General Motors engine plant on Walker Road, circa 1956.

The engine line at General Motors, December 1957. By year's end, the plant employed more than 1,000 workers, turning out 150,000 engines a year.

February 28, 1962: GMC workers set a new record in the Community Fund drive for the United Way, with 97 percent of employees participating. Reviewing the results, from left to right, are Cec McGinnis, general foreman; William Evans, assembler; Leo Butnari, union member; and Alix Sinkevitch, chairman of the union shop committee.

August 22, 1962: Workers add finishing touches to the engines on the conveyor before they are tested and painted.

The Windsor Star

Windfall
SNOW
5 a.m. 8, 9 a.m. 13, 2 p.m. 19
Low tonight 12, high Wed. 28

VOL. 89, NO. 137   30 Pages

WINDSOR ONTARIO TUESDAY FEBRUARY 12 1963

FINAL
★★★★

SEVEN CENTS

GM TO MAKE AUTOMATICS HERE

General Motors announced on February 12, 1963, that it would build automatic transmissions in Canada for the first time in Windsor. Engine production was shifted to McKinnon Industries in St. Catharines.

February 12, 1963: Called the "Pretty Miss with Transmission" by *The Star*, Mary Capik shows what a completed Powerglide unit looks like, with her thumbs up of approval.

Automatic transmission assembly line at the Walker Road plant, 1963. McKinnon Industries Ltd., a GMC subsidiary, took over Windsor's plant, replacing engine production with a full range of automatic and manual transmissions.

"New Look": The former General Motors of Canada engine plant on Walker Road completed its transformation to a transmissions plant under McKinnon Industries Ltd. with updated signs in 1964. McKinnon Industries operated the plant until the company was dissolved into General Motors of Canada in 1969.

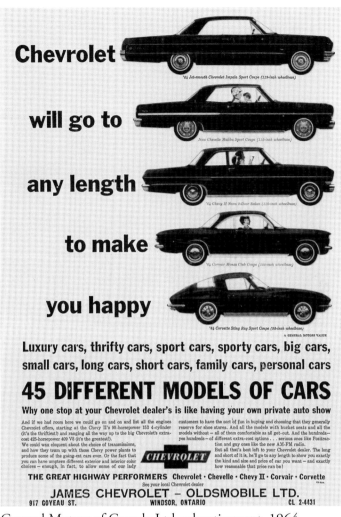

August 18, 1964: Edwin H. Walker, president of General Motors Canada, at left, and Reeve Louis Parent of Sandwich East Township, tighten the ceremonial last bolt for the framework of the new $20 million GM trim plant, under construction on Lauzon Road.

General Motors of Canada Ltd. advertisement, 1964.

July 14, 1965: Millwright strikers use their signs for rain protection outside the GMC trim plant. After a week off the job, the construction workers accepted interim contracts so they could resume work.

Reeve Louis Parent, GMC president Edwin H. Walker, and Mayor John Wheelton, from left to right, cut their way into the new trim plant at its grand opening on November 25, 1965. Holding back the makeshift door made of automotive interior fabric are plant employees Valeria Graham, at left, and Louise Wiper.

"Industrial Innovation": Workers enjoy a Windsor 'first' at the new trim plant on November 25, 1965: an escalator. *The Star* reported that it was able to carry 5,000 people per hour.

A two-shift birthday party was held at the General Motors trim plant on April 5, 1966 to mark its first anniversary. Ann Provost, at left, and Janet Hastings—two of the plant's 38 original hires—cut the cake with A. Grant Warner, plant manager.

The new General Motors trim plant, 1965. The plant was considered one of the most modern facilities in Canada.

December 31, 1965: The GM trim plant differed from Windsor's other major industries in that the majority of their hourly workers were female. According to *The Star*, it took a "woman's touch" to trim a new car's interior properly. Here, an employee tacks the lining on a door panel.

Cutting fabric at the trim plant, circa 1966. After one year of production, the plant had grown to 1,380 employees.

June 29, 1968: Winston D. Morris, at far right, collects his prize from foremen W.E. Sol, at left, and M.D. MacMillan after coming up with a winning idea for the GM Suggestion Award program. His proposal for quality control improvements for door trim assembly earned him a cheque for $2,136.

Strikers mill around entrance of General Motors' trim plant on Lauzon Road

Cec Southward

CHARGES FOLLOW GM INCIDENT

March 20, 1968: Members of Local 195 staged massive demonstrations at the two General Motors plants, resulting in 13 arrests over two days. Picketers were charged with obstructing police as they attempted to block supervisory personnel from entering the plant. The UAW strike, in both Quebec and Ontario, began February 9th over contract negotiations.

Trim plant workers listen to the details of a new contract agreement at Teutonia Hall on March 28, 1968. In a victory for the union, the contract featured wage parity with American workers and was quickly ratified, ending a 48-day strike.

September 19, 1970: Pat Bachalo, a door trimmer, pauses in her picket duties to apply lipstick on the fifth day of strike action against General Motors of Canada.

November 11, 1970: Raymond Present, 18-year-old picket captain at the trim plant, tears up his sign as news that the Americans and General Motors had reached an agreement. While this did not end their strike, local workers hoped it would induce a settlement in Canada. Unfortunately, the strike in Windsor stretched on for over a month longer.

Windsor business and government leaders toured the trim plant on May 18, 1976. Pat Howe operates a sewing machine while Mayor Donald Lappan of Tecumseh, J.A. Pegg, plant manager, and Bob Duddy, president of Windsor Chamber of Commerce look on.

Adolph Mallat guides the 5-millionth automatic transmission off the line on September 14, 1978. Production at Windsor's plant was on track to double by 1980.

January 29, 1980: An aerial view of the General Motors transmission plant, with Kildare Road in the foreground. Note the plant's signature stack and water-tower. The transmission plant closed in 2010 and is in the process of demolition in 2016.

A Windsor industrial landmark for 50 years, the art deco General Motors administration building on Walker Road fell to the wrecking ball in February, 1980. The demolition was part of GMC's massive expansion of the transmission plant, which would increase the workforce from 1200 to 3810.

BUSINESS
& INDUSTRY

Windsor's forte was making cars, but despite its one-trick reputation, it boasted lots of other business interests to keep the city busy over the years. Fuelled by the economic boom of wartime production, Windsor entered the 1950s with promise, as automotive production continued to spawn a variety of parts manufacturers and create a climate for business to thrive.

Windsor and Essex County's growing size—and increasing industrial might—created the need for shipping, in and out. Several railways serviced the area, including the Essex Terminal Railway which carried goods from east-end factories through to Amherstburg and the Canadian National Railway station downtown, which closed in 1961. However, this meant that when they were hit by work stoppages, local business suffered, as was the case during a 1950 national rail strike which the *Windsor Daily Star* said held "a paralyzing grip on the nation's economy." The Detroit River, long a conduit

for business and pleasure alike, continued to feed industry in the post-war period—aided by the opening of the St. Lawrence Seaway in 1959. Canada Steamship Lines operated out of a busy dock in the 1950s. The Morton Terminal in Ojibway opened up in the 1958. But CSL also had a local connection: Paul Martin Jr.—the future prime minister and son of one of Windsor's most popular politicians ever—became president of the international shipping company in 1972. He endured an eight-week strike in 1974 and bought the company with the help of two partners in 1981.

The Big Three carmakers, of course, continued pumping out products, marking the city's largest industry, but also stimulated the rapid growth of parts industries. Windsor Tool & Die, which started in 1927, enjoyed several expansions along the way, including a major one in 1964 at its Kildare Road site. Kelsey Wheel (later Kelsey Hayes) added a $1.6-million expansion in the mid-1960s, nearly doubling its Windsor operations. International Tool Limited, founded by Peter Hedgewick in 1945, is considered the predecessor to much of Windsor's current tool, die, and mould making industry. Other automotive feeder industries, like Champion Spark Plug, Walker Metal Products, and many others helped Windsor power along in the 1950s and later.

Many other companies, big and small, also contributed to the local economy, through good times and bad. Hiram Walker & Sons, the local king of whisky, which expanded its offerings and continued sending spirits abroad in the post-war days, celebrated its 100th birthday in 1958 with a number of events. Another major local industry, The Canadian Salt Company, (which started its first mine in 1893 at 30 Prospect Avenue as the Windsor Salt Company), was bought by Morton Salt in 1954 and opened a second mine at 200 Morton Dr. in 1955. Other businesses helped maintain the "Made in Windsor" brand, from Purity Dairies, International Playing Card Company, Holiday Juice, Jamieson Laboratories, and Welles Corporation—even Willys of Canada Ltd.

Another major sector of Windsor's economy was retail and shopping. Downtown was the area's mecca of consumerism in the first part of the 20th century, but as time went on, shopping expanded. Ottawa Street and Drouillard Road were popular spots to shop in the 1950s and later, as were Erie Street, Wyandotte Street, Huron Church Road, and a growing number of strip malls farther and farther from the city core. In 1970, Devonshire Mall emerged as the juggernaut that stole many customers and spelled the end for certain downtown businesses in particular.

Some notable stores provided Windsor with more than just good shopping and variety, but iconic shops. Nate Tepperman started his door-to-door business in 1925, though he soon turned his efforts into a successful Ottawa Street furniture store. He opened a 30,000-square-foot warehouse at Dougall and Ouellette when the area was rather barren, and expanded again in 1973 and 1978. Gray's Department Store, opened on Ottawa Street in 1925 by Harry Gray—father of Canada's first Jewish cabinet minister, Herb Gray—underwent a 7,000-foot expansion in 1964. Founded in 1929 by Sam Freed as Sam's Place, the Ottawa Street clothier now known as Freeds went on to become Canada's largest independent men's store, growing through the '70s and beyond. The Brotherhood Department Store opened in 1940 on Ottawa Street, and upgraded to a "bigger and brighter" version with a 3,500-square-foot addition in 1963. A group of struggling pharmacists joined forces in 1962 and formed what would grow into a string of Big V pharmacies, now Shoppers Drug Mart. Woolco's $1.3-million building opened in Eastown Plaza in 1968, prompting *The Star* to declare, "this type of centre is the new general store." It was an era when name stores in Windsor served almost as cultural hubs, local ones and chains alike, such as F.W. Woolworth, S.S. Kresge's, Zellers, and Kmart.

As a car town, Windsor always endured ups and downs with the ebb and flow of the auto industry. Highs and lows were inevitable. But the only way the city could truly survive is through a diversity of business and commerce, which Windsor served up with flair, wearing overalls or suits alike.

Stan Brown Transport Ltd. makes a delivery, circa 1953.

The Windsor Bedding Company Ltd., circa 1950. A 1959 city directory places the company at two locations: 90 Wyandotte Street and 620 Glengarry Avenue.

August 25, 1950: It was business as usual for Essex Terminal Railway, ordered by the union to stay on the job despite a nationwide strike. The ETR line, founded in 1902, connected Windsor's industries with larger railway lines, running from factories in East Windsor to Amherstburg.

A fleet of Checker Cabs in front of the company's garage and service station at Park Street West and Pelissier Street, circa 1950s.

The receiving entrance of Gotfredson Truck Corporation at 2470 Wyandotte Street East, circa 1950. The plant produced trucks in the '20s and '30s, but continued to manufacture parts until 1960. Complete Packing Inc. now occupies this site.

The Seely Building on Church Street, 1950. The company based in Windsor and Detroit produced perfumes and extracts, but the building was sold that year to the Bell Paper Company.

Nate Tepperman in front of Tepperman's Furniture Store on Ottawa Street near Pierre Avenue, circa 1950. Tepperman started out as a door-to-door salesman in 1925, and grew his company into a furniture giant and a fixture on Ottawa Street.

Advertisements for Sam's Department Store, 1950s. These billboards were located on Gladstone Avenue, around the corner from the storefront at 1526 Ottawa Street. Sam's Department Store, famous for its one-cent sales, was founded by Sam Freed in 1929. The family business exists today as Freeds.

A neighbourhood clothing store, Morris Dry Goods was located at 1012 Drouillard Road, pictured here in June 1951.

August 21, 1951: The official company flag of Hiram Walker & Sons Ltd. was lost for 20 years before being located by an employee. Around the flag, from left to right, are Cecilia Tessier, Margorie Allen, Pat Marchand, J.P. Carr, and Wilfred Downes.

Standard Paint and Varnish Company Ltd. at 845 Wyandotte Street West, 1952. The factory, which produced household paints and industrial coating, was sold to Rinshed-Mason Company in 1952. It would burn down in 1953 and be quickly rebuilt. The factory exists today as BASF Windsor.

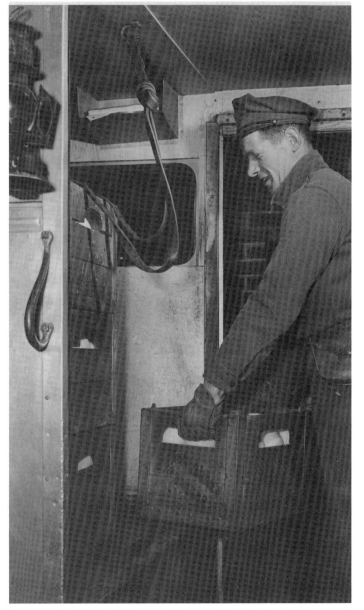

An aerial view of Hiram Walker & Sons Ltd., circa 1954.

January 9, 1954: Milkman George Minello loads his truck at 6 a.m. for his morning run. Purity Dairies Ltd. delivered milk daily to 16,000 customers from their facility on Howard Avenue.

The Windsor Daily Star EXTRA

Couldn't Last
Colder, damper
6 a.m., 32; 2 p.m., 48
Low tonight 38, high tomorrow 46
High yesterday 50, low 29
Sun sets 6.09, rises tomorrow 7:22

The Canadian Press—Associated Press—United Press—Reuters—Associated Press Wirephoto

Weather page 19, financial page 36
Theatres, amusements page 35

VOL. 71, NO. 144   44 PAGES   WINDSOR, ONTARIO, CANADA, FRIDAY, FEBRUARY 19, 1954   Authorized as Second Class Mail, Post Office Department, Ottawa   FIVE CENTS

C.I.L. PLANT BUILDINGS SINKING

February 19, 1954: A sudden cave-in at the Canadian Industries Limited plant on Windsor's west side suspended all operations at the chlorine manufacturing plant. Pictured at top, the sinkhole developed from a cave-in of abandoned underground mine shafts 1,000 feet below the surface, used for salt-brining 50 years previous. Buildings, pipelines, and even Essex Terminal rail lines, pictured at bottom left, were destroyed in the subsidence. At bottom right, a group of workmen use a heavy pump to drain the sinkhole's lake during the months-long cleanup. As a result, CIL ceased its operations in Windsor and 300 employees lost their jobs.

Champion Spark Plug Company of Canada Ltd. unveiled its 1955 production secrets for a select few automotive journalists on September 30, 1954. Examining the new spark plugs, in the hands of employee Pauline Brunelle, are Charles A. Speers, Roly Pepper, and Remy Le Poittevin, from left to right.

The Ojibway Rock Salt Mine opened in 1955. At left, workers operate a diesel-power loader, which loads salt onto waiting shuttle cars at a rate of 12 tonnes per minute. At right, workers bag the "highway salt," one of the mine's products. By 1957, 175 persons from Windsor and LaSalle were employed at the new mine, which had a yearly output of 750,000 tonnes a year.

Monarch Mattress Manufacturing Co. on Wyandotte Street East and Gladstone Avenue in the late 1950s. Monarch opened in 1948 and remained in business until 2015.

Fabrication Bay at the Canadian Bridge Company plant on Walker Road, 1957. One of Windsor's oldest industries, the plant shifted from wartime production of tugboats and marine engines to building steel for construction projects.

February 7, 1957: Goodwill Industries in Windsor opened a new clothing outlet at 1067 Drouillard Road. From left to right are E.W. Lancaster, Joseph Peltier, M. Frank Brobst, Betty Hill, and W. Rae Burnie.

December 31, 1957: John Morocko trims a crankshaft at one of the large furnaces at the Dominion Forge plant. An feeder industry for Windsor's automotive plants (primarily for Ford of Canada), Dominion Forge employed 900 workers at its height in the 1960s.

December 31, 1955: This advertisement announced the opening of a new Beaver Gas Station on Tecumseh Road East. Started by Donald Plumb, Beaver Gas Stations were locally owned and operated until they were sold to Shell Oil in the '60s.

December 31, 1957: Surrounded by wheels is James Brown, an employee of Kelsey Wheel Company Ltd., which specialized in making steel wheels for the automotive industry. The company, which became Kelsey-Hayes, closed its doors in 2009 after 96 years in business.

Workers package up Windsor Salt table salt, circa 1957. The Canadian Salt Company Ltd.'s mine at Prospect Avenue produced household grade salt, employing 150 persons who work on the brine wells and evaporators. It is still in operation.

September 5, 1958: Executives of Hiram Walker & Sons Limited autograph the first barrel of Canadian Club Whisky produced in the firm's second century of operations.

Windsor's first two-storey commercial brick building dating back to the 1870s on Riverside Drive at Louis Avenue was home to a pest control service in 1958. This commercial building is still standing and remains unoccupied after its last tenant, *The Drive* magazine, vacated in 2007.

January 19, 1963: The Meretsky & Gitlin Furniture storage building, located at 255 Riverside Drive East, was Windsor's first town hall. The cornerstone from 1856 is shown inset. The building was demolished in 1963.

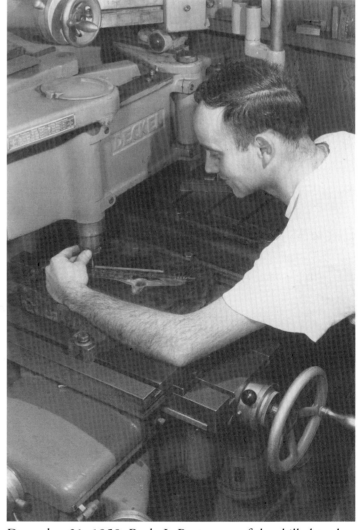

December 31, 1958: Rudy LaPorte, one of the skilled tradesmen employed at Windsor Tool & Die, sinks a steel die for a vehicle name plate.

The staff stand outside Sadler's Highway Market in Essex, circa 1959. Note the prices in the windows, including jam for 47 cents or bacon for 39 cents.

The Willys of Canada Ltd. plant, at 2525 Central Avenue, was retooled to manufacture Jeeps in 1959. The existing plant was established in 1954 for assembly and distribution, but was projected to produce 1,000 Jeeps a year, starting with the "open-type Jeep," pictured at right. The plant was closed 10 years later.

Border Cities Wire & Iron Ltd. at 861 Walker Road, circa 1963. The company manufactured railings, grill work, and other types of fencing from 1919 to 1985.

Ottawa Street, pictured here in 1959, was one of Windsor's main shopping districts in the '50s and '60s. Visible storefronts include: Halmo Jewellers, Whiteman's Furniture, Louis Berger, Dominion Cigar Store, F.W. Woolworth Co., Sunshine Confectionary, Merlo Bros. Hardware, Kozak's, Dowlers, Sam's Department Store, Gray's Department Store, and the Park Theatre, from left to right.

The Woollatt Industries and Construction Limited building on Ottawa Street between Argyle Road and Walker Road, circa 1960.

Passengers mill about the CNR platform on June 29, 1961, waiting for the last boarding call ever at the downtown station on the riverfront, east of Dieppe Gardens. From then on, passengers boarded trains at the new station in Walkerville.

January 16, 1964: Gray's Department Store expanded by a third in 1964. Watching the excavation on Ottawa Street, from left to right, are D.M. Levi, owner; Mayor Michael J. Patrick, and Nate Shapiro, general manager of the store.

Brotherhood Department Store, owned by Al and Sam Vexler and located at 1535 Ottawa Street, ran this ad in *The Star* on December 10, 1964. Brotherhood was famous for stocking "husky sizes."

The corner of University Avenue and Pelissier Street was full of retailers in 1961. From left to right are Mabel & Smith Millinery and Vincente Hair Styles, with Niagara Restaurant below. Today, this building houses Wedge Hair Salon, Full Circle Vintage, and Craft Heads Brewery.

Shiny new SW&A buses were ready to hit the road in March 1966. As of 1965, the fare was 25 cents with fourteen bus routes across the city. Transit Windsor took over SW&A in 1977.

Windsor Tool & Die Ltd. moved into the plant at 1680 Kildare Road in 1948 and underwent multiple expansions. Pictured here in 1964, the company employed over 200 workers.

August 4, 1965: Hiram Walker & Sons hired three special security guards to roam the grounds of its Pike Creek plant: Mr. Club, Belinda, and Scott—security geese from Scotland. At left, Mayor John Wheelton welcomes the leader of the geese, Mr. Club, who is held by Mr. and Mrs. Les Higgins of the Humane Society. At right, H. Clifford Hatch and Paul J.G. Kidd look over blueprints in front of Pike Creek "maturing" warehouses, each with a 1,000,000 gallon capacity.

"Salt City:" Jack MacKenzie, safety director, walks away from Windsor's Ojibway Mine in 1966. At right, Phil Specht and David Labelle plant explosives to loosen some of the 1,000,000 tonnes of salt mined annually.

The Dominion Forge plant on Seminole Street, 1968. The company expanded into cold forging in the 1960s, and added a new wing to the plant to house the new machinery. Dominion Forge ceased operations in 1989 after a protracted labour dispute.

August 27, 1969: Brotherhood Department Store, at 1535 Ottawa Street, changed hands after 28 years in business. Here, retiring owners Al and Sam Vexler hand the keys over to incoming businessman Louis Rosenberg, from left to right.

September 18, 1967: An aerial view of Morton Terminal Limited slip on Windsor's west side shows there's no room for more than eight lake freighters while, at right, two salties (ocean-going vessels), take on cargo for overseas ports.

June 19, 1968: The "new general store," Woolco was called a "thrill for most shoppers because of the vast array of merchandise and convenience." Pictured here at Eastown Plaza, at the corner of Tecumseh and Lauzon, this Woolco was opened in 1967. Walmart Canada purchased Woolco in 1994.

Jack Shanfield of Shanfields-Meyers Jewellery and China Shop stands amid construction on the downtown strip on September 24, 1970. One of Windsor's most enduring downtown businesses, Shanfields opened at 188 Ouellette Avenue in 1946 and is still open to customers today.

November 14, 1975: Mary Coombs works away at the new Champion Spark Plug plant on Lauzon Parkway. The plant produced over 200,000 plugs a day, and was the second largest industrial development in Windsor in the mid-1970s, surpassed only by the new Chrysler truck plant.

"Just Like Florida": Essex County Warden Bob Pulleybank, Mayor Frank Wansbrough, Joseph Colasanti, and Reeve Dick Thompson, from left to right, examine fruit at Alex Colasanti's tropical greenhouse in 1971. Started as a fruit stand in 1941, it grew into Colasanti's Tropical Gardens, an indoor entertainment and shopping centre—a favourite county attraction today.

July 25, 1972: David Percy and Paul Parent demonstrate their skills to foreman Gerry Pohle (far left) and acting manager Paul Macko (far right) after completing a 16-week training program at International Tools Limited. ITL was founded in 1946 by Peter Hedgewick. An estimated 80 percent of Windsor's current tool and die shops can be traced back to this company.

Windsor's tenth Dominion Store opened at Dougall and Cabana on February 11, 1969.

Discount department store Sayvette was slated to close on October 22, 1975. Opened at Tecumseh Mall back in 1972, the store was the sixth in the store chain to close as Sayvette struggled to compete with Kmart and Woolco.

Bus chassis move down the line at the Welles Corporation on June 11, 1975. Welles reached a record production level of 1,000 units in 1975, and primarily manufactured school buses. The business closed in 1990.

Quality control manager Walter Gazo (far right) shows Charles Jamail the Holiday Juice bottling line at the Jay-Zee Food Products plant located on Walker Road. In 1977, the operation was renamed Holiday Juice Limited. When purchased by the John Labatt Ltd. in the '80s, the plant would produce Everfresh Juice.

January 28, 1976: Josephine Siefker, an employee of International Playing Card Company Ltd., "deals herself a winner." The plant, located at 1123 Mercer Street, cut and processed 5 million decks of Bee and Bicycle cards each year. After 71 years in business, the plant was shuttered in 1989.

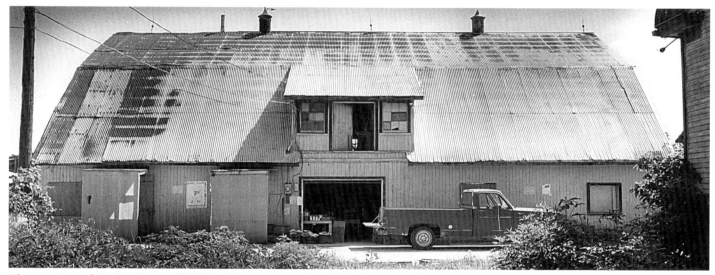

The exterior of the last barn of Walker Farms, 1980. Established in 1904 by Hiram Walker & Sons, the farms covered thousands of acres at their peak but were largely closed by the '60s.

Bill Tepperman, pictured here in 1977, took over the family business after his father's passing in 1970. After Tepperman's moved to Dougall Avenue in 1980, the store on Ottawa Street housed the Local 195 union headquarters.

LABOUR RELATIONS

If Windsor's formidable labour movement was cemented in the 1940s with the infamous Ford Strike, it wasn't until the 1950s and later that it really gained strength.

Workers at the Kelsey Wheel (later Kelsey-Hayes) plant in Windsor formed the first United Auto Workers union local in Canada in 1936 with the creation of UAW Local 195—in an era of bitter acrimony between companies and employees. Jimmy Napier and four others were fired for trying to organize a union at Kelsey Wheel, though he and his group persisted, winning their jobs back while giving hope to fellow workers.

Windsor Ford workers voted in 1941 to join the UAW, followed in 1942 by Chrysler workers. The dominoes began to fall. With growing labour unrest across the country, when workers did not have basic benefits such as unemployment insurance or medicare, the growing manufacturing powerhouse of Windsor was set for change. The 99-day Ford Strike in 1945 achieved what workers were striving for across Canada: union check-off. In unionized workplaces, all workers had to pay union dues whether they signed a union card or not. Then the real work started.

Union membership ballooned in Windsor. So too did expectations.

It seemed at times that Windsor was always on strike. A particularly hostile labour dispute festered during the long, hot summer of 1953, when Local 880 of the International Teamsters Union showed that they do not mess around. Among many altercations during the six-week work stoppage, non-union trucks were pelted with rocks, despite a police escort; a 100-car blockade formed in front of the Great Lakes Die Casting Plant where non-union shipments were arriving; and workers overturned a rogue truck.

Unions contributed much more than muscle to battle companies, of course. Critics say a union-town reputation scared away investment, though the union movement produced skilled labour and helped raise wages and improve benefits for many. The 1950s brought something desperately needed for unionized workers—pension plans, helping people live well in retirement. Topping up unemployment insurance through the Guaranteed Annual Wage Program was big as well, as were annual pay increases. Union members also gave back to the community, with famously generous charitable contributions. Plus, they embraced civic engagement and came out by the hundreds—sometimes thousands—to support barbecues, picnics, fundraisers and, the big one, the annual Labour Day parade. Marching bands, speeches, beauty queens, and tons of fun, the event was often attended by political leaders who knew how much power came with the growing union movement.

In 1957, thousands attended the 75th anniversary edition of the local Labour Day parade in Canada. Demonstrations of unemployed workers, protests, and union parties all attracted throngs in a show of solidarity between labour and Windsor at large. The winning 1959 Labour Day parade slogan, "Be Union, Buy Union," represented a mindset of the day. That said, a 1964 proposal to build an impressive tower called the Greater Windsor Labour Centre never materialized. Other dreams did, however. The '60s brought added benefits, including a much-needed dental plan.

Plus, the biggest deal of all came in 1965 with the advent of the Auto Pact. The Canada-United States Automotive Products Agreements—better known as the Auto Pact—was signed by Prime Minister Lester B. Pearson and US President Lyndon B. Johnson in Texas, removing tariffs on vehicles and parts between the two countries. American car companies benefited greatly, but so did workers in Canada, especially southern Ontario. The Big Three automakers agreed not to let automobile production fall below 1964 levels, assuring relatively high production sales ratios. Canada began producing fewer models of cars, but many more of the ones it did. Canadian plants grew in size. In 1964, only seven percent of cars made in Canada were sent south of the border, but by 1968 that number had jumped to 60 percent. Car and car-part production surpassed pulp and paper as the most important industry in Canada. Jobs seemed plentiful and wages great. In 1968, controversial wage parity was introduced—meaning Canadian workers earned what their American counterparts did.

In the '70s, strides were achieved in vision and hearing care, the right to refuse unsafe work, voluntary overtime, and the 30-and-out pension—allowing employees who had toiled 30 years at the company to retire long before age 65. But the Auto Pact did not stop labour unrest. It emboldened workers more. In 1968, for instance, workers struck for 111 days at Dominion Forge, where picketers and police clashed. As *The Windsor Star* reported, "Windsor police, wearing newly acquired riot gear, this morning engaged in shoving matches with strikers in front of Dominion Forge."

Other strikes erupted during the 1970s, with such diverse groups as A&P employees, postal workers, garbage men, and much more. And in terms of pure political pressure, nothing quite matched the Day of Protest organized by the Canadian Labour Congress on October 14, 1976—all to critique the Liberal government's Anti-Inflation Act, which implemented wage and price controls. Some 30,000 workers in Windsor alone stayed off the job that day. Talk about influence! It was possibly the peak of union power. But times were changing.

On January 17, 1977, the era came to a crashing halt when popular labour leader Charlie Brooks was shot dead at age 61 by a disgruntled Chrysler employee fired from the company. Not liking what he heard at the union hall, the man retrieved a shotgun from his car and put five shots into a door before kicking it down and firing four more times, killing Brooks. The president of UAW Local 444's funeral was the largest the city had ever seen, with 8,000-plus people in attendance. Brooks's contribution to the community was great. In the words of Local 444: "Charlie Brooks was elected President in July of 1956, and from that point on, it was full speed ahead." Windsor even created the floating Peace Fountain at the foot of Coventry Gardens in his honour.

Without Brooks at the helm, the Windsor union movement nevertheless pushed on, with increasing pressure from corporations to cut labour costs. In 1979, under the leadership of Bob White, the Canadian region of the UAW began pulling away from the American union, setting the stage for the creation of the Canadian Auto Workers in 1985. Of course, along the way many more locals of many more unions popped up in Windsor. As Carl Morgan and Herb Colling say in *Pioneering the Auto Age*, "Pound-for-pound, the skilled hands of Windsor have contributed more towards the Canadian economy than any other manufacturing centre in the country."

Though unionism always had a way of triggering strong reactions for or against, like it or not Windsor developed a long-lasting affair with the labour movement. But make no mistake: the gains in wages and conditions that unions won did not come easily. In Windsor, virtually every union advance saw hard fights and, often, labour stoppages, unrest, strikes. It all created havoc and acrimony, yes, but also a city where working-class people didn't just manufacture things, they bought what they built.

The union headquarters of the UAW Local 200 on Wyandotte Street East in 1950. Local 200, which represented workers at Ford Motor Company of Canada, received its charter in 1941 and rapidly grew into one of the largest and most influential locals in Canada.

September 6, 1950: Visitors look at educational literature during an open house at the Local 195 hall on Chatham Street. From left to right are: Lillian Patridge, Frank Dodd, James Hollerhead, Stanley Wochuk, Theodore Brown and his son Kenneth, and Robert Ullman. The union members are Gladys Marshall, Alvin Decaire, and Charlie Brooks.

"Labour Town": Crowds pack into the Jackson Park grandstand on Labour Day, 1951. The annual Labour Day parade drew thousands of Windsorites downtown for the event.

September 3, 1952: The rocket, representing the swift progress of the labour movement, won first place in the "profession division" at the Labour Day parade in 1952. The float was an entry by the 15 building trades, all affiliates of the American Federation of Labor (AFL).

In what the *Star* called "a display of strength," crowds stood six people deep to watch the Labour Day parade in 1951. Here, men representing UAW Local 195—an amalgamated union for workers from Kelsey Wheel, GM, and many others—march past Wyandotte Street.

July 21, 1953: A shattered truck window was the prize won by Ollie Mastronardi for running a gauntlet of striking truck drivers from Local 880 of the International Teamsters Union AFL. He succeeded in reaching the safety of the customs area on the Ambassador Bridge, despite the pursuit of five cars full of strikers and three police cruisers. With Mastronardi, at centre, are his two companions Bob Anderson, at left, and Robert Maisonville (plus a load of fresh lettuce). The labour dispute over wages began on July 19.

A ring of policemen guard a moving van that was hijacked and overturned by strikers during the Teamsters Union labour dispute in 1953. A wrecking crew from N.E. Curtis put the M.J. Campbell moving van back on its wheels without protest or further incident.

July 31, 1953: Striking members of Local 880 run along the east fence of Chrysler Plant 2 in a vain attempt to stop two Hamilton trucks from leaving the company grounds. The strikers had kept a two-hour vigil at the south gate, waiting for the trucks to attempt to leave with their police escort. However, in a coordinated stunt, the trucks suddenly sped northward inside the fence to a second gate about 200 yards away, with their police escort, at far right, keeping pace outside the fence.

August 10, 1953: Reminiscent of the infamous Ford Strike of 1945, striking members of Local 880 Teamsters Union commandeered cars to form a barricade in front of the Great Lakes Die Casting plant at 875 Tecumseh Road East. Inside a "renegade" truck owned by McKinlay Transport Company was unloading its cargo of 12 tonnes of zinc alloy. The blockade had more than 100 vehicles, including several city buses.

News that the six-week-long strike by Local 880 Teamsters Union was over reached the truckers on duty at the Ambassador Bridge on August 28, 1953. Reading the paper, from left to right, are Jim Gagnon, Cecil Scriver, Ernest Williamson, Pat Battaglia, Ronald Wilson, and Don Damiamakas, with John Lebeznick and Samuel Hannah behind them. They celebrated on the spot by opening a bag of peaches.

Windsor faced a milk shortage on January 8, 1954, when milk deliverymen and plant workers, members of Local 440, Dairy Workers' Union, went on strike for higher wages. Pictured here is the picket line outside Purity Dairies Limited, with local president Thomas Rees, at far right.

The Windsor delegation at the UAW convention in Cleveland, 1954. The Local 200 contingent, for Ford workers, pictured here voting on a resolution, are Lloyd Allen, Jack Liddle, Leo Pare, James Orem, Frank Quinlan, Dave Watson, Harvey Patter, and Harry Ford, from left to right. As one of the largest union chapters in Canada, the Local 200 was always able to make its voice heard at international gatherings.

September 6, 1954: Windsor's Unemployed Association only had 30 parade members when they lined up to start, but their ranks doubled in size by time they reached Jackson Park.

Miss Local 61 sits proudly with her 'chaperones' for the Labour Day parade in 1954. According to a *Star* reporter, with "all its natural beauty, the Local 61 Distillery Workers Union float was a natural for top honours."

The first collective bargaining agreement covering City Hall workers was signed on September 10, 1954, by Mayor Arthur J. Reaume. Standing, from left to right, are W.A. Acting, negotiator; Thomas McNaull, president of the Local 543 for Municipal Office Workers; Nelson Bradd from the Trades and Labor Council; C.V. Waters, city clerk; and Frances Lenar, union secretary.

The Local 195 float from the Labour Day parade, 1955. The float featured the figure of progress, and carried the theme of unity between craft and industrial unions.

July 11, 1955: Albert Rutt awards prizes to Danny Williams, Bobby Taylor, and Ronnie Jones, from left to right, the winners of the 50-yard dash at the Local 195's annual union picnic. Union chapters often hosted community events like picnics and barbecues or raised money for charities. Ronnie Jones would grow up to be better known as Ron Jones, Windsor firefighter and city councillor.

"Busmen Say 'No'": Striking Windsor SW&A bus drivers voted down a proposal which would have sent them back to work on May 29, 1956. Here, Tom Murphy casts his ballot under the watchful eye of one of the official scrutineers. Transit service returned to Windsor on June 4th, after a 14-day walkout, making it the longest bus strike in the city's history up to that point.

"Windsor Loves a Parade": One of the most colourful and best-attended Labour Day parades in Windsor's history was held in 1957, the 75th anniversary of the event in Canada. At top, the American Federation of Musicians band, from the Windsor local, treated the crowd to a song and dance as they marched down Ouellette Avenue. Pictured below is the marching column led by the Essex Legion Colour Guard, followed by the Sea Cadet Band and the Boy Scout Colour Party. The largest marching unit was Local 880, Teamsters Union, at bottom left, who turned out 13 riders on horseback and 17 trucks. At bottom right, Local 793 for Operating Engineers towers over the competition in a giant earth mover.

December 20, 1957: Between 300 and 400 unemployed persons marched through the city as a demonstration to back up their demands for more work. Here, the line-up, walking east on Pitt Street, turns onto Ouellette Avenue.

Chrysler Local 444 Christmas Party, 1957. This was no small affair: 1,400 children attended and 1,500 pounds of candy, 225 dozen oranges, 2,800 small toys, 25 bushels of apples, and 2,800 balloons were handed out.

When Prime Minister John Diefenbaker made a campaign stop in Windsor on March 5, 1958, he was greeted with a political protest by members of Local 444. Area unions opposed the government's stance on unemployment and feared that the auto industry was being dominated by American interests.

The slogan "Be Union, Buy Union!" won the Windsor Union Label Council first prize during the Labour Day parade in 1959.

September 8, 1964: Members of Local 444 revealed their political allegiances as they carried signs supporting New Democratic candidate Bill Riggs in the coming Windsor-Sandwich by-election. Riggs finished second to Progressive Conservative candidate Richard Thrasher. Alderman Bill Riggs was a longtime printer at *The Windsor Star* and was well-known for his involvement with local unions.

This float was a joint effort of Locals 195, 200, 240, and 444, which represented workers at the Big Three automotive companies. Some 50,000 Windsorites lined the streets downtown for the Labour Day parade in 1964.

November 27, 1964: Wilfred J. Sefton, president of the Greater Windsor Labour Centre, holds an architect's drawing of the proposed downtown labour centre, backed by 30 local unions. Work was scheduled to begin in 1965, but the plans never came to fruition.

Auto-matic
WINDY, COLD
Low tonight 4, high Sunday 23
a.m. 10, 9 a.m. 10, 2 p.m. 10
(Complete weather, Page 6)

The Windsor Star

FINAL
★ ★ ★ ★

VOL. 93, NO. 115   72 Pages   Including Weekend Magazine   WINDSOR ONTARIO SATURDAY JANUARY 16 1965   SEVEN CENTS

SIGN AUTO AGREEMENT

January 18, 1965: President Lyndon B. Johnson and Prime Minister Lester B. Pearson sign the historic automotive agreement at Johnson's ranch in Texas. Sitting in the foreground from left to right are Paul Martin, minister of external affairs; Pearson, Johnson, and Secretary of State Dean Rusk. The Auto Pact was a free-trade agreement for motor vehicles and automotive parts between Canada and the United States. The increased market is credited with sustaining Canada's automotive industry into the 21st century.

Windsor joined a wildcat walkout of postal workers across Canada on July 21, 1965, bringing local mail service to a halt for over a week. Al Brown, Conrad Williams, Kenneth Langbridge, Colin Campbell, James Coghlin, and John Edwards, from left to right, walk the picket line while reading up on sister strikes in 30 other cities. Pictured at right, letter carrier Robert Longmuir makes a point with his pet squirrel monkey, Cheetah, who joined him on picket duty. This watershed strike resulted in Lester B. Pearson extending the right to strike and collective bargaining to public sector employees.

The Local 444 hockey team, made up of Chrysler workers, in the mid-1960s.

300 tractors from Essex and Kent Counties took to the highways in support of the Ontario Farm Union on June 20, 1966. The tractors pictured here wait to turn onto Highway 2 from side roads to form the "motorized picket." The farmers were supporting a brief on milk prices and other agricultural issues presented by the farming union to the provincial government.

November 6, 1966: Walter Reuther, international president of the UAW, officially opened the new union headquarters for the Local 200, Local 444, and Local 240 on Turner Road. At the ribbon cutting, from left to right, are Charles Brooks, Local 444 president; George Burt, Canadian regional director; Emil Mazey of the UAW, Reuther, and Henry Renaud, president of the Local 200. Reuther is remembered as one of America's greatest union leaders for his social justice initiatives and the massive growth of the UAW during his tenure, from 1946 to 1970.

Stop Over
GETTING WARMER
6 a.m 56, 9 a.m. 67 2 p m 78
Low tonight 57 high Sat 82
(Complete weather page 6)

The Windsor Star

FINAL
★ ★ ★ ★

VOL. 96, NO. 150   42 Pages   WINDSOR ONTARIO FRIDAY AUGUST 26 1966   TEN CENTS

CANADA HIGHBALLS INTO CRISIS

The Windsor Star declared a national crisis on August 26, 1966, as trains across Canada sat idle when a general strike by Local 185, the Brotherhood of Railway Trainmen, forced a shutdown of all rail transportation. In Windsor, the local chapter decried the Liberal government's scramble to pass emergency legislation, including a deadline for compulsory arbitration. The back-to-work bill came into effect on September 2nd, but Windsor's workers defied the order for three more days in protest.

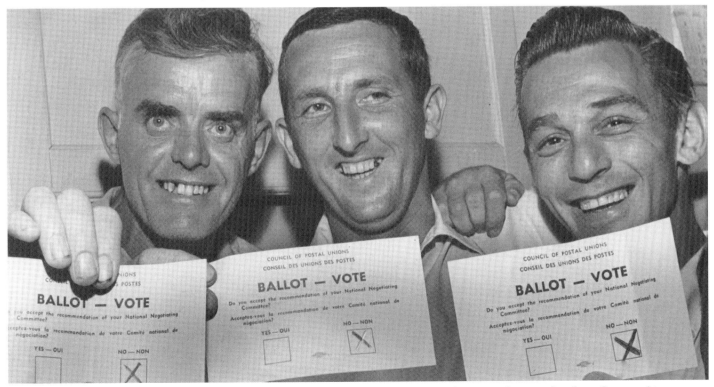

"234 Times No!": Postal workers and letter carriers in Windsor overwhelmingly rejected terms for their first working agreement with the Canadian government on August 7, 1968. These 'posties,' Charles Dawe, Roger Emslie, and Fred Hole, from left to right, did not hide their feelings, though the ballot was supposed to be secret. Despite voting 234 to 12 against ratification in Windsor, the contract was approved by 60 percent of union voters across Canada and postal workers returned to work the following day, ending a 23-day strike.

POLICE TANGLE WITH PICKETS

September 5, 1968: Riot-helmeted Windsor police line the sidewalk outside the Dominion Forge plant after a shoving match with picketers while a truckload of dies was removed from the plant on court order. From there, strikers held "spontaneous" demonstrations in front of the truck driver's residence and at City Hall. The strike over contract negotiations lasted for a staggering 111 days.

Leading the Labour Day parade in 1969 were the following personalities, from left to right: Herb Gray, MP, Mayor William C. Riggs, Ed Baillargeon, president of the Windsor and District Labour Council, Hugh Peacock, MPP, former Alderman Roy Perry, Alderman Roy Moore, and Bernard Newman, MPP. In the second row are Mark MacGuigan, MP, Senator Paul Martin, Fred Burr, MPP, Alderman Peter Mackenzie, Alderman Thomas Toth, and Alderman Roy Battagello. In the third row are Eugene Whelan, MP, and former mayor Arthur Reaume.

Canadian postal workers continued their fight for better wages and protection against automation in 1970, holding a series of rotating 24-hour strikes in cities across Canada. On May 27, Windsor's local walked out early, before their designated turn, and maintained their strike for 12 days. Here, Brian Renaud informs Doris Vermette that she need not bother with her mail, as it won't go anywhere despite her "pretty smile." Ultimately, the payoff was worth it, as postal workers received above-average wage increases.

September 24, 1973: Dave Westwood, Ruth Shuel, and Jimmy Gordon, from left to right, brandish placards in favour of their local executive, including president Richard Tighe. Local 61 Distillery Workers Union voted to defect from their international parent union based on their concerns over the lack of Canadian autonomy.

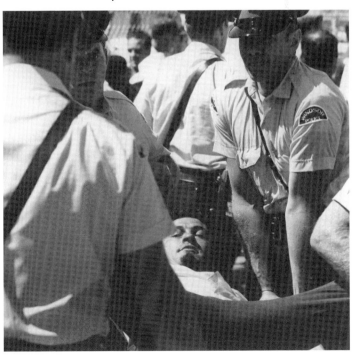

Garbage started to pile up around Windsor as civic employees went out on strike in June 1971. At left, the picket line guards a line-up of garbage trucks on Victoria Avenue. At right, a CUPE picketer is removed by Windsor police during skirmishes between police and union members as supervisory personnel attempted to move a fleet of garbage packers. The strike, over issues of job security, cost of living, and compensation, ended after 15 days—much to the relief of Windsor residents.

Classrooms were empty on January 3, 1973, after the mass resignations of teachers from the Essex County Separate School Board, pictured at left, and Windsor's secondary schools over contract negotiations. At right, county teachers give their approval of the settlement, returning elementary students to the classroom after three days of extended Christmas holiday. High schools in Windsor did not reopen until January 23rd, after the intervention of Education Minister Thomas Wells.

March 9, 1973: Murray Whelpton, Windsor Utilities Commissioner and union member, conducts a meeting via walkie-talkie, after he refuses to cross the picket line of his sister union, Local 911, Brotherhood of Electrical Workers, that was ironically striking against the WUC.

"Angels of Mercy Rebel": Nurses protest outside IODE Riverview Unit on July 15, 1974. The nurses' demonstration was not an official picket line, but a "good cheering section" according to nursing representative Lois Fairley. The nurses aimed to gain public support in their contract negotiations.

"First Ever": Two Windsor legal secretaries made history on September 19, 1974, when they began a strike against the law firm of Weingarden and Hawrish. Here, Mary Anne Fox maintains the small picket in front of the Canada Building, while Arthur Weingarden quickly crosses the picket line on his way to his office. According to *The Star*, it was the first strike ever undertaken by law firm employees in Canada.

The Windsor Board of Education imposed a lockout after a one-day walkout by high-school teachers on March 30, 1976. A sign at Forster Collegiate Institute explains the empty class-rooms. At first, teachers showed up without pay until the doors were physically locked. Makeshift classrooms were set up around the city until the lockout ended on May 11th.

On October 14, 1976, The Canadian Labour Congress declared a collective "Day of Protest" to demonstrate against the Liberal government's Anti-Inflation Act, which introduced price and wage controls. At left, Windsor "postie" Gord Hunt protests in his long johns, while at right, Charles Brooks leads the Local 444 contingent in a parade down Ouellette Avenue. More than 30,000 workers stayed off the job in Windsor.

Local 444's Charles Brooks slain; suspect arrested

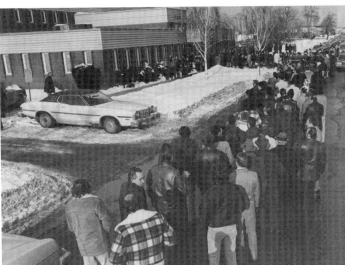

On January 17, 1977, longtime Local 444 leader Charles Brooks was fatally shot to death in his office by disgruntled autoworker Clarence Talbot. At top left, the body of Charles Brooks is removed from the union hall on Turner Road, while the door that Talbot fired several shots through and kicked down is removed as evidence at top right. Talbot was found not guilty by reason of insanity and spent 10 years in a mental institution. At bottom left, thousands of mourners line up to pay their respects at Brooks' funeral—one of the largest in Windsor's history. A legendary leader, Brooks led the Chrysler workers of Local 444 from its inception in 1956. His legacy is enshrined in the Charlie Brooks Memorial Peace Fountain in Reaume Park. The plaque unveiling with UAW president Douglas Fraser is pictured at bottom right.

CULTURAL LIFE

Many of Windsor's most important cultural institutions took root in the 1940s, but they didn't really blossom until the decades that followed.

The Art Gallery of Windsor, for instance, was born in 1943 at Willistead Manor and was known as the Willistead Art Gallery. In 1946, the gallery came under the direction of its first full-time curator, Kenneth Saltmarche. By the '60s, however, the gallery became a victim of its own success, and both crowds and collection had outgrown its space. Plus, without proper temperature control and burglar-proof facilities, some larger art galleries such as the Detroit Institute of Arts would not lend major works. But what to do, where to go? Build onto Willistead Manor? That didn't seem right. In 1970, Mayor Frank Wansbrough came up with a creative solution: what about using the abandoned Carling Brewery warehouse on Riverside Drive? The city sold the building to the gallery for a token $2 and the new Art Gallery

of Windsor opened in September of 1975, moving into its big new home next to the riverfront—and displaying an impressive collection for a museum of its size.

Another local cultural institution, the Windsor Public Library started in 1894 and in 1903, moved into the Carnegie Library building, now demolished, at Victoria Avenue and Park Street. It moved into its 100,000-square-foot modern home on Ouellette Avenue in 1973 to general acclaim.

Meanwhile, in 1941, CKLW staff musician Ernest Rennie formed the Windsor Concert Orchestra to raise funds for local servicemen overseas. Violinist Matti Holli took over the following year, with live CKLW broadcasts from the Prince Edward Hotel Ballroom. In 1948, the ensemble took the name the Windsor Symphony Orchestra, and after a couple of different locations, settled on the Tivoli Theatre (now the Walkerville Theatre) as their home venue. It moved to the Capitol Theatre

179

from 1959 to 1960. Then on October 22, 1961, the WSO gave its first performance at the newly built Cleary Auditorium (now Chrysler Theatre). Maestro Holli continued to lead the orchestra through its years of growth until his death in 1977. In 1979, Hungarian-born Laszlo Gati took over as Windsor Symphony Orchestra conductor. Gati, according to the WSO, was "noted for his fiery performances," and helped the orchestra continue to advance, leading it to its first commercial recording in 1983 and a higher standing in the community.

A number of dance and acting troupes added to the area's cultural life, such as the Windsor Light Opera Association (later the Windsor Light Music Theatre), founded in 1948 by Dr. John H. L. Watson. The group produced two major musicals a year, a tradition still carried on today. The group's first home was the Walkerville Collegiate stage, though in 1960 it moved to the Cleary Auditorium, always keeping its combined love of music and drama.

A number of artists stood out during the '50s, '60s and '70s. Windsor-born Emilia Cundari became a star of the Metropolitan Opera in New York City in the mid-1950s and in Europe through the 1970s. Pat Sturn, born in Romania, became Windsor's pre-eminent portrait photographer until her retirement in 1981. Jack Scott was born in Windsor but moved to Michigan before becoming the first white rock 'n' roll singer to achieve fame from Detroit, signing with ABC-Paramount Records in 1957. Scott sometimes played with the Windsor group The Chantones.

Teaze was a hard-thumping band from Windsor that rocked from 1975 to 1981, recording successful albums while touring in Canada and the US and, perhaps most notably, in Japan in 1978. Alexander Zonjic, who released his first self-titled album in 1978, went on to become a renowned flutist, playing light jazz and gigging with big names from the US, as well as a Detroit radio personality.

Acclaimed American author Joyce Carol Oates, affected by the Vietnam War and the Detroit riots, moved from the Motor City in 1968 to teach at the University of Windsor, before moving on to Princeton in 1978. Writer Eugene McNamara founded the University of Windsor Review in 1965, while author Alistair MacLeod, who started teaching at the University of Windsor in 1969, went on to win many prestigious literary awards.

Venues also played an important role, creating spaces for audiences to participate in the local cultural scene. At the turn of the century, there was the Windsor Opera House, which eventually became CH Smith Department Store. In the era of the silent screen, which peaked in the '20s, more playhouses started popping up: The Royal, The Princess, The Empire, The Windsor, The Favorite, The Wyandotte, and The Home. The Howard Crane-designed Walkerville Theatre (called the Tivoli by 1930), offered a smorgasbord of films and live productions. The Vanity Theatre, opened in 1937, was designed by Albert McPhail

and offered a stylish, modern design and an impressive 966 seats. Perhaps its finest hour came in 1968 with the worldwide premiere of *The Devil's Brigade*. Some 1,000 people showed up seeking autographs at the Vanity when Hollywood heartthrobs such as Cliff Robertson and Jeremy Slate graced the red carpet.

But the granddaddy of all the venues is the Thomas White Lamb-designed Capitol Theatre, born in 1920 as Loew's Windsor Theatre with 1,995 seats, then the most in Canada. It originally served as a vaudeville venue, though it went on to become much more—a community gem, really. In 1975, it was split into three smaller theatres by Famous Players Cinema. And in 1993, facing demolition, three levels of government provided grants to renovate the facility to its former glory.

In 1950, the Capitol Theatre hosted a particularly special performance: a one-hour live broadcast to mark the beginning of Windsor's own full CBC station, CBE. The station began in 1935 as CRCW, a Canadian Radio Broadcasting Commission station on affiliate CKLW. But CBE graduated to its own station at 1550 AM in 1950. It expanded to FM in 1977.

CKLW—which began as CKOK in 1932—went on to make its own history, thanks to the advent of rock 'n' roll. For much of its early life, CKLW had an American flavour, developing affiliations with a changing roster of US stations. But Windsor's Radio Eight-Oh, or Radio 8, or the Big 8, as it became known, hit its glory years when it traded its variety format for hits of the day in the mid-'60s. Featuring on-air personalities over the years such as Gary "Morning Mouth" Burbank, Walt "Baby" Love, Byron MacGregor, and many more, the station found its groove, thanks partly to the large transmitter that sent its airwaves far abroad into the United States. In 1967, CKLW claimed top spot in Detroit-area radio ratings. But another reason for the station's success was its long-time programming director Rosalie Trombley, who ascended to the position after working her way up from station librarian. With a reputation as a hit-maker, she chose a popular selection of R&B and Motown music. However, with the advent of Canadian content requirements in 1971 and increased US competition, the station's popularity declined somewhat, though it remained a local radio force.

Locally produced television made its debut in 1954, thanks to CKLW-TV, also known as Channel 9. Originally operated as a CBC affiliate, it also maintained affiliations with the American-based DuMont Television Network until that network's demise in 1956. The station started to broadcast in colour in 1968, and went on to become the CBC station CBET, which has covered the local community for decades.

Through it all, culture survived in Windsor, sometimes influenced by the other side of the border and sometimes the other way around. An auto town, yes, but an arts town, too.

April 7, 1949: The Windsor Light Opera's first performance was a concert of selected pieces from Gilbert and Sullivan's *Pirates of Penzance* for the patients of the Essex County Sanitarium. In the foreground, from left to right, are Dr. John Watson, director of the association, Veronica Reich and Yvonne St. Laurent, patients; and A.J. Gervais, association president, with the rest of the cast behind them.

Toby David, a well-known radio personality on CKLW's morning show, signs autographs for fans in July 1950. David would famously go on to become CKLW-TV's "Captain Jolly" on *Popeye and Pals* in the late '50s and early '60s.

The headquarters of the Windsor branch of the American Federation of Musicians, 1950. One of the oldest unions in Windsor, Local 566 received its charter in 1911.

"Father of the Blues": W.C. Handy plays his most famous composition, "St. Louis Blues," on the trumpet for members of Assumption High School's band on May 17, 1952. The students, from left to right, are Robert Shary, Clyde Jacob, and Gary Docherty.

Jaclie Beauchamp, theatre cashier, on the job at Capitol Theatre in downtown Windsor, 1954. Note the admission prices of 65 cents and 40 cents.

June 28, 1954: Miss Centennial Doris Crawford sings "Alice Blue Gown" while ballerina Annette Brand executes a dance interpretation of the song for Music Under the Stars. At right, overflow crowds of nearly 20,000 people fill Jackson Park for what *The Star* called "the most ambitious show to date." Music Under the Stars were summer concerts sponsored by Ford Motor Company of Canada in the 1950s.

CKLW Radio and CKLW-TV moved into their new station on Crawford Avenue in 1954. With a 650-foot broadcasting tower, CKLW Radio had the strongest regional signal, able to reach Detroit and much of the American midwest. CKLW-TV hit the airwaves for the first time on September 16, 1954. Pictured at right, President J.E. Campeau and Operations Director S. Campbell Ritchie show off the brand-new set to *The Star*, which called it a "miniature Hollywood."

The "Wild Mouse" or "Wilde Maus," a wood roller coaster imported from Germany, was opened in 1957. It was the first such ride in the Detroit-Windsor area. The Bob-Lo Island Amusement Park ran from 1889 to 1993.

Pictured here in 1955, Windsor-born soprano Emilia Cundari applies last-minute touches before a performance, as her parents look on. An internationally renowned opera singer, Cundari was engaged at the Metropolitan Opera in New York City the following year.

November 22, 1956: Don Piper, at left, and Jim Welsh are a pair of gangsters in the Windsor Light Opera Association's production of "Kiss Me Kate."

Windsor's own Dorothy Collins was a familiar face on the popular TV program "Your Hit Parade" on NBC in the 1950s.

Maestro Matti Holli, conductor of the Junior Symphony Orchestra, helps two young violinists, Angela Hrachovi and Beatrice Helin, as they rehearse for the final concert of the 1957–58 season. Holli, also the conductor of the Windsor Symphony Orchestra, founded the Junior Symphony in 1957, which became the International Youth Symphony in 1966.

The Windsor Symphony Orchestra string section, 1958. From left to right are Harry Schram, bass; Celia Hardcastle, cello; and Jack Stone, viola; with Lasse Pohjola, the concert master, kneeling in front. Hardcastle, one of Windsor's best known local musicians, owned a sheet music store on Pitt Street West and was heavily involved with the American Federation of Musicians.

July 1, 1958: Hundreds of Windsorites made the trek to Bob-Lo Island for the Dominion Day holiday, after the ferry made three special stops at the Government Dock at the foot of Church Street. Here, Irma Bernard and Mac Macintosh wave from the deck with Joe Short—better known as Captain Bob-Lo.

April 7, 1959: Delmer Willick, Adrian Verhulst, and Leonard Warner, from left to right, load paintings en route for storage. After a year of fighting with the Library Board for control, curator Kenneth Saltmarche resigned and the Windsor Art Association moved the paintings out of Willistead Manor with the intention of opening an independent gallery.

April 18, 1959: These civic players could hardly wait until the Cleary Auditorium was opened and decided to test it out a little early with a rehearsal of their next play, "Blithe Spirit." From left to right are Virginia Benton, Shirley Taylor, Ron Steele, Jessica Klein Lebink (on floor), Marie Simpson, and director James Benton.

Jerry Booth, better known to Windsor's children as Jingles the Clown, poses with his Herkimer Dragon and Cecil B. Rabbitt before his live show at the Capitol Theatre on February 12, 1960. Jingles the Clown was the star of "Jingles in Boofland," a popular children's show from CKLW-TV in the '50s and '60s.

The South Branch of the Windsor Public Library, April 1960. The experimental branch was located in a converted hardware store at 1425 Tecumseh Road East, instead of within a school, as an effort to reach the public. From left to right are Diana Wilk, Raffaella Brancaleoni, Jane MacRae, Linda Richards, Don Fleming, and Philip Carley.

A newly renovated Willistead Art Gallery of Windsor opened on October 6, 1960. In the months following the director's resignation and the removal of artwork, the Windsor Art Association received the support of the city to run an independent art gallery on the second floor of Willistead Manor.

The Carnegie Library, 1963. The library's annex, pictured at right, was constructed in 1957 to house a children's library and non-fiction titles.

One of Canada's most famous authors, Morley Callaghan, at far left, addressed students at Assumption University on March 28, 1960. Here, he answers questions from Professor Eugene McNamara, centre, and student Bruce Keele.

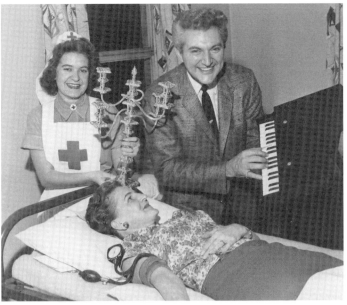

Liberace made a stop at the Red Cross blood clinic on October 20, 1961, to sign autographs while in Windsor to perform at Elmwood Casino. Here, Mrs. J.K. Holden gazes up at her surprise visitor, while clinical assistant Laura Davidson holds Liberace's candelabra.

October 8, 1960: Mayor Michael J. Patrick tries his hand at conducting the Windsor Symphony Orchestra, which would soon be performing their first show in the newly opened Cleary Auditorium.

The Tivoli Theatre, located at 1564 Wyandotte Street East, showed its last film and closed its doors on March 2, 1963. Originally opened as a vaudeville house in 1920, the building would be resurrected later as a bingo hall. In 2014, the theatre was restored and reopened as The Walkerville Theatre.

November 26, 1963: This dancing quartette—Lois Martin, Dorothy Dombkowski, Betty Houghton, and Helen Mady, from left to right—prepare for the Windsor Light Opera's presentation of *Oklahoma* at Cleary Auditorium.

April 12, 1966: Windsor high-school students took to the picket line to demand a "modern public library," arguing that Carnegie Library (opened in 1903) was outdated and unsafe. The building, at 450 Victoria Avenue, was demolished in 1974, one year after a new main library branch opened. Carnegie apartment building stands on the site.

August 30, 1965: Despite a fatal accident on the "Bug" ride a few days previous, *The Star* declared it "business as usual on the midway" as the crowds continued to come to Bob-Lo Island.

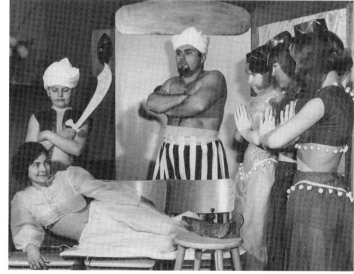

March 27, 1966: The Windsor Little Theatre's production of Aladdin, featuring Juanita Sandford as the Princess (reclining); Bryn Schofield as Guard; William R. Dolishny as the Genie; and Pauline Oshar, Linda Hersche, and Sandra Bellaka as harem girls.

September 27, 1967: The Brothers-in-Law, a satirical band made up of police officers, serenade in the background while Mrs. Donald Jeannette registers Meyrick Stanton, right, for courses at the YMCA. The Brothers-in-Law, from left to right, are Alec Somerville, Larry Reaume, and Bob Lee. The Brothers-in-Law released several successful albums in the '60s, the most popular being 1965's "Oh! Oh! Canada!"

Close to 1,000 people crowded in front of the Vanity Theatre on Ouellette Avenue for the world premiere of *The Devil's Brigade* on May 14, 1968. The film, about the exploits of the first Special Forces Brigade, a joint Canadian and US team from World War II, premiered simultaneously in Windsor and Detroit. Veterans from the brigade came from all across Canada to attend the event. Pictured at bottom, autograph hunters wave their paper bait at actor Jeremy Slate as he leaves the theatre.

Bozo's Big Top entertained a generation of local children when it debuted on CKLW-TV in 1967, with an innovation—a live audience. The Bozo the Clown pictured here (with his sidekick, Mr. Calliope) is Art Cervi, who acted in the role on CKLW-TV from 1967 to 1975.

Jimmy Durante at the Elmwood Casino, 1968. A favourite of local audiences, Durante, an American comic and entertainer, made Elmwood one of his regular stops on his tour circuit, calling it "real high class."

Eugene McNamara reads some of his original poetry at Peter K. Ryan's interiors shop on Goyeau Street on October 9, 1968. A prolific poet and author, McNamara was an English professor at the University of Windsor from 1959 to 1995. He founded *The Windsor Review* in 1965 and served as it editor until 1987.

June 13, 1970: The Park Theatre, at 1377 Ottawa Street, would close as soon as its run of *M*A*S*H* was finished in July. The theatre, then owned by Famous Players, was closed at the same time that two brand new cinemas were opening at Devonshire Mall. The building was sold to the next-door Bank of Commerce and demolished for a parking lot.

Kenneth Saltmarche, pictured here in 1972, was the director and curator of the Art Gallery of Windsor from 1946 to 1985. He was instrumental in the creation of an independent gallery and shaped the collection with his strong commitment to feature Canadian art.

Detroit rockers The Rationals give a free concert in Dieppe Gardens during the International Freedom Festival on July 6, 1970.

Art in the Alley, 1973. A response to Art in the Park (then in its fourth year), *The Star* described it as "a revolt by a band of disgruntled artists against the garden party atmosphere." Here, area artists Bert Weir, Gary Findlay, Bob Rudkin, and Bob Monks, from left to right, prepare the event, held behind the Mushroom Gallery on Riverside Drive, while Mark Monforton, standing at far left, examines one of Monk's works.

Canadian artist, illustrator, and writer William Kurelek poses with his "Self-Portrait" at the Art Gallery of Windsor in 1974.

Chris Guriancik, of the Hot Morley rock group, performs for the 2,500 people who attended the "Battle of the Bands" at Jackson Park during the Firefighter's Field Day in 1972. Local group Amitrof were declared the winners out of the twelve bands from Windsor and Essex County who competed that year.

Musicians (including Alexander Zonjic on the flute) wound their way through Art in the Alley on July 2, 1974. Over 150 craftsmen set up displays during the three-day exhibit, which drew up to 10,000 Windsorites.

"The Girl with the Golden Ear" Rosalie Trombley was Windsor's own hitmaker for CKLW's Big 8 Radio. Pictured here in 1974, Trombley was the music director during the golden age of CKLW radio in the 1960s, when it was one of the leading stations in North America. She picked out hit singles from bands like Earth, Wind and Fire, Kiss, Ted Nugent, The Guess Who, and Bob Seger.

The Art Gallery of Windsor moved into its own space, the former Carling Breweries Bottling Plant at 445 Riverside Drive, on September 27, 1975. At right, Mayor Bert Weeks prepares to hand the deed for the new Windsor Art Gallery building to gallery president Charles Donaldson, during the opening ceremonies, jokingly reminding him that the gallery still hadn't paid the $2 it owed for the building.

Art in the Park, 1975. The annual art exhibit and sale was founded in 1969 by Kenneth Saltmarche and the Art Gallery of Windsor to provide local artists with an opportunity to showcase their work for the public. At top left, Robert Lyons fashions a broom. At top right, an art enthusiast examines a painting. David Partridge, pictured at bottom left, works on a mural of nails, made with a technique called "naillies," while watched by a young fan, while Lieutenant-General Pauline McGibbon, and her husband Donald, study wood carvings at bottom right.

Joyce Carol Oates in her office at the University of Windsor, 1976. An award-winning writer, Oates taught in the English Department from 1967 to 1977, along with her husband Raymond Smith, before moving on to Princeton University. Together, they founded the *Ontario Review* in 1974.

"Mr. Light Opera": Dr. John Watson, pictured here in 1976, founded the Windsor Light Opera in 1948. Watson, a scientist by trade, wore many hats as a producer, director, and actor, and produced 79 shows before his retirement in 1989. The theatre company continues on today, under the name Windsor Light Musical Theatre.

The Log Flume ride was one of Bob-Lo Island's most popular attractions in 1976. The amusement park remained open until 1993.

The Vanity Theatre, at 671 Ouellette Avenue, reopened on June 14, 1977 after extensive renovations. Once a downtown hot spot, sales declined, and unable to compete with multi-screen venues, Vanity closed in 1987. The building was demolished in 2016.

Gil Grossutti, at left, and Alexander Zonjic perform in 1977. Zonjic would find international fame as a professional flutist, releasing a self-titled album in 1978—the first of many.

Famed Canadian author Alistair MacLeod began teaching at the University of Windsor in 1969. He would go on to publish his award-winning novel, *No Great Mischief*, in 1999.

"Alley Ballet": Members of the Metropolitan Ballet Company of Michigan, the Windsor City Ballet, and the Windsor Light Opera pooled their talent to present a rendition of *West Side Story* in Richmond Landing, between Riverside Drive and Pitt Street, on August 28, 1977.

The brand new Windsor Public Library was officially opened at 850 Ouellette Avenue in September 1979. A replacement for the Carnegie Library, the ultra-modern building was designed by Windsor architects Johnson & McWhinnie.

The Nitty Gritty Dirt Band had the crowd roaring along during a free concert for the Freedom Festival Jamboree in Dieppe Park on July 2, 1977.

August 30, 1980: Amaranth, a local rock group, show their stuff at the annual Battle of the Bands, during the Firefighter's Field Day at Mic Mac Park.

BLACK HISTORY

It wasn't just a parade, it wasn't just a get-together, it was the "Greatest Freedom Show on Earth." It connected two countries and two races. And above all, it illustrated Windsor's proud role, as one of the final stops in the Underground Railroad, in the hard-fought emancipation of slaves. In its heyday, Windsor's annual Emancipation Day celebration, which marked the passing of the Abolition Act in the British Empire, drew tens of thousands of people from Canada and the United States with one main goal: to celebrate freedom.

The Emancipation Day Parade and celebrations also showed how important the African-Canadian community was to the founding of Windsor. Black people began arriving in Windsor in the 1700s, largely as part of the Loyalist migration from the United States in the wake of the American Revolution—some as the slaves of Loyalist owners and others freed for their service to the Crown. But the influx became a tide after August 1, 1834,

when the Slavery Abolition Act came into effect in all British colonies, making Canada the destination for freedom. Abraham Lincoln did not make his Emancipation Proclamation until January 1, 1863. Black people turned to the Underground Railroad, the now famed series of safe houses that allowed escaping slaves to spirit away under cover of night to places such as Windsor, Amherstburg, Maidstone, Gosfield, Chatham, and Buxton.

A century later, local businessman and bon vivant Walter Perry spearheaded the revival of Windsor's Emancipation Day celebrations—but with an audacious idea: a grand cross-border celebration of freedom. As Perry said in a 1935 edition of *Progress*, an Emancipation Day publication: "I want all people to know that the main reason for starting this show was to acquaint the Negroes with the whites." And it worked! Everyday folk came out, as did mayors, councillors, and business people. African-Americans came to Windsor in droves, mostly from Detroit, but many coming from Ohio or as far as Georgia and Alabama. Some big names who attended Windsor's Emancipation Day Parade included: Martin Luther King

Jr., Adam Clayton Powell, Joe Louis, Satchel Paige, Jesse Owens, Mary McLeod Bethune, W.C. Handy, Martha Reeves, and Eleanor Roosevelt. Stevie Wonder reportedly gave his first public performance during one of the celebrations while a young Diana Ross entered a talent competition—and finished second. The Miss Sepia contest was the first international Black beauty pageant in North America. Ribs, rides, speakers: the Emancipation Day party was a cultural force. But it was put on hiatus in 1967, when the Detroit Riots left 43 dead and smoke from a city on fire sent an ominous message across the river. Emancipation Day resumed in 1969, though it never returned to its former glory. Nevertheless, it remains a reminder of the proud legacy of Windsor's Black community.

The celebration that at its peak attracted more than 100,000 participants, however, is far from the only such legacy of Windsor's African-Canadian community. A number of historic churches tell a story of both struggle and success as centres of gospel music and community life, many acting as Underground Railroad stations. The Sandwich First Baptist Church started as an informal parish in the 1820s by escaped slaves and is the oldest active Black church in Canada. First Baptist Church was founded in 1853 on McDougall, though it moved to Mercer and Tuscarora streets in 1915. The British Methodist Episcopal Church was built in 1856 on McDougall Street, but was replaced by a new church on University in 1963. Churches such as the Nazrey African Methodist Episcopal Church in Amherstburg, the Mount Zion Church of God in Christ, and the Tanner African Methodist Episcopal Church all overflowed with history.

Though African-Canadians faced many barriers, from poverty to discrimination, many still managed to transcend these obstacles. Like Mr. Emancipation himself, Walter Perry, another Perry also made his mark: Roy Perry. In 1949, Roy Perry became Windsor's first African-Canadian alderman, and went on to become a well-loved community advocate. He started a popular annual skating party at Windsor Arena that at its peak in the late 1950s attracted as many as 2,000 participants. There was also Alton "Uncle Al" Parker, who in 1942 became Windsor's first Black police constable, and in 1951, Canada's first police detective. Howard Homer Watkins—from the storied Watkins family, which saw several generations living in Sandwich on what is now called Watkins Street—followed suit, becoming a Windsor detective in 1960. Watkins' father, Homer, was an old-time vaudeville actor who sat on Sandwich Town Council and owned a local confectionery, who was celebrated annually by the community with Homer Watkins Day.

But it wasn't all fun, of course. African-Canadians had to overcome many hurdles. The McDougall Street Corridor, where a majority of the Black community lived, served as its own sort of living archive to the African-Canadian experience. The City of Windsor undertook a series of "redevelopment" projects in the '40s, and again in the '60s, which targeted this area, east of City Hall, as a type of urban slum. The demolition of old homes, churches (like the British Methodist Episcopal Church), and African-Canadian businesses in favour of subsidized housing destabilized the McDougall neighbourhood, dispersing African-Canadians from the core. However, the neighbourhood is still considered by many to be the historic heart of Windsor's Black community.

As days of protest against the establishment raged across North America in the counterculture 1960s and 1970s, so too did the push for justice in Windsor. On March 29, 1965, Windsor has its first civil-rights demonstration when 700 protestors walked to City Hall Square to hear speakers address racial discrimination. On August 31 of the same year, officials in Amherstburg confronted "alleged anti-Negro incidents," according to *The Windsor Star*, and formed a citizens action group, as some feared that the Ku Klux Klan was attempting to infiltrate the town. It was the year Amherstburg was hit with cross burnings.

Leading the civil-rights charge was one of Windsor's most prominent activists: Howard McCurdy. In 1959, he became the first African-Canadian to hold a tenure-track position at a Canadian university when he started as a University of Windsor biology professor (he would go on to become department head from 1974–79). In 1962, he founded the Guardian Club, a civil rights organization in Windsor, and in 1969, he created and became first president of the National Black Coalition of Canada. He was elected a City of Windsor alderman in 1980, and an NDP MP for Windsor-Walkerville from 1984–88—and never stopped fighting for justice.

In 1975, in an attempt to preserve the African-Canadian legacy in southwestern Ontario, Melvin "Mac" Simpson helped spearhead the creation of the North American Black Historical Museum—now called the Amherstburg Freedom Museum.

"The '50s to the '80s was really a renaissance for the local African-Canadian community," Elise Harding-Davis, a local historian of Black culture whose electrical contractor father was prevented from joining a union and buying property in the 1950s, said in 2016. "You saw a lot of Black businesses opening and you saw a lot of families moving out to the suburbs from the core. You also saw a lot of advancements with civil rights. There were still struggles, especially with legalities. But as a whole, it was a good time for African-Canadians. We progressed."

There is no Windsor-area history without Black history. African-Canadians were part of this region's story from the very beginning, helping mold a more vibrant and just community.

"Greatest Freedom Show on Earth": The three-day Emancipation Celebrations were underway in Windsor on July 28, 1952. The featured speaker, Dr. Archibald Carey Jr., a well-known civil rights activist from Chicago, shakes hands with Mayor Arthur J. Reaume, at left, while Walter 'Mr. Emancipation' Perry, founder and organizer of the festival, looks on. Carey spoke on racial discrimination to a crowd of 10,000 people.

January 29, 1953: Local school children crowd around Alderman Dr. Roy Perry during the annual Ice Carnival held at Windsor Arena. Beginning in 1949, Perry organized the skating parties—with free hot dogs, pop, and hot chocolate, for area youth. Over 1,000 children attended the 1953 event.

These three majorettes were but a small part of the mile-long procession that wound its way from City Hall to Jackson Park during the Emancipation Day parade on August 2, 1953. The Emancipation Day celebrations commemorated the abolition of slavery in the British Empire.

Over 30 people were baptized in the Detroit River by Bishop C.L. Morton, pastor of the Mount Zion International Church of God in Christ, on July 5, 1954. Morton was a prolific preacher, famous for his broadcasts on CKLW radio. His annual baptismal services in the '40s and '50s drew thousands of witnesses.

August 3, 1954: The Silk Hat Boosters of Detroit's Elk Lodge, one of many American entries into that year's parade. Note the spectators sitting on the roof of Imperial Shoes.

A highlight of the Emancipation Day celebrations was the Miss Sepia International pageant, where young, talented Black women from Windsor and Detroit competed for a crown and cash prize. Pictured here on August 3, 1954, contestants travel down Ouellette Avenue on a special float celebrating Windsor's Centennial.

Emancipation Day in 1954 boasted two highly distinguished speakers: Eleanor Roosevelt, at left, and Mary McLeod Bethune, at right. Hugh Graybiel, publisher of *The Windsor Star*, stands between them. Roosevelt as former First Lady was a strong advocate for human rights, and widely outspoken about racial issues. Educator and civil rights activist Bethune was well known at the time as the founder of the National Council of Negro Women.

"I had just as much fun as the youngsters," admitted Alderman Dr. Roy Perry, after his annual Ice Carnival on February 9, 1955. Here, Perry is surrounded by some of the 2,000 city children who attended the event.

July 9, 1956: Mayor Michael J. Patrick and James E. Watson, city solicitor, clear books out of the legal library in preparation for the demolition of old City Hall. James E. Watson was appointed in 1950, and is believed to be the first African-Canadian city solicitor in Canada.

First Baptist Church was originally founded in 1853 by escaped slaves but moved to Mercer Street at Tuscarora in 1915. The church, pictured here in 1957, is still active today.

August 7, 1956: Torrential downpours failed to dampen the spirits of the marchers who waited patiently before they took part in the annual Emancipation Day parade. A *Star* photographer snapped this shot of a hallway of the Windsor Police station crowded with performers seeking shelter.

Reverend Martin Luther King Jr. was the guest speaker at the Emancipation Day celebrations on August 7, 1956. At the time, King was largely unknown, having led the Montgomery Bus Boycott only one year previous. Discussing the program, from left to right, are Russell Small, president of the Emancipation Committee; Reverend King, Reverend Theodore S. Boone of Detroit, and Walter Perry.

The contestants for the Miss Sepia beauty pageant, 1956. The judges picked Miss Illinois, Joyce Felton, 19, of Detroit, who is at extreme right in the front row. The ladies were allowed to choose a city or state of their fancy to represent, even though the majority of participants were from Windsor or Detroit.

Joe Louis' former trainer Alter 'Duke' Ellis, at left, and chef Ray Horn battle the heat as they load ribs onto the grill on August 3, 1957. Barbecued spareribs and chicken were popular fare at the annual festival.

After the Jackson Park Grandstand burned to the ground on July 12, 1957, Walter Perry (with his signature cigar in his mouth) assured everyone that the Emancipation Day festivities would go on as planned. Here, he surveys the fire with Alton C. Parker, holding a young Dianne Steel.

Freedom Awards for 1956 went to Paul Martin, minister of national health and welfare; Louis C. Blount, vice president of the Great Lakes Insurance Company of Detroit; and E.C. Row, former president of Chrysler Canada, from left to right. Alderman Dr. Roy Perry, at far left, made the presentations.

More than 100,000 people from both sides of the border lined Ouellette Avenue on August 2, 1959, to view the 28th annual Emancipation Day parade. The girls pictured here were among 60-odd marching groups and 20 bands that took part.

The Windsor Community Band of Canada was formed in the Mercer Street area in 1957 by Harry "Gramps" Land, a retiree of the Charles Young Post Band of Detroit. Starting with only his grandchildren, the band quickly grew to more than 22 members by 1960. At left, young majorettes Carol Glenn, Barbara Ann Scott, Karla Taylor, Annette Ivens, Deborah Tolson, Brenda Strain, Valerie Porter, Thasia Chase, and Karen Elliot, from left to right, are ready for their next gig: leading the Knights of Pythias parade in Pontiac, Michigan. At right, Harry "Gramps" Land listens closely as three of his protégés, Kachwellyn Breaux, Mitchell Hall, and Elaine Penn, from left to right, practise their latest piece.

August 29, 1961: Reverend L.O. Jenkins stands in front of Tanner African Methodist Episcopal Church on the occasion of its 71st anniversary. The church, located at Assumption Street and Mercer Street, used to be Mercer Street Baptist. It was demolished in October 1962 as part of the city's redevelopment scheme.

Windsor's own Joan Hurst, 17, of 1097 McDougall Street, shows off her trophy (and balancing ability) after winning the Miss International Sepia beauty pageant in 1961. The contest was typically dominated—and won—by entrants from Detroit.

July 29, 1961: Walter Perry, organizer of the Emancipation Day celebrations, samples his famous "secretive sauce." With Perry, from left to right, are Jim Steele, Sarah Horn, and Ray Horn.

"Crowd Pleasers": For over two hours, bands and other marching units from Michigan, Ohio, and Ontario marched down Ouellette Avenue to Jackson Park for the Emancipation Day parade in 1961. The parade was led by the famed Sarnia Lionettes drum and bugle band, seen with its colour party above.

Beauty queens ride in a 1962 Impala convertible during the Emancipation Day parade. The Prince Edward Hotel on Ouellette Avenue is in the background.

Constable Howard Watkins of the Windsor Police Youth Branch speaks to more than 100 children about citizenship at Tanner African Methodist Episcopal Church on April 23, 1962.

Windsor's 107-year-old British Methodist Episcopal Church on 363 McDougall Street was torn down in 1963 as part of the city's redevelopment building scheme. The original building, pictured at left, with Reverend I.H. Edwards on its front steps in 1961, was built in 1854 by emancipated slaves. The new church on University Avenue is pictured at right in 1967. It is still active today.

October 1, 1962: Sandwich Baptist Church held its third annual "Homer Watkins Day" celebration to honour Watkins as the oldest deacon of the church. Here, he receives a flower from pastor Thomas Garel. The Watkins are one of Windsor's oldest African-Canadian families, dating back to the 1830s. Watkins Street in Sandwich was renamed in Homer's honour in 1963.

Thomas Traylor and Carol Dean exhibit their twisting talents for the camera after dancing to first prize over 50 couples in a "frantic" twist contest at Jackson Park as part of the Emancipation Day celebrations in 1962.

August 7, 1962: The Brewster Kadets of America, from Detroit, were a crowd favourite at the Emancipation Day celebrations.

Dr. Martin Luther King Jr. receives a citation for "promoting human relations around the world" from Mayor Michael J. Patrick at the annual Brotherhood dinner on March 15, 1963. T. Stewart Anderson, chairman of the dinner, is at right. Dr. King would give his famous "I Have a Dream Speech" only months later at the March on Washington.

The cornerstone laying for a new Tanner African Methodist Episcopal Church, June 3, 1963. From left to right are George Coates, Grand Lodge officer; Reverend G.A. Coates; Allen R. Millben; A.D. Caldwell, chairman of trustee board; and Darfield W. Parker, Grand Master. The church, which had its roots in the Mercer Street Baptist from 1877, moved into its new building on McDougall Street in 1964.

July 21, 1965: Walter "Mr. Emancipation" Perry hands a placard promoting the 34th annual Emancipation Day celebrations to Garry Eaton of the boys' club of First Baptist Church, who would distribute the signs around the city.

Dorothy Dandridge, at centre, appeared at the Elmwood Casino with Latin music icon Xavier Cugat in April 1964. She is pictured here at a party hosted in her honour by Dr. Roy Perry and his wife Charlotte. Dandridge is perhaps most famous as the first African-American woman nominated for an Academy Award for Best Actress in 1954.

700 Windsorites marched to City Hall Square during a civil rights demonstration on March 29, 1965. Carrying signs that read "March for freedom in Selma and Windsor," the group listened to speakers on the struggle for racial equality in the United States and at home. The march, the first of its kind in Windsor, had "Negro and White demonstrators walking side by side" in the words of *The Windsor Star*.

August 31, 1965: A citizens' action group was formed to address alleged "anti-Negro incidents" in the town of Amherstburg. Committee members, from left to right, are Dr. Daniel Hill, Mayor Murray Smith, George McCurdy, and Mrs. Howard Harris in the front row, and Michael Marentette, Ontario Human Rights Commission Officer; Dr. E.M. Warren, James Cake, and Ralph McCurdy in the back row. Rumours were flying that Amherstburg had its own Ku Klux Klan chapter, after a cross burning and KKK signs appeared around town.

"Last Telegram": In 1967, Dr. Martin Luther King Jr. sent a telegram to Walter Perry declining an invitation to that year's Emancipation Celebrations (which ended up being cancelled) due to a schedule conflict. Here, his nephew William Perry Jr. reads the telegram on April 5, 1968—a day following King's assassination in Texas.

The Windsor Star reported a strong emphasis on militancy among many of the entries from the Emancipation Day parade in 1966. This group, the French Dukes of Ann Arbor, Michigan, were clad in black uniforms and red berets, while performing a precision drill for the crowd.

WINDSOR ONTARIO THURSDAY JULY 27 1967

Emancipation festivities out
Perry cancels week's program

In the wake of the Detroit Riots in 1967, Walter Perry decided on July 27 to cancel the annual Emancipation Day celebrations that were scheduled to take place the following week. The cancellation came as a relief to many Windsorites who, according to *The Star*, were "petrified" that the event could spark "lawlessness or violence." City council controversially denied the festival key permits in 1968, so the event was not resumed until 1969—though many say it was never the same.

The funeral of Walter Perry, August 21, 1967. "Mr. Emancipation" died at age 68 and was buried at Grove Cemetery. At the service, the band played *When the Saints Go Marching In* and *Birth of the Blues*, as was Perry's last request.

Funeral services for Windsor detective Howard Watkins were held on June 17, 1968. Only 40 years of age, Watkins succumbed to a heart condition, and was remembered for his dedicated service, particularly to Windsor's youth.

September 9, 1968: Members of the Church of God in Christ march into their new building, at Mercer Street and Cataraqui Street, singing *We're Marching Upward to Zion* as they made their way from their old rented quarters at 900 Mercer Street.

July 24, 1969: Detective Alton C. Parker ("Uncle Al," as the neighbourhood children called him) is surrounded by children who attended his first annual Kid's Party at Broadhead Park.

July 29, 1969: Mrs. Howard McCurdy, left, and Mrs. George Crowell polish a plaque from 1928 that they discovered on the Ouellette Avenue branch of the Toronto Dominion Bank. The women were leaders of the Black Heritage Club of Windsor, which was formed that year to rediscover the contributions made by the local Black community to Essex County.

Dr. Howard McCurdy, pictured here in his laboratory at the University of Windsor, became the first African Canadian to hold a tenure-track position when he joined the biology department in 1959. He was Department Head from 1974 to 1979. A long-time social activist, McCurdy co-founded the National Black Coalition of Canada in 1969. He went on to serve on city council and as the MP for Windsor-Walkerville. He was inducted into the Order of Canada in 2012.

A precision group marches past People's Credit on Ouellette Avenue during the Emancipation Day parade in 1970. According to *The Star*, marching entries provided a change from the usual drums and bugles typical of past parades.

Debbie Milburn, 20, sheds tears of joy after being chosen Miss Sepia of 1974. She was given a shot at the Miss Western Ontario contest that Labour Day weekend.

"Uncle Al" Parker helps two young neighbours with their pony ride during his Kids Party at Broadhead Park in 1975.

Charlotte Watkins, community advocate and daughter of Homer Watkins, stands in front of Sandwich First Baptist Church on January 5, 1974. The oldest Black church in the Windsor area, Sandwich First Baptist was a stop on the Underground Railroad for fugitive slaves fleeing to Canada.

Bishop C.L. Morton Jr. carries on the family tradition, as pastor of the church that his father established: Mt. Zion Church of God in Christ on McDougall Street. He is pictured here in 1975 with his brother, Reverend Paul Morton, of New Orleans, Louisiana, behind him.

Paul Martin, long-time Windsor MP, and Alton C. Parker, Canada's first Black detective, were both inducted into the Order of Canada on April 7, 1976. Then retired, Parker was honoured for his community work with children and ex-convicts.

August 1, 1977: 'Miss Sepia' Tammy Taylor of Windsor is given her trophy by festival director Edmund "Ted" Powell, who took over the Emancipation Day celebrations after Walter Perry's death in 1967. In 1977, City Council moved the festival to Mic Mac Park—a decision that Powell blamed for the festival's poor attendance, drawing around half of its normal attendees.

September 23, 1978: Melvin "Mac" Simpson, founder and executive director of the North American Black Cultural Centre, stands on the future museum site, designed to record the rich heritage of Blacks in Essex County. The building on the left is the Taylor log cabin from the Fort Malden Reserve, which would be restored to resemble the home of a freed slave circa 1855. On the right is the Nazery African Methodist Episcopal Church, built in 1848, which would retire as an active church and be restored. The museum is still open today as the Amherstburg Freedom Museum.

MULTICULTURALISM

Though Windsor has long struggled to diversify its economy, its people are a different story. The city's history is one of multiculturalism, given that Windsor is the fourth most ethnically diverse city in Canada. Proudly so, as well.

As a border city next to Detroit, a major US urban centre in the heart of the Midwest, Windsor was well situated for an influx from a wide variety of places. According to Statistics Canada, only the country's biggest cities have higher proportions of ethnic diversity: Toronto, Montreal, and Vancouver. Windsor therefore stands out for a city its size.

The Detroit River Region's original settlers were First Nations, with indigenous tribes such as the Huron, Ojibway, Wyandot, and more. When the French first arrived in the area—Detroit was settled under the direction of Antoine de la Mothe Cadillac in 1701 while European settlements began on what would become the Canadian side of the Detroit River in 1747—other nationalities were not far behind. The Border Cities were unique for their early French Catholic heritage (in a province dominated by Anglo-Protestant settlers), but English, Irish, Scottish, and African-American immigrants soon diversified the

Windsor area, eventually overtaking the French in sheer numbers.

Windsor's various ethnic communities—which flourished in the post-war decades—had their roots in early immigration patterns, from as early as the 18th century. For example, Chinese labourers began arriving on Canada's west coast in 1788 to help with the building of trading posts, and then the Canadian Pacific Railway, though that work eventually dried up. Facing unemployment and institutionalized racism, many of these Chinese Canadians began heading east. Windsor, with its burgeoning industries, was an attractive location. According to a 1901 census, among the first to arrive in Windsor was Kee Chong Lee in 1897, when he set up a hand laundry business. The Chinese community only grew from there, forming the Chinese Benevolent Society in 1918 and starting a growing Chinatown business district on Riverside Drive East, until it was expropriated by the city to make way for Le Goyeau apartments in 1960.

Another early community, the Italians formed a major part of the Windsor story, growing up around Erie Street—known as Little Italy—but also in other areas of the city and county. The Italian community grew so large it spawned several clubs. The Border Cities Italian Club (which would become the Giovanni Caboto Club) formed in 1925, becoming the first Italian club in southwestern Ontario. Its first building at Parent Avenue and Tecumseh Road was erected in 1950, and would be expanded in 1972, 1978, and 1986. Other clubs, like Fogolar Furlan, the Ciociaro Club, and the Calabria Club, would follow.

Other immigration continued apace: Irish, Scottish, German, Polish, Middle Eastern, Ukrainian, African, Jewish, and much, much more. Many ethnic groups had created their own houses of worship or clubs prior to World War II, though immigration picked up after hostilities ended. During the war, after all, and even for a few years afterward, some people of German, Italian, and Japanese ancestry—and "any particular person... acting in a manner prejudicial to the public safety," according to the 1939 Defence of Canada Regulations—were interned in camps and their property seized.

Prior to the war in the Windsor area, as with much of the country, few agencies were dedicated to newcomers. In Windsor, only IODE Memorial Hospital and the YMCA served new Canadians' cultural and citizenship needs in the Windsor area. By the '50s, other civic organizations were started, as Windsor's population grew and continued to diversify. The Essex County New Citizens Association, for instance, started in 1949, while the Windsor Ethnic Council began in 1954. Other organizations included: the Catholic Immigration Centre on Cadillac Street, the Lutheran Immigration Centre on Parent Avenue, the Interchurch Council and the Citizenship Council of Greater Windsor, the Canadian All Nations Cultural Association, the Windsor Ethnic Council, and the Essex County All Nations Association. All these organizations helped new arrivals integrate and stage cultural events. Brotherhood Week, observed across Canada in the 1950s and 1960s, celebrated different cultures. St. Clair College offered English as a second language classes in the 1970s. The world was coming to Windsor.

As Windsor became recognized as an increasingly cosmopolitan city, it became a destination for refugees, who could often integrate more easily with the help of existing ethnic communities. One immigrant wave of note stemmed from the Hungarian Revolution of 1956, when Soviet forces violently suppressed an uprising and more than 200,000 Hungarians fled as refugees. Many arrived in Windsor, where citizens pitched in to assist. Windsor accepted refugees as part of the Canadian government's special Chinese Refugee Program (a response to famine in mainland China) in 1962. Another large

influx came in 1978, 1979 and 1980 when refugees, who became known as Vietnamese Boat People—fleeing their country after the Vietnam War—began arriving in North America, including in Windsor.

In 1967, Canada opened the doors more to immigration. As a *Windsor Star* front-page headline declared on September 12, 1967, "Immigrant Laws Liberalized: Family, Skills Stressed." The changes featured a new point system to evaluate potential immigrants, focused on categories like age, education, and employment potential. This meant that laws were being applied equally to all nations, whereas before certain countries benefited more than others. And though annual immigration was expected to climb only from 200,000 to 220,000, Windsor was one of the cities that enjoyed increased immigration.

However, 1971 stands out as the year the country truly embraced diversity—when Canada became the first country in the world to officially adopt multiculturalism as an official government policy. The 1971 Multiculturalism Policy of Canada also enshrined the rights of Aboriginal people and the country's two official languages of English and French. "Canadian multiculturalism is fundamental to our belief that all citizens are equal," according to the federal government. "Multiculturalism ensures that all citizens can keep their identities, can take pride in their ancestry and have a sense of belonging." Given some people criticized the idea at the time, and that Canada had been less welcoming in the past, the multicultural policy represented a notable change in public thinking.

In 1973, partly as a response to Canada's new multiculturalism policy, the Multicultural Council of Windsor and Essex County was born, with Dr. Rudolph Helling as the group's first president. It moved offices a number of times but always stuck to its mission of helping new Canadians. In 1975, the Multicultural Council's most popular event began as a type of bazaar with ethnic food and cultural items on display at the Cleary Auditorium. It would go on to be called the Carrousel of Nations, and would expand greatly, with various "villages" across the city annually showcasing everything from Lebanese to Jamaican culture, and lots more in between. In the words of the Multicultural Council, "the 1970s were really the heyday of folkloric activity."

Between 1961 and 1971, Windsor's population jumped 83 percent, to 209,000—much of that thanks to immigration from around the globe. Windsor and Essex County truly embraced Canada's official policy of multiculturalism and grew because of it, in numbers and in culture.

The new Giovanni Caboto Club building, at 2175 Parent Avenue, was dedicated on June 19, 1950, coinciding with the 25th anniversary of the club. At right, Colonel William Griesinger, MPP for Windsor-Sandwich, officially opens the new club rooms, surrounded by some of the 800 club members who attended the event.

The van Erp family, newly arrived Dutch immigrants, ended up on the doorstep of Reverend H.J. Storm of Windsor on April 9, 1952, having gotten lost in their search for their new home. The next day, they were on their way to their farm in Tilbury.

Members of Windsor's Chinese community stand in front of their float, sponsored by the Chinese Benevolent Society, for the Windsor Centennial Parade on July 1, 1954.

October 27, 1958: Gordona Budimir, Milrad Radovic, and Libby Bacuvcik prepare for the Canadian Festival of Serbian Singing Federation of America, held at the Prince Edward Hotel. More than 1,000 attended the two-day festival.

These students at Frank W. Begley Public School point out their countries of origin on a map to commemorate Brotherhood Week in 1956. At the time, Begley had the most diverse student population of any school in Windsor. From left to right are Lee Fong, China; Winada Talbot and Betty McLaughlin, Canada; Aurelia Erescu, Romania; and Sam Jadhout, Lebanon.

Hungarian refugees arrive in Windsor, December 1956. Thousands of refugees fled Budapest after the Red Army invaded to quell a rebellion. The Canadian government accepted 37,000 refugees, most of them settling throughout Ontario—including Windsor. At left, refugees touch the safety of Canadian soil after arriving by charter flight from Vienna, while Mr. and Mrs. James Zobor, and their son John, arrive at the CNR station, pictured at right.

The second annual Jewish Music Festival featured a concert at Shaar Hashomayim Synagogue on January 31, 1957. From left to right are Frank Ugrits, viola; Celia Hardcastle, cello; Wayne Townsend, piano; Ann Grayson, second violin; Ruth Irwin Pohjola, piano; Sidney Levine, clarinet; and Lasse Pohjola, violin.

April 4, 1959: Larame Filipek and Carolyn Czwornog, from left to right, are twirled by their partners, Tony Wolanski and Edward Dydo. The couples are wearing traditional costumes representing different regions in Poland.

February 16, 1959: Students from Gordon McGregor School, dressed in their national costumes, greet the beginning of National Brotherhood Week. From left to right are Marlee Jackew, Polish; Marvin Crawford, Ukrainian; Brenda Holsey, Russian; Hans Zaborek, Swiss; Armin Lippman, German; Anne Pecnick, Croatian; Dianne Virga, Serbian; and Elizabeth Stelzer, Austrian.

The Jewish Community Centre, at 1641 Ouellette Avenue, opened in 1959. Designed by J.P. Thompson and Associates, more than 10 years of planning by Windsor's Jewish Community Council went into the construction of the building. The community centre is still open today, though it underwent a major renovation in 1993.

In 1962, the Canadian government accepted 109 families as part of a special Chinese Refugee Program, responding to the mass exodus of people fleeing famine in mainland China. Pictured at left, Lee Dean, a prominent member of Windsor's Chinese community, welcomes Yuen Ha, Kin Bun, and Bing Tong Yan, from left to right, upon their arrival at Windsor Airport. Pictured at right, U Kwong laughs at his mother, Mrs. Sau Yim Wah, as she tries to use an "American knife and fork the same way she uses chopsticks," in the words of *The Star*. Similar photo-ops were staged across Canada, arranged by the federal government, to ensure that Canadians would receive the refugees positively.

May 9, 1959: Angeliki Lambracon and Anastasia Stefanopoulou listen to Philip Vacratis play the pipe, the national instrument of Greece, as they prepare for a festival held in Windsor and Detroit. According to *The Star*, Windsor had 750 Greek immigrants in 1959, who were making plans to build a Greek Orthodox church.

A *Star* feature on Windsor's Little Italy in 1964 declared the Italian community to be 30,000 strong, and concentrated in the Erie Street and Parent Avenue corridor. At left, parishioners come out of St. Angela Merici Church after a Sunday service. The church was built by Italian immigrants and opened in 1940. At right, men play a traditional hand game called "Morra", which according to *The Star*, was banned in Italy because of "flaring tempers" and intense rivalries.

Windsor's Hungarian community commemorated the 1956 Hungarian Revolution in front of City Hall on October 22, 1962. Holding the flag—with the Russian hammer and sickle cut away—are Elizabeth Mandics and Helen Szabo, both former refugees, helped by Mrs. William Stefan and Albert Horvath, from left to right.

The "Year of the Monkey" would be celebrated on February 4, 1968, by Windsor's Chinese residents with an opera sponsored by the Chinese Benevolent Society. Rehearsing, from left to right, are: Keith Lee, Mrs. Po Anne Gan, Ken Gean, and Diane Gene.

May 9, 1966: Over 200 members of Windsor's Polish community march to Holy Trinity Church, at 1035 Ellis Avenue, for a memorial mass to commemorate two anniversaries: the 175th anniversary of the signing of the Polish constitution and 1,000 years of Christianity in Poland.

May 1, 1965: A group of would-be pipers puff enthusiastically into a set of practice chanters during the Scottish Society of Windsor's beginners bagpipe course. From left to right, in the front row, are Jamie Hogg, Bryce Ramsay, Gordon Ramsay, and Ian Murray, with Dermot Ganley, Michael Mayne, Ciaran Ganley, and James Ganley in the back row.

In 1967, the Canadian government overhauled its immigration policy to introduce the points system, designed to increase sponsorship rights, stop discrimination against certain countries, and tie immigration to economic conditions in Canada. After its introduction, immigration from Africa, Latin America, the Caribbean, and Asia dramatically increased.

October 19, 1967: Jewish children Blaine Speigel, Gordon Morse, and Janice Weingarden celebrate the Festival of Sukkot at Temple Beth El.

Last year's queen, Eleanor Mamaril, at left, presents the trophy to the newly crowned Miss Independence, Carol Urbayan, on June 23, 1969 at Caboto Hall. The annual celebration of Philippine Independence Day, held by the Filipino Organization of Windsor, marks the date when the Philippines gained freedom from Spanish rule.

November 30, 1968: Piper Jock McEllan hoists a toast to the haggis as part of the St. Andrew's Day dinner and dance held at the Teutonia Club, sponsored by the Border Cities Burns Club. Watching are chef Horst Volesing (at left) and Robert Murray, who later addressed the haggis in the words of Scottish poet Robert Burns.

October 22, 1970: Members of the Filipino Association of Windsor perform a traditional dance for the University of Windsor's United Nations Club.

September 4, 1973: The Fogolar Furlan tug-of-war team digs in to beat Fullarton Township and take second place overall during the last day of the Italia Sports Weekend. The highlight of the weekend was the "Tour of Windsor" bicycle race, an event that exists today as the Tour di Via Italia.

More than 200 Ukrainian Canadians gathered in City Hall Square on March 25, 1973, to commemorate the seven million Ukrainians who starved to death from famine in 1933. Here, Reverend Basil Dzurman, at left, of Sts. Vladimir and Olga Eastern Rite Catholic Church and Reverend Witaly Metulynsky, at right, of St. Vladimir's Ukrainian Orthodox Cathedral, lead prayers.

Karneval, German 'Mardi Gras', 1973. At left, the party-goers help toast Karneval, held at the Teutonia Club, while at right, Teutonia Club president Helmut Mueller is "capped" with *narrenkappen* (fool's cap) during the festivities. The Teutonia Club building, opened at 55 Edinborough Street in 1954, closed in 2016, but the German club still exists.

June 15, 1974: Roman chariots and soldiers paraded through downtown Windsor on their way to the Caboto Club on Parent Avenue to celebrate the sixth annual Roman festival held by the Windsor Italian Business and Professional Association.

July 20, 1974: Tibor and Elizabeth Kleinacs show off their wares in front of their newly opened Hungarian restaurant, the Blue Danube, at 1235 Ottawa Street. Many Hungarians settled near Ottawa Street during the 1920s, but by the '70s, only remnants of that original neighbourhood remained.

July 31, 1974: Around 100 of Windsor's 500 East Indian immigrants taught at the University of Windsor. Pictured leaving University Centre are Dr. O.P. Chanda, Davinder Singh, Harjit Sethi, and Thair Omar, from left to right.

December 1, 1973: Members of the Ukrainian Women's Association of Canada form an assembly line to make *pyrohy* (Ukrainian perogies) for the *pushynia* or smörgåsbord dinner and dance at St. Vladimir's Ukrainian Orthodox Cathedral. In the early '70s, the Ukrainian community exceeded 6,500 people.

February 26, 1974: Shirley Zokvich leads an "English as a Second Language" class for new Canadians at St. Clair College's Patterson facility. More than 150 new immigrants took advantage of the classes that year.

October 27, 1974: Members of Windsor's Ukrainian community march outside Cleary Auditorium during a concert by Ukrainian opera stars Yevhenia Miroshnichenko and Dmytro Hnatiuk. The protest was aimed at the Soviet Union's control over Ukrainian artists and urged Windsorites to boycott the concert.

Windsor's first refugees from Vietnam arrived on August 14, 1975. Thanh Ha Le, Amh Hoa Le, Hiep Doan, and Hinh Doan fled Saigon only one day before the city was captured by the North Vietnamese forces and were sponsored by Mrs. Richard Graybiel to settle in Windsor.

August 7, 1976: Nine Kurdish refugees from Iraq discuss their first eight weeks in Windsor for a *Star* feature. The Canadian government accepted Kurdish refugees for the first time in the wake of violent conflict between Kurdish rebels and Saddam Hussein's regime. Twenty-three of the 100 Kurds accepted were settled in Windsor. Their major complaint? The unexpected Windsor humidity, instead of the cold they expected from Canada.

May 30, 1977: Teams from all over the city competed in a bocce tournament at the opening of the Ciociaro Club, an Italian club on North Talbot Road. A three-day festival marked the club's official opening with government speakers, a banquet, and an open house for the public.

June 7, 1977: Joe Gan stands in front of his 10-year-old establishment, the Mai Mai Restaurant, at 754 Ouellette Avenue. Gan immigrated to Windsor in 1930 and became one of Windsor's best known restauranteurs, owning spots like Hotel Commodore, Gan's Restaurant, Jo-Lim's, and the Mai Mai, among others.

Fire-eater Tunka Abdurama causes a stir at the Caribbean Village during the Carrousel of Nations on June 20, 1977. The Carrousel of Nations was created after the Multicultural Council of Windsor and Essex County held a highly successful Multicultural Festival in 1974.

October 30, 1978: Members of the Canadian Lebanese League participated in a walk-a-thon to buy supplies for refugees displaced by fighting in Lebanon. Here, they march past the Toronto Dominion Bank at the corner of Ouellette Avenue and Riverside Drive. The league represented 6,000 people in Windsor and Essex County.

June 10, 1978: Wilmer Nadjiwon, of the Cape Croker Indian Reserve, works on a wood carving at the North American Indian Village at Willistead Park. That year, there were 31 Carrousel 'villages' around the city and county.

November 20, 1978: Dancers celebrate the annual Kirchweihfest festival, an old German church custom, at the Teutonia Club. A tradition hundreds of years old, all church members would grow a rosemary bush, the largest of which would be donated to the church to be auctioned off.

November 15, 1979: Six-year-old Vietnamese refugee A-Mui Moc, who arrived in Windsor three weeks previous, experiences his first snowfall.

The Calabria Club, an Italian club on Howard Avenue, held its first Grape Harvest in September 1979. Here, celebrants "get into the spirits" with a wine-chugging contest.

Darlene Trojansek and other members of the Slovenian Village Dance Group prepare for the Festival of Dances to be held on May 27, 1980. The cultural extravaganza focused on fashion and dance from the 22 countries involved in that year's Carrousel of Nations.

Vietnamese refugees, known as 'Boat People', arrived in Windsor in the late 1970s, some of the 60,000 refugees accepted by Canada during the international crisis. Here, newly arrived immigrants, awaiting housing, pass the time watching television in a hotel room on December 10, 1978.

The Nhon Thai family escaped Vietnam in the freighter *Hai Hong* and were settled in the Windsor Housing Authority's St. Joseph Avenue project in West Windsor in 1979. From left to right are Nhon Thai, his wife Quach Kim Tien with their grandchild Praharita (who was born on the *Hai Hong*); and Praharita's mother, Tran Ten Thai. Behind them are neighbours Pat Westwood, Jo-Anne Jones, and Helen Demers, who helped the new family settle in.

June 18, 1979: Carole Ng performs a classical ribbon dance at the Chinese Village, held at St. Andrew's Presbyterian Church.

December 17, 1980: Over 600 immigrants, including 200 refugee children, attended a Christmas party thrown by Operation Lifeline, a local group that helped new families settle in Windsor. Examining their presents, from left to right, are: A Kiu Moc, Xao Khen, Oy Khen Ly, and A Di Moc, with A Pao Moc held by A Mui Moc in the back row.

THE SPORTING LIFE

Windsor has long enjoyed a love affair with sports, even before the city had many facilities to support them. Not just one or two sports, either, but a full fans' paradise.

The main team round these parts today is the Windsor Spitfires, which had some starts and stops before taking off for good, eventually winning back-to-back Memorial Cup championships in 2009 and 2010. The junior hockey franchise, among the oldest in the Ontario Hockey League, began in the Ontario Hockey Association in 1945. The original Spitfires folded in 1953, unleashing the Windsor Bulldogs squad in the Senior A League. Perhaps the Bulldogs' greatest claim to fame came under captain Lou Bendo, beating a touring Soviet team in Canada on November 21, 1962, then going on to claim the Allan Cup in the 1962–63 season—though the team would fold in 1964. But the Spitfires would fly again, re-launching in 1971 as part of the Southern Ontario Junior A Hockey League—winning the championship in the 1973–74 season. At first, the squad fought more than opponents. It also battled the league, which for a while excluded the Spits from moving up to a higher league because Windsor Arena was deemed an "inadequate facility." The Spits came out on top, joining the Ontario Major Junior Hockey League in 1975 (which later became the Ontario Hockey League). In the 1979–80 season, they won their first Emms Division title before a raucous home crowd. Windsor hosted the Memorial Cup in 1981, though did not place.

Hockey was far from the only sport in Windsor and Essex County. The AKO Fratmen football squad also attracted fans from around the area, with the help of some hard-hitting on-field success. The team started as an offshoot of the AKO Fraternity, playing in the Canadian Junior Football League in the 1940s, winning national titles in 1952, 1954, and 1999. Fratmen Field was built in 1953, now better known as Windsor Stadium. Multi-position player Tommy Grant was the star. Grant went on to play with the Hamilton Tiger-Cats and Winnipeg Blue Bombers from 1956–69 before being inducted into the Canadian Football Hall of Fame.

The quintessential American game, baseball, was also big just across the border from Detroit. The Tecumseh Indians started in 1943. The first game in Memorial Park in 1946 drew 4,000 fans, thanks in part to new grandstands. Over the years, the club went through many evolutions, becoming the Tecumseh Red Caps in 1954, with the sponsorship of Carling Brewery. In 1959, they morphed into the Tecumseh Green Giants, named after the town's biggest employer, though after the plant was taken over by Family Traditions in 1996, the team became the Tecumseh Thunder. In 1979, their home turf was renamed Lacasse Park after Mr. Baseball himself, Bert Lacasse, a longtime player and coach.

The 1950s and 1960s brought Olympic gold home to southwestern Ontario. Marksman Gerry Ouellette won gold for Windsor by recording the first perfect score in Olympic prone shooting, firing 60 shots in half the allotted time—all with a borrowed rifle. His rifle was damaged in transit to the 1956 Games in Melbourne, Australia, so a teammate loaned Ouellette a gun he had never used, and helped to make history as a result.

Other noteworthy local Olympic achievements also invigorated fans. The 1952 Canadian Olympic basketball team included a significant Windsor contingent: Woody Campbell, Bill Coulthard, J.S. (Red) Curren, Bill Pataky, Bob Phibbs, Bob Simpson, and Harry Wade. As well, Windsor-born Ernestine Russell made it into the record books by becoming the first person to win the Velma Springstead Award as Canada's female athlete of the year three years in a row: 1953, 1954, and 1955. Plus, Russell became Canada's first female Olympic gymnast when she competed in Melbourne in 1956. That year the whole Canadian Olympic gymnastic team hailed from the Windsor area: Russell, Ed Gagnier, and coach Bernard "Bernie" Newman. Incidentally, Newman later turned his competitive spirit to politics, serving first as a Windsor alderman then as the Member of Provincial Parliament for Windsor-Walkerville from 1959 to 1987.

Windsor's Olympic dream didn't stop there, but caught fire in the 1970s. Mary Grant of Cottam participated in the 1972 Munich Games in archery. Windsor-born Cathy Priestner was not just a two-time Olympian, but the first Canadian woman to win an individual medal in Olympic speed skating. After competing with the Canadian Olympic team in 1972 in Sapporo, Japan, she captured the silver medal in the 500-metre event in 1976 at the Innsbruck Games. Swimmer Doug Martin, of the Windsor Aquatic Club, made it to the 1976 Summer Games in Montreal in his signature butterfly event, placing 22nd. Local fencing wonder Eli Sukunda, known for his deftness with the sabre, also competed in the Montreal Games and would go on to become a three-time Olympian. Windsor did itself proud on the world stage, putting forth elite athletes who could compete with the best of them.

Other notable sports milestones include: the creation of the Windsor Badminton and Bowling Club in the 1950s, in the days when members met at Sunnyside Tavern; the establishment of the Windsor Gymnastics Club in 1953 (thanks to Bernie Newman); the establishment of the Windsor Warlocks lacrosse team in 1960; the founding of the Windsor Aquatic Club in 1970; the birth of Rose City Gymnastics in 1976; and the establishment of the Windsor Amateur Boxing Club in 1968. In 1973, the WABC won the Michigan Golden Gloves championship, becoming the only Canadian team to beat the notoriously tough Detroit Kronk and Brewster Clubs.

Also, from a fan-heaven point of view, the star-studded 1976 Canadian Open was held at the Essex Golf and Country Club. Jerry Pate won with a competitive course record of 63, while none other than Jack Nicklaus came second, ahead of a who's who of golf, including: Arnold Palmer, Gary Player, Tom Watson, Johnny Miller, Tom Weiskopf, Ben Crenshaw, and most of the day's best players.

And when it comes to sports in Windsor, bowling is never far behind, especially in the 1960s and 1970s. Bowlero opened in the 1960s with 50 lanes. When it later bumped up to 74 lanes, it became the largest 10-pin establishment in the country, in an era when bowling alleys dotted Windsor and Essex County like so many pins on a map, though it ended up closing in 2015. Indeed, for many in Windsor, good-old recreation was as much of a sport as the rest of them. The opening of the Windsor Raceway was the biggest story of 1965, bringing patrons from all over Essex County and beyond to bet on their favourite steeds. The Windsor Flying Club put on an annual spectacle, drawing crowds for their air shows that featured daring aerobatic feats. And one can't forget the day that Miss Supertest III claimed the Harmsworth Cup. Windsorites celebrated on the shores of the Detroit River as the speedboat took top honours for Canada for the first time in history.

Finally, you can't talk about sport in Windsor without a mention of Killer Kowalski. Born Wladek (Walter) Kowalski in 1926, the Polish-Canadian wrestler hit the ring professionally in 1948 and toiled as one of the most popular villains of the day until his retirement in 1977—wrestling in many top leagues, including the WWF. His nasty ring character, however, contrasted sharply with his friendly, polite demeanor in real life.

Whether it was about teams, Olympic aspiration, or plain-old recreation, devoted Windsor and Essex County fans always cherished their sports.

April 28, 1959: This water lily, performed by the Herman Collegiate water ballet, took months of hard practice to perfect. The girls were members of the only synchronized swim team in the city.

Members of the city's newly formed competitive swim team, the Windsor Aquatic Club, dive for the water as they trained in the Adie Knox Herman Swimming Pool for the Swimathon, held February 13 and 14, 1971. From left to right, the swimmers are Doug Martin, 15; Chris Service, 15; Steve Friis, 7; and Patricia Roy, 8. Doug Martin, a Windsor Essex Sports Hall of Famer, went on to compete in the Ontario Games, Pan-Am Games, and the 1976 Montreal Olympics.

The winners of the Windsor Secondary School Athletic Association's swim meet in December, 1976, line up at the pool's edge. Front to back are Jill Trotter, Beth Carmichael, Lori Scott, and Greg Hemstreet. Lori Scott became one of Windsor's finest swimmers, qualifying for the Moscow Olympics in 1980. However, like all of Canada's team, she did not attend due to the American-led boycott.

Windsor's own Major Leaguer Reno Bertoia was out on the diamond at Assumption High School to offer a few tips to Father Ronald Cullen's baseball team on May 17, 1958. Here, he displays the proper fielding stance to infielders Ken Long and Frank Flanagan. After retiring from baseball, Bertoia became a longtime Windsor high-school teacher.

The 1962–63 Green Giants were the 20th edition of the Tecumseh Baseball Club, and continued to be a power in the Essex County Senior League. Season favourites, they narrowly lost to the Maidstone Shamrocks in game five of the finals.

August 2, 1977: Karen Allen of Malden Centre, left, slides into both the home plate and Lisa Sajatovich, pitcher for the Riverside club, in the final game of the Turtle Club of LaSalle's softball tournament. Malden Centre won the game, taking the tournament over 13 other teams from Windsor, Essex County, and Chatham.

July 4, 1969: President Bert Lacasse of the Tecumseh Baseball Club, at left, and Club Director Ray Beausoleil, at right, try out their very own "Iron Mike" pitching machine with team member Tom Trepanier, up to bat. A first for the Windsor area, the machine was used to give batting instruction to about 400 Tecumseh ballplayers that year.

The Windsor Chiefs brought the Tecumseh Green Giants' reign as champions of the Essex County Senior Baseball League to a crashing halt with their victory on September 26, 1977. Sharing a celebratory squeeze are Chief stars, from left to right: Ris Massetti, pitcher Roger Doe, and Bruce Walker. Bruce Walker is better known as a CFL football star, who played six seasons as a wide receiver for the Ottawa Rough Riders.

From left to right, Gerard Lapierre, Tony Chibi, Tony 'Red' Glasser, and John Allenby—one of these keglers would become the next Canadian 10-Pin Singles bowling champion in April 1959. Tony Chibi was one of the region's strongest bowlers, most famous for his hat trick of Canadian championships in 1960, 1961, and 1963. Even though a painful inflammatory condition called bursitis forced Chibi to retire prematurely, his remarkable career earned him a spot as one of the few bowlers in the Windsor Essex County Sports Hall of Fame.

Leamington's Lou Matassa, a "Canadian professional pin king," shows off his form in 1966. A regular on the bowling circuit, Matassa held many local records and was inducted into the Windsor-Essex Chatham-Kent Bowling Association Hall of Fame in 1975 for superior performance.

March 15, 1969: The Windsor Alumni pose with the Montreal Sportsmen's Cup after they won the Canadian Amateur Basketball Association Senior A men's championship. Captain Bob Turner and coach Bob Hanson hold the trophy, which returned to Windsor for the first time since 1936. Flanking Turner and Hanson are Mario Baggio and Greg McCollough, while the other teammates are Steve Rogin and Paul Carter (foreground) and manager Ed Fedory, Angelo Mazzuchin, assistant coach Mike Gloster, Wayne Curtin, Jon Elcombe, and Dexter Robinson (middle row); Gerry Schen, Rick Cloutier, and Mike Taranczuk (back row), from left to right.

Raiders' Dennis Kelly is wary of Brennan's Mike Nipinak during the opener of the 1972–1973 high-school basketball season. The Brennan Cardinals were defending provincial champions, but 10 of their star players graduated. They lost this game to their traditional rivals from across town, the Assumption Purple Raiders, 53–45.

Members of the 1980 All-City first-team smile down at the camera, from left to right: Janine Casagrande, Jackie Pidgeon, Misty Thomas, Mary Leixner, and Celeste Harris. Misty Thomas, here a sixteen-year-old Massey student, became a key member of the Canadian National Basketball Team from 1982 to 1989. She led Canada to a fourth-place finish at the 1984 Los Angeles Olympics and a bronze medal at the 1986 world championships.

In 1973, the Windsor Amateur Boxing Club became the only Canadian club to win the Michigan Golden Gloves championship, defeating the infamous Kronk and Brewster clubs of Detroit. Seen here are four of the five WABC members crowned Golden Glove kings, from left to right: manager Harry Marshall, Tom Marshall, Mark Wilson, Ron Morris, coach Jerry McCarthy, and Peter Reschke. Harry Marshall, a Windsor Essex County Sports Hall of Famer, co-founded the WABC in 1968 after a successful boxing career in the 1940s.

Tony Mellor blasts right, but lacks reach while Bill Noble, on the left, connects on his way to a TKO triumph. Noble, of the WABC, registered a second round knockout against his clubmate, Mellor, during a heavyweight matchup at Windsor Arena on April 17, 1973.

July 11, 1973: These young WABC fighters were on their way to Edmonton for the Junior Olympics. Chris McCauley, 13, was in the flyweight division; Bud Lishenki, 15, was the province's bantamweight champion; and Robert Hudson, 15, was the lightweight king.

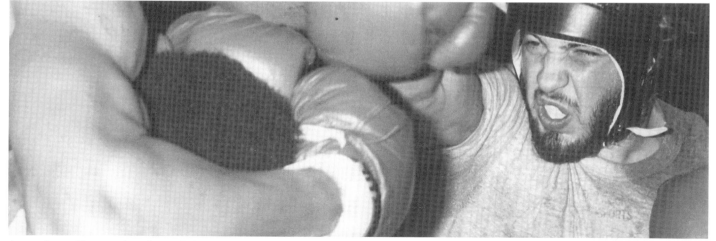

A snarling Chris Kolonelos, of the WABC, wades in against a ducking Dominique Bradford of Detroit Considine in their heavyweight matchup for the Golden Gloves boxing championship on February 27, 1978. In front of a crowd of 600 at Elmwood Casino, Kolonelos won all three rounds in a unanimous decision for his eighth straight victory.

Windsor's Tommy Grant, star player for the Hamilton Tiger-Cats and Winnipeg Blue Bombers, is seen here upon winning the Schenley Award for the Most Outstanding Canadian Player in 1964. Grant played an impressive fourteen seasons in the CFL, participating in nine Grey Cup games and winning four. He was inducted into the Canadian Football Hall of Fame in 1995.

Meet the Star's Tier 1 All City football team for 1980, selected from senior players of the Windsor Secondary School Assocation. Left to right, back row: Scott McLauchlan (Massey), Gino Castellan (Lowe), Tony Dennis (Centennial), David Lovegrove (Massey), Gino Lomazzo (Brennan); front row: Kevin Reaume (Brennan), Paul Bridgeman (Centennial), Howie Hasking (Herman), John Thys (Lowe), Kelvin Proctor (Lowe), Peter Lynn (Centennial), Dan Mooney (Brennan), and John LeFler (Herman).

The AKO Fratmen and Coach Al Newman, far right, with the *Leader-Post* Trophy, after winning their first national championship in 1952. The AKO Fratmen, established in 1929, took home national titles from the Canadian Junior Football League in 1952, 1954, and 1999.

Windsor native, Walter "Killer" Kowalski was one of the most notorious 'villains' in the WWF from 1948 to 1977, known for his signature Iron Claw move.

August 16, 1966: Mayor John Wheelton dropped by to greet members of the Ontario and Quebec junior golf teams upon their arrival in Windsor for a two-day match at Beach Grove Golf and Country Club. Showing the mayor how, from left to right, are captains Brian McLean of Quebec and Gary Hamilton of Ontario; Bill Curry, Windsor's only player on the Ontario team; and Eric Reid, Quebec's junior champion.

February 2, 1976: Heralded as "Windsor's best bet to win a spot on the Olympic team," Eli Sukunda is the "man behind the fencer's mask," practising his cuts with his coach and mentor, Istvan Danosi, in preparation for the Montreal Games. Brandishing his sabre at right, Sukunda would do Windsor proud by participating in three Olympic Games in 1976, 1984, and 1988 as both an athlete and a coach. In 1977, he made an amazing recovery after being stabbed five times by a disgruntled patron at his family's business, the St. Clair Tavern.

Canada's first female gymnast Ernestine Russell poses with her teammate Ed Gagnier and their coach Bernard Newman before the 1956 Olympic Games. Training partners at the Windsor Gymnastics Club, Russell and Gagnier were the only two members of Canada's first Olympic gymnastic team since 1908.

Ernestine Russell completes a successful dismount during the 1960 Olympic Games in Rome.

This line-up of young skaters took to the ice at the big revue staged by the Windsor Figure Skating Club at Windsor Arena on March 8, 1957. Around 400 amateur skaters participated in the show, including Carol Maran, Mary Ellen Macauley, Margaret Walker, Vivian Tutton, Joan Harris, and Pat Nawitsky, from left to right.

Fifteen-year-old Carolyn Skoczen took the world of figure skating by storm in 1977, winning at both the Canadian Figure Skaing finals in Calgary and the World Junior Figure Skating Championships in Paris.

Pee-wee hockey players make a mad dash for the dressing room after completing their playoff schedule on February 25, 1967. More than 180 boys battled in the bitter cold weather for top honours in the bantam and pee-wee leagues.

The Windsor Minor Hockey Association kicked off its 1971–72 season with a puck drop by Siro Martinello, president of the WMHA and manager of Windsor Arena, for team captains, Dave Hennessy of the Mavericks and Greg Parent of the Dusters. Martinello, a lifelong proponent of hockey, lacrosse, and figure skating, was recognized by the Windsor Essex County Sports Hall of Fame in 1993 for his support of young athletes.

December 28, 1974: Windsor Club 240's Brad Smith and Sandy Ross are awarded top forward and best defenseman, respectively, during the annual International Midget Hockey Tournament at Windsor Arena. Smith would graduate to the Spitfires, followed by a long playing career in the NHL. Smith was affectionately known as "Motor City Smitty" for his tenacious, physical style of play. He is currently Director of Player Personnel with the Colorado Avalanche.

Star photographer Bill Bishop caught this moment during the juvenile hockey playoffs in Riverside Arena in April 1966 for the all-Ontario championship.

"Reds Learn, Appreciate 'Our Game'" declared a *Star* reporter, after an exhibition game on November 24, 1957 between the touring Russian Selects and the Windsor Bulldogs ended in a amicable 5-5 tie. Above, Russia's Nikolai Khystov, left, checks Windsor's Lionel Heinrich as they jostle for the puck. Despite Cold War tensions, local fans and the visiting Russians reached an early détente, with friendly cheering as the Selects earned respect for their determined play and shared love of the game.

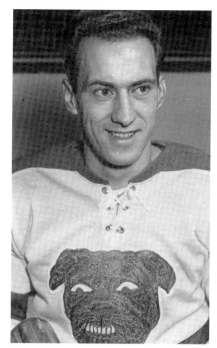

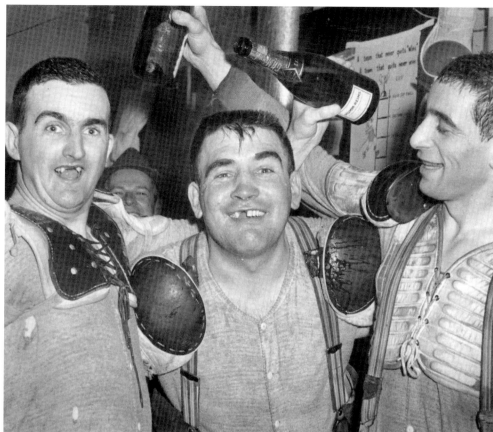

Lou Bendo, captain of the Windsor Bulldogs and perennial fan favourite, in his first year with the team in 1956. Bendo led the Bulldogs in career playoff points (113) and goals in a single game (6), and was rewarded for his success with the Andy Bellemer Trophy for sportsmanship and exemplary play in the 1961–62 season.

April 26, 1963: Windsor Bulldogs Jack Costello, Real Chevrefils, and Tom Micallef, from left to right, celebrate after winning the Allan Cup. They defeated the Winnipeg Maroons in the Senior A national hockey championship four games to one. The city erupted into days of celebration with two parades: one planned and the other an impromptu jaunt through the streets on the arena's zamboni.

The 1962–63 Windsor Bulldogs with Allan Cup, centre. Embolded by their success, the Bulldogs joined the International Hockey League for the next season. However, after a disappointing season and due to financial woes, the Bulldogs folded in 1964.

January 25, 1973: An off-camera shot by Spitfire defenceman Wayne Zawisza finds the back of the net, beating Detroit Jr. Red Wings goalie Dennis Declercq. With a good view of the first period goal are the Spitfires' Morris Elsley (15), Mark Smith (16), and Frank Beaton (19), as the Wings' Pete Feamster (21) checks Elsley. The Spitfires joined the Southern Ontario Junior A Hockey League from 1971 to 1975, when they moved up to the Ontario Major Junior Hockey League.

September 8, 1973: Former player Eddie Stankiewicz greets Spitfire candidates Ken Bracken, Lou Gagnon, and Jim Ferguson, from left to right, upon his return to Windsor as the new head coach. Stankiewicz resigned his post within 48 hours of the announcement, citing personal reasons, and was replaced by Wayne Maxner.

This Spitfire quartet of Bill McCreary, Mark Smith, Gary Armstrong, and Scott Miller, from left to right, deposited 10 pucks in the Michigan Americans' net on January 3, 1974. McCreary, here in his only season with the Spitfires, would find fame as an NHL referee. He was enshrined in the Hockey Hall of Fame in 2014 for his storied career, which included officiating fifteen Stanley Cup Finals.

The Spitfires' Ian Campbell (19) takes down his opponent, Dave Rowse during a game against the Welland Sabres on November 8, 1974.

April 2, 1975: John Tavella's Spitfire linemates, Mark Smith (centre) and Scott Miller (right), help him celebrate winning the league scoring championship by pouring bubbly into the Pat Patterson Trophy.

Coach Wayne Maxner gives a pep talk to Spitfires Jim Mellon, John Kwant, and captain Joel Quenneville during training camp in 1977. Quenneville would go on to a successful NHL playing career, but is best known as "Coach Q" of the Chicago Blackhawks, who have won three Stanley Cups under his leadership to date.

March 5, 1979: Hundreds of fans line up outside of Windsor Arena for tickets to the Spitfires' playoff game against the London Knights. The supply of 3,700 tickets was gone by 10 a.m.

April 17, 1980: Eager fans camped overnight outside Windsor Arena hoping to score tickets, at $4.50 apiece, for the deciding game of the OMJHL Emms Division final series between the hometown Spitfires and the Branford Alexanders. While tickets were limited, fans were ultimately not disappointed, as the Spitfires won their first Emms division title that night.

December 5, 1980: A game between the Windsor Spitfires, in the dark jerseys, and the Oshawa Generals quickly escalated into a bench-clearing brawl only 13 minutes into the first period. Referee Rob Good needed a 45-minute delay to sort out the 10 ejections and other penalties which totalled 442 minutes. The game was eventually won by the Generals.

September 10, 1973: The Windsor Warlocks lacrosse team celebrate capturing the President's Cup and their third national championship in four years. Carrying the cup are captain Jim Hinkson, left, and rookie sensation, Duffy McCarthy (7), followed by a convoy of Bruce Belland (2), Ron Martinello (9), and Ron Liscombe (12). Ron Martinello is a member of the Windsor Essex County Sports Hall of Fame along with his father Medo and brother Terry, all inducted for their contributions to the game of lacrosse.

August 25, 1980: Local stock car racer, Wayne Monk, leads a line of cars readying for the running of the Coca Cola Invitational 100 at Windsor's Checker Flag International Speedway on County Road 42, near Lesperance Road.

A Harvard from the RCAF impresses the crowd with an aerobatic run at the Windsor Flying Club's air show in 1951. A special exhaust, the same that is used by aerial sign writers, was used to trace the movement of the aircraft through the sky.

Story of Year: Racing Returns to Windsor

Al Siegel, owner of Elmwood Casino, built the Windsor Raceway in Ojibway in 1965, bringing harness racing back to Windsor for the first time since 1936.

November 17, 1966: The Windsor Raceway debuted a midweek matinee, which was quickly declared a success. In the fifth afternoon race, Faber's Penny (5) gallops towards victory for Harold Fisher, followed by Clement Hanover (8) with Larry Walker coming in second place.

October 9, 1967: Mistie Bondella (2) hits the finish line first in front of record-breaking crowds at opening night for Windsor Raceway's third season. A Thanksgiving night, a crowd of 5,816 showed up for the return of winter harness racing and bet a handsome $263,837.

CANADA GRABS HARMSWORTH

August 24, 1959: Bob Hayward piloted the powerboat Miss Supertest III over a 45-mile course on the Detroit River to "one of the most amazing triumphs in world speedboat racing history," bringing the Harmsworth Trophy to Canada for the first time. Coming across the finish line at 160 mph, Hayward took the title away from the Americans, who had won for the previous 39 years. Miss Supertest III would successfully defend her title in the 1960 and 1961 races, making her the first vessel to win the Trophy three times in a row.

Canada's "First Lady of Tennis", Faye Urban, strokes back-hand to claim a gold medal win at the Canada Games in 1969. Urban was a champion tennis player in the 1960s, competing at Wimbledon five times and captaining Canada's team at the Federation Cup in 1968.

Lou Veres, pictured here in 1954, was a tireless promoter of tennis in Windsor-Essex, serving as a high-school coach and a City of Windsor summer instructor. He co-founded Southwestern Ontario Tennis Training, as well as numerous tournaments. In his Lancer days, he was a star basketball player known as "Captain Lou" for heading up the varsity team for three years. He was inducted into the Windsor Essex County Sports Hall of Fame in 2009.

Marksman Gerry Ouellette, at right, became Windsor's first and only individual gold medalist when he posted a perfect score in the small-bore rifle prone event at the 1956 Olympic Games in Melbourne. He went on to become a decorated marksman who regularly represented Windsor on the inter-national circuit.

Art Grundy checks out his shooting awards in 1964, after winning the Canadian Open and Closed Championships for marksmanship. Grundy qualified for the Olympics in 1976 and 1980, but missed the Games both times—once, due to team downsizing and the other because of the Moscow Games boycott. He was awarded the Distinguished Marksman Award from the NRA, one of few Canadians to be recognized by the American organization.

SCHOOL DAYS

Schools went through a rebirth in the latter half of the 20th century in Windsor and Essex County. Though schoolhouses had been built in the area since the 1800s—at a time when the buildings were still known as numbered "School Sections"—many were never replaced, even though they were badly out of date and out of shape. Then came the 1950s.

One of the oldest still standing at the time was a little white schoolhouse, School Section 7 at Inman Side Road, which welcomed students for the last time on November 4, 1952. The long-time Highway 3 landmark was replaced by a fancy new schoolhouse with two rooms instead of one, built at a cost of $43,000. In 1951, the historic Glengarda Academy, designed in 1938 as the Glengarda Ursuline School, went on a fundraising campaign for upgrades, seeking $100,000—a princely sum at the time.

Even by 1960, many schools remained terribly antiquated, such as School Section 11 in Maidstone that had a large heating plant in the middle of the classroom. Others

were cramped with furnaces in closets, not to mention other deficiencies. St. Peter's Union Separate School, on Highway 2 east of Lesperance, was condemned as a "fire trap" by Sandwich East Township Council in 1960. The updating of old school buildings only escalated from there, as the push for modern facilities that consumed much of Windsor in this time period reached the area of schooling. LaSalle's landmark Sacred Heart Separate School disappeared in 1962, the old Leamington District High School in 1965, St. Alphonsus School on Park Street in 1966, St. Clare School in 1970, Holy Rosary on Drouillard Road in 1971, Mercer Street School in 1972, John Cahill School in 1977, St. Joseph School in 1977, Western Public School in 1979, and the stately Patterson Collegiate in 1979. But for pure architectural loss, the grand St. Mary's Academy stands out from the rest. In order to make way for a subdivision, the grand St. Mary's Academy was imploded in dramatic fashion on April 29, 1977, though the date wasn't publicized at the time in order to limit onlookers. Built between 1927 and 1929 at a cost of $1 million, the large five-storey building featured a chapel, classrooms, oak staircases, stained-glass windows, ornate detailing, and a majestic gothic tower. "Almost immediately the decision to demolish St. Mary's was regretted," reads a school history. "It became Windsor's biggest historical and architectural loss."

Thanks in part to the post-war baby boom, new school construction exploded in the '50s and '60s. The philosophy was that modern surroundings, featuring innovations like open-concept classrooms and increased use of natural light, would help create a better generation of better students and modern citizens. As the *Windsor Daily Star* said in 1956: "New schools are appearing everywhere in the city." The new buildings included: Belle River High School in 1949, Essex District High School in 1950, St. Christopher's School in Sandwich East Township in 1952, Leamington District High School in 1953, Assumption High School's new unit in 1955, Coronation School in Sandwich East in 1955, Immaculate Separate School in 1955, St. Gabriel School in 1956, W.F. Herman Collegiate Institute in 1958, Vincent Massey in 1960, St. Anne Senior High School in 1961, St. Peter's Union Separate School in 1961, Millen Public School in 1963, Oakwood Public School in 1965, St. Alphonsus School across from Carnegie Library on Victoria Street in 1965, St. Jude Separate School in 1966, Centennial Secondary School in 1969, and Sandwich Secondary 1975. L'Essor French-language secondary school opened in 1979, but not before protests as far back as 1974 calling for a French high school in the area. One school that deserves special mention for its unique offering is Walkerville Collegiate Institute, which opened in 1922 but enjoyed a major renovation in 1957 that added a gym, cafeteria, music room, and rifle range (which, not surprisingly, is no longer in use).

In 1968, *The Star* declared that "the one-room schoolhouse went modern," but by the '60s and '70s, more than just school buildings changed. So did what was in them—and not simply with school uniforms and the shortening of hemlines. Many schools started diversifying with different curricula, such as music, environmental arts, and drama programs, plus more sports and technical departments, including typing and home economics and even computer classes. It was an era of trying different things in education, having more special events and unique projects. More schools, yes, but also more programs. As society expanded past the traditional, so did the school system in Windsor and Essex County.

November 4, 1952: Students line up outside their one-room schoolhouse, School Section 7, a landmark on Highway 3 since 1888, for the last time before moving into their new modern school in Essex.

October 8, 1954: Over 700 students of St. Mary's Academy gather in the chapel to welcome Mother Marie-Gustave, Superior General of the Sisters of the Holy Name of Jesus and Mary, during her official visitation to the school.

Pictured here in 1952, Father Charles Armstrong was the Athletic Director at Assumption High School from 1938 to 1972. Remembered as the "Spirit of Assumption," he was one of the original inductees to the Windsor Essex County Sports Hall of Fame in 1981.

October 25, 1954: Gymnast Ernestine Russell, one of Canada's top female athletes and a Kennedy student, vaults through the stretched legs of Leissa Krol.

November 2, 1955: Practical classes in homemaking were a main feature of Windsor high schools' "opportunity classes" for girls. Similarly, the boys received lessons in carpentry and mechanics. Three members of the senior girls' class are seen here in the well-equipped kitchen of Forster Collegiate.

The Walkerville Collegiate Pipe Band, led by Pipe Major "Jock" Copland, in 1957. According to *The Star*, many of the young cadets joined the Essex and Kent Scottish regiment following their high-school graduation.

High demand led to the construction of many new elementary schools in the 1950s, including Coronation School in Sandwich East Township (at left) and Sacred Heart Separate School in LaSalle, both completed in 1955 and still in use.

Cast members rehearse a scene of *Charley's Aunt* at Walkerville Collegiate on February 23, 1956. From left to right, in the front row, are Bob Gieswein as Lord Fancourt Babberly and Medora Sale as Amy Spettigue, with Bill Roddy as Charles Wykeham, Ted Smith as Jim Chesney, and Adele Wachna as Kitty Verdun in the back row.

Riverside High School Glee Club, 1957. Among the musicians are Ann Ferry, Merrie-Lee Wilkinson, David Phillips, and Lois Carswell, from left to right.

"Gals Approve": Forster Collegiate cadets showed off their new uniforms on March 30, 1957. From left to right are Lorraine Allen, Helen Silk, Maureen Fisk, Sergeant Major Wayne Hutchinson, Staff Sergeant Tom Painte, and Bugle Sergeant Wayne Brown.

December 17, 1959: Old and new styles of school architecture stand side by side at 1124 Monmouth Road, where the original St. Anne School was being razed to make way for a playground.

When W.F. Herman Collegiate Institute opened in 1958, it was called one of the most modern schools in Canada. Named after W.F. Herman, *The Star*'s owner and publisher from 1918 to 1938, the building was an example of "functional simplicity" with its large classrooms and use of natural light.

St. Peter's Union School, one of the area's last one-room schoolhouses, located on Highway 2, was condemned as a "fire trap" in 1960. At right, eight-year-old Linda Baillargeon is ready for her first day at the new St. Peter's Separate School.

September 6, 1960: Some of the 625 students at Vincent Massey Collegiate Institute take a peek inside the cafeteria on their first day of school in the new building.

An aerial of Vincent Massey Collegiate and the surrounding neighbourhood, 1961. The school would rapidly expand, peaking at 2,200 students by the mid-1960s. In 1966, a major expansion was added, including a "Stonehenge" styled library.

"Meet the Champs": The General Amherst High School football team won the SWOSSA Senior A championship in 1964. The team members are, in the front row: Jim Foreman, Tom Durocher, Bill Atkinson, George McCurdy, Victor Budiak, Gene Masney, Terry Hall, and Bob Taylor, from left to right. Second row: Terry Mosey, Bill Richardson, Barry McCurdy, Victor DiNardo, Tony DiNardo, Tony D'Aloisio, Bill Halstead, West Paisley, Greg Wigle, and Gerald Grondin. Third row: Murray Fox, Rocco Mancini, Doug Knight, Frank DiTomasso, Tony Capaldi, Dennis Averill, Gary McNanemy, Dennis Baudoin, and W.J. Wilson (coach). Back row: Jim White, Ivan Iler, Tom Bates, Roy Fells, Earl Duckworth, and Howard Renaud. Note that there is an extra name listed in the second row, as it was printed in *The Star*.

April 15, 1964: The Harry E. Guppy High School of Commerce senior typing team finished second in a provincial typing competition with an average of 66.4 words per minute. From left to right are Dorothy Awad, who won an individual medal for her typing speed of 71.76 wpm, and Susan Lomas.

October 16, 1964: Charles Valliere wears a new, bright red safety vest given to Windsor's school patrols, while he helps young students cross the corner of Wyandotte Street East at Marentette Avenue.

Industrial Arts at Harry E. Guppy High School of Commerce, 1965. Here, students Dan Higgins and Chris Lusk, both students from Kennedy Collegiate taking shop classes at Guppy, receive advice from their teacher William Weir.

Featuring a unique hexagonal design, Oakwood Public School was opened in 1965. An adjoining community centre was built in 1976. The school was closed in 2012 and both properties were sold to the French school board in 2014.

Kindergarten students at Frank W. Begley Public School donned hats with the new Canadian Maple Leaf flag to celebrate citizenship day on May 22, 1965.

St. Alphonsus students rush through the school's main doors for the last time on November 29, 1965. The old building, located at 75 Park Street, was demolished in 1966 and turned into a municipal parking lot. The students went to school the next day at the new St. Alphonsus School, located on Victoria Street, which was Ontario's first round-shaped school building.

Harrow High's senior girls' basketball team won the Essex County B Secondary School championship in 1966. Kneeling from left to right are Mary Anne Pollard, Sue Baldwin, Sharon Bedal, Sally Meek, Francine Philcox, Patti Holmes, Betty Ann Balags, and Mary Ann Peter. Back row: Mrs. Edward Young, coach; Lila Murray, manager; Margaret Palmer; Peggy Wright; Ilene Strachn; Martha Mathews; Bernice Shepley; Cathy Duransky; Jo Anne Grant, timer; and Linda Graf, scorer. After 112 years, Harrow District High School was closed in 2016.

Girls from Brennan High School in their bright red blazers and plaid skirts take part in the annual Mary Day Parade in 1966.

The last day of school stampede and paper throwing ritual for children at Queen Victoria Public School, June 28, 1966.

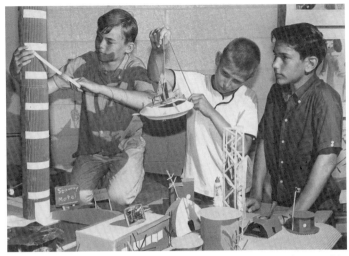

June 24, 1966: Students from St. Hubert's School assemble an arts and crafts project depicting "Windsor 2000 A.D." From left to right are Larry Austin, Douglas Monforton, and Larry Belanger.

March 9, 1967: William Hands Vocational School's carpentry shop featured a full complement of equipment, including band saws and planers. Here, principal Gordon Aitchison, left, watches student Jim McLeod at work. William Hands would become Century Secondary School (which was closed in 2014) and now houses Westview Freedom Academy.

May 21, 1966: English classes at St. Mary's Academy studied *The Windsor Star* as part of their curriculum. The girls wrote regular letters to the editor to express their opinions.

Canada's first manned space venture took off from Southwood Public School in 1967 as three young "exponauts" launched into a 30-hour simulated flight on the school's front lawn. A Centennial school project, they emerged from the capsule the next day.

93 Forster Collegiate students board the train to Expo 67 in Montreal on May 17, 1967. The school's concert band was among 250 other schools from across Canada chosen to perform at Expo.

Computer science was offered for the first time at Walkerville Collegiate in 1967. Here, E.H. Skelly, the teacher for the pilot project, shows two Grade 10 students, Reinhold Roth and Shirley Schmidt, the basics of computer programming.

June 2, 1967: Joseph Or stands by the unveiled Centennial Obelisk, which was designed and built by the students, at W.D. Lowe Technical School. Lowe was an all-boys school until 1974 when students from a closed Patterson Collegiate transferred over.

February 9, 1968: The Grade 5 class at Queen Victoria Public School put on a play to illustrate the novel *Call it Courage*. From left to right are narrator Myra Tadic, bird Beverly Michalik, drummer Karla Kielman, "island" Judy Fitzsimmons, and the hero (in his imaginary canoe with his pet dog) Randy Middleton. The school counts a famous novelist, Farley Mowat, in their alumni.

Brennan's 440-yard relay team—Don Robichaud, Tony Minardi, John Minardi, and Mike Chalut, from left to right—prepares for the 20th annual Kennedy Relays on May 9, 1968. The athletic director at Kennedy, Archie Green, established the Kennedy Relays in 1949 and the meet is still going strong today.

The Forster Spartans prepare for the start of the football season in 1968, hoping to unseat the top-seeded Massey Mustangs. From left to right are Tom Lovell, guard; John Yascheshyn, fullback; Tom Bishop, centre; Doug Middleton, flanker back; and Dennis Bacon, guard.

March 27, 1969: Walkerville Collegiate music teacher Bruce Curry leads the student orchestra in a rehearsal for the Kiwanis Music Festival. Bruce Curry would also serve as the director of the International Youth Symphony after founder Matti Holli's death in 1977.

April 28, 1969: 200 St. Anne Senior High School students protest the possible closing of their school outside Ste. Anne Parish in Tecumseh. With their school needing funds, the students wanted the parish to increase their monetary support to keep the school open—and they succeeded.

Cheerleaders from Massey Secondary School show off their prize-winning form after taking the top spot at a regional championship at the University of Windsor in 1969.

October 23, 1969: Elsie Morely, assistant head of the English department, was one of thirty teachers who participated in Riverside High School's first annual tricycle race. Riverside (then called Riverside Composite High School) opened on Jerome Street in September 1963.

November 9, 1970: Thirty female students from the Harry E. Guppy High School of Commerce (now Catholic Central) were sent home to change from their "slacks" into dresses as per the school's business attire policy. From left to right are Nancy Falkner, Sandra Chabot, Marlene Gagnier, Anita Gordon, Marilyn Stanciu, Sheila Carroll, Shelley Walker, Debbie Matejicek, Judy Ashley, and Judy Clayton. Principal Lewis Cook declared that the girls were "out to make a bit of trouble."

Contestants for the title of Kennedy Karnival King show off their costumes in anticipation of the coronation on May 8, 1970. From left to right are George Lucschuwit (mouse), Robert Craig (prophet), George Hudacek, Randy Berdan (uncle), and Mark Buller (Tarzan).

Homecoming at Centennial Secondary School, early 1970s. Announced as a centennial project in 1967, the school operated from 1969 to 1986, at which time it merged with Massey Secondary School (which integrated Centennial's orange into their school colours). The Centennial school building at 1400 Northwood Avenue currently houses Holy Names Catholic High School.

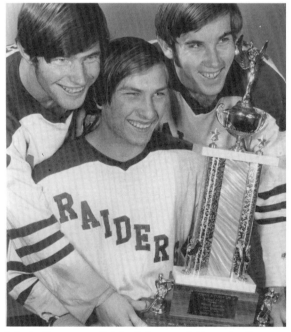

Mark Boisvert, Eddy Mio, and Dwight Barron helped lead the Assumption Purple Raiders to their second consecutive championship on February 23, 1971. Eddy Mio would go on to a long career as a goalie in the NHL, most famously playing with Wayne Gretzky in the Edmonton Oilers.

March 3, 1971: Holy Rosary students Donald Green and Sherry Belleau watch the demolition of their school on Drouillard Road. The old school was replaced by a combined school-community centre. The new Holy Rosary was closed in 1990, but the building is now the Gino A. Marcus Community Complex.

"The Mud Bowl": It's hard to tell the Herman Collegiate Green Griffins apart from the Assumption Purple Raiders, as a slippery Assumption ball-carrier John Girard attempts to run past his would-be tacklers during the championship game on November 19, 1972. At right, the victorious Raiders Dan Dupuis, John Campigotto, Mike Hogan, Bruno Limarzi, and Ron Reaume celebrate their victory—and third straight season on top.

April 7, 1972: Evacuated students at St. Anne Junior High School watch volunteer firefighters battle the remainder of an electrical fire which destroyed the school's new library.

November 22, 1972: Members of the Drama Club at Assumption High School rehearse for their production of *West Side Story*.

December 6, 1973: Students cheer on student prime minister Connie Hinch, as she breaks ground for the Sandwich Secondary School building on Malden Road. The new high school was opened in 1975.

April 28, 1973: Cyril Hallam, left, and Principal Alex Liddel check over the final reunion program in front of Patterson Secondary School. Patterson closed at the end of that school year and its students were transferred to Lowe Secondary School. The school, built in 1888, was demolished in 1979, pictured at right.

Demonstrators, chanting "*Vive L'École Française*," marched outside of the Holiday Inn on February 9, 1974, to demand a local French secondary school from provincial cabinet ministers meeting inside.

November 7, 1975: Massey Secondary School students Russ Gessner and Jim Dibe give Morris the Horse a final hug, after the mascot was banned from football games by school officials for inciting too much mischief.

Pictured here in 1976, Father Ronald Cullen holds legendary status at Assumption High School, where he coached hockey, baseball, and other sports for nearly 40 years.

June 28, 1978: Students at St. Joseph School wave goodbye to their school on Jos Janisse Avenue after their last day of classes. The school, which was built in 1925, was permanently closed due to low enrollment.

Lacrosse was introduced into the girls' physical education program at Kennedy Secondary School in 1976. *The Star* explained that the girls were taught a modified version of the sport so that "it is not as rough as the style used by the boys."

November 20, 1976: A farewell mass was held for St. Mary's Academy, which was set to be demolished the following Spring to make way for a housing development. At right, rubble and glass from broken windows litters the chapel of the former school on March 22, 1977, weeks before its demolition.

St. Mary's Academy was imploded by Controlled Demolition Inc. on April 29, 1977. Built in 1928, the school was one of Windsor's finest examples of Gothic Revival style architecture. While many in the community, including a newly formed Windsor Architectural Conservation Advisory Committee, were against the demolition, St. Mary's Gate, a subdivision of single-family homes, was built on the school grounds.

St. Joan of Arc, built in 1956, was also closed at the end of the school year in 1978. The building, at 2330 Somme Avenue, now houses the offices of several Unifor locals, including Local 195.

March 21, 1977: Coach Gerry Brumpton, at centre, is surrounded by his two-time Ontario basketball champions, the Lowe Trojans. Lowe's sport teams were formerly known as the "Rough Riders," but rebranded as the Trojans after the school was amalgamated with Patterson Secondary School. W.D. Lowe was closed in 2000, and reopened in 2012 as Giles Campus French Immersion Public School.

October 10, 1978: Kennedy's cheerleaders show off after winning a cheer competition at Devonshire Mall. The members of the team are Chris Herold, back; Nada Borcic, Benita Talbot, and Sherry Wright, middle row from left to right; and Lyn Schoolet, Jane Osborne and Wendy Long, in the front row.

Essex County's first French language high school, École Secondaire Catholique l'Essor, in St. Clair Beach, is pictured here, mid-construction, in December 1978. The school was hotly debated in Windsor for years, from the need for a French school in the first place to the budget and location. Despite the controversies, l'Essor opened its doors to students in 1979.

April 20, 1979: Student president Dave McKay holds aloft the sign of the newly named street, Griffin Court, running along one side of Herman Secondary School in front of an excited student body. In 2016, Herman and Percy C. McCallum Public School merged to form a K–12 school called W.F. Herman Academy.

The flag was flying at half-mast during Western Public School's final assembly on June 26, 1979. Families were angry at the Peter Street school's closing, many of them calling it the end of a "west-end tradition."

COLLEGIATE LIFE

The '50s and '60s were an important era for higher education in Windsor, which graduated to another level of schooling. Assumption College, previously associated with the University of Western Ontario, became an independent institution in 1953. And St. Clair College, which had its roots in the Western Ontario Institute of Technology, held its first classes in 1967. Both schools helped bolster area smarts, but in different ways.

Windsor's march towards full university status was a long time coming. Education started as an offshoot of Assumption Parish in 1786 with two schools, one for boys and one for girls. In 1857, Assumption College opened, though it struggled for years with different administrations and unstable funding before gaining a sure foothold. In 1919, Assumption College formed an affiliation with Western University in London. It wasn't until 1953, after years of lobbying and rising costs, that the Ontario legislature finally granted denominational Assumption College its own university powers. In 1956, the growing school changed its name to Assumption University of Windsor, with Reverend Eugene Carlisle LeBel as its first president. Essex College, a recent creation at the time, joined the university with responsibility for science, business, and nursing. The storied school had to wait until 1963, however, before it would officially

be called the University of Windsor. It had to leave its official religious status behind in order to qualify for public support, which it greatly needed to expand. According to a history written by Father Thomas Rosica, former president and vice-chancellor of Assumption University, "the development of a non-denominational provincial university out of an historic Roman Catholic university was unprecedented."

John Francis Leddy took over as president in 1964, overseeing a period of sustained growth. From 1967 to 1977 the school jumped from roughly 1,500 students to 8,000 and undertook a massive building campaign. It was an impressive coming-of-age story for one of the most historic schools in the country, given it sat at the foot of the Ambassador Bridge next to the busiest border crossing in North America, in the gateway of Canada.

The university also chipped in its share of sports over the years. At first, the school's basketball team played friendly skirmishes with Detroit counterparts early in the 20th century and other sports rolled out in casual leagues, as well. Things didn't really take off until 1952, when under the leadership of Father John "Jocko" Hussey as moderator of athletics and Frank DeMarco as intercollegiate and intramural director, the school joined the Ontario-Quebec Athletic Association—launching a more developed sports tradition with the Purple Raiders, then Lancer Athletics. In the 1953–54 season, Assumption won the men's basketball championship, but that was only the beginning. They developed into a powerhouse in the 1960s and early 1970s, winning the national title five times. Their success was infectious, and more teams blossomed every year, partly thanks to the input of the school's first athletics director Richard Moriarty. In 1975, the Lancer men's football team captured the Yates Cup, making them national co-champions. In the 1960–61 school year, women's sports started on campus, with the help of Sis Thompson who initially coached the basketball team.

The school transformed in other ways, as well. As the University of Windsor evolved, so too did its student body, going on to mirror much of the social unrest happening on college campuses across the continent, with rallies, protests, and sit-ins forming part of the normal course of events into the 1970s. It was the day of outdoor convocation ceremonies and free love, though gender roles were still rather entrenched—considering that women were only allowed to enroll in 1950. Still, over the years as society evolved, so did the school, with increasing enrollment and a prestigious place in the community.

St. Clair College, meanwhile, started more as a concept than its own school. The Western Ontario Institute of Technology began in 1958, a part of the then Ryerson Institute of Technology (now Ryerson University) in Toronto. Under the direction of Doug McRae, the school attracted 104 male students for its first-year technology program, at 815 Mercer Street in an 1890 building that was once a two-room schoolhouse. According to school records, the first graduating class of 47 students had an impressive hiring rate: 100 percent. After Ontario created 19 Colleges of Applied Arts and Technology, the local path was set. St. Clair was founded in 1966—part of a provincial drive to create career-oriented diploma and certificate courses, not to mention continuing education programs across the province. The concept soon proved popular in Windsor. WOIT merged with St. Clair in 1967, when Richard C. Quittenton—a trained nuclear engineer who had smelted aluminum and brewed beer—was appointed president.

Classes started for about 300 St. Clair students in a little building—affectionately referred to as Green Acres—on Talbot Road West, where the main campus now sits, and in the former WOIT site. In 1970, the entire School of Technology moved to the main campus from its former WOIT site. And in 1977, St. Clair opened the Thames Campus in Chatham—part of a sustained growth in students and physical amenities over the years. All the while, the school's teams, the Saints, added a welcome sporting element to the collegiate life.

As the area grew, so did both the University of Windsor and St. Clair College with enrollment, programs, and buildings boosting higher education in a city known more for its car culture, helping set the stage for diversification later on. As it turns out, diversifying wasn't just smart for students, it was smart for the whole area.

Reverend A.J. Grant CSB and Dr. William Phillips, immediately behind the bearers, lead the procession of graduates from the Administration building to Assumption Church for the annual Baccalaureate Mass during convocation on June 4, 1955. As women were only accepted into Assumption College in 1950, this was one of the first ceremonies with female graduates.

The newly elected officers of Assumption College Student Council admire their campaign posters from March 1956. The council members, at the bottom, from left to right, are Bill Stephen, second vice president, and Jim Hartford, junior class president. In the middle row are Gerry Dittrick, senior class president, Nancy Hogan, Holy Names Association president, and Marilyn Miller, vice president, whose poster adorns the wall beside them. At the top are Norm Rice, sophomore representative, and Michael Maloney, president.

The academic year at Assumption University formally opened with a parade to the celebration of mass on September 27, 1956. That year, Assumption College changed its name to Assumption University of Windsor. Enrollment was at an all-time high with 800 students, bolstered by the new affiliation with the non-denominational Essex College. Essex College initially offered degrees in science and mathematics, eventually adding business and nursing.

April 16, 1958: Campus greetings from Reverend N.J. Ruth CSB, Dean of Arts and Science; Very Reverend Gerard Owens CSR, president of Holy Redeemer College; Very Reverend E.J. Lajeunesse, vice president of Assumption; Reverend Robert Spencer Rayson, principal of Canterbury College; Sister Pauline of Mary SNJM, acting principal of Holy Names College; and Dr. Frank DeMarco, staff chairman of Essex College, from left to right. DeMarco was a central figure in the university's development, serving as the University of Windsor's inaugural vice president, a post he held until 1979.

September 26, 1959: Seventeen-year-old Carolyne Walling receives a congratulatory kiss from her boyfriend, Harvey Grigg, after she was announced Frosh Queen of Assumption University.

The opening ceremonies for Holy Redeemer College, a seminary for Redemptorist priests on Cousineau Road in Sandwich West Township, were held on May 11, 1958. Cardinal James Charles McGuigan, archbishop of Toronto, presided over chapel dedication service. The college's affiliation with Assumption University, signed in 1956, marked the first time in the world that an Anglican college was affiliated with a Roman Catholic university. Designed by Francis Barry Byrne, the mid-century modernist building is a designated heritage site in Windsor, and currently houses Académie Ste. Cécile International School.

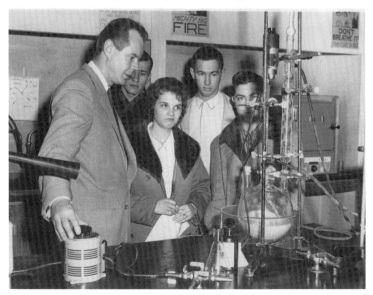

January 14, 1960: Dr. Kenneth G. Rutherford explains an organic chemisty experiment to Bill Kostyniuk, Nancy Skov, John Trott, and Allan McCoy, from left to right, all grade 13 students at Herman Collegiate. Over five hundred students from Windsor and Essex County came for the campus tour of Assumption University, including displays and exhibits like the one pictured here.

October 18, 1961: Premier Leslie Frost, at right, gets a little help from Gary S. Dunlop, president of the Assumption University engineering society, to cut the ribbon and officially open the Essex College engineering building.

The new engineering building for Essex College, located at University Avenue West and Patricia Road.

Governor General Georges Vanier presided over the official opening of the new University Centre at a special convocation service on December 4, 1961.

September 23, 1961: A group of registrants gather in front of the new men's residence under construction, Cody Hall. From left to right are: Nasware Nazaruddin of Indonesia, Lise Fournier of Saskatchewan, Phyllis Peterson of New Brunswick, Cory Burgis of Panama, Martha Gosling of New York, Liz Dettman of Quebec, and Dave Ramdoesingh of Trinidad. Designed by Windsor firm Johnson & McWhinnie, Cody Hall was an example of mid-century modern architecture. It was demolished in 2012.

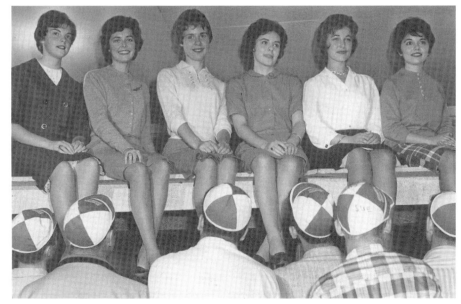

A throng of male freshmen kneel before the six co-eds at Assumption University seeking the title of Frosh Queen for the 1961–62 school year. From left to right are Anne Delaney, Sue Callaghan, Gloria Grondin, Linda Belanger, Nelly Hirsch, and Madelyn Nardella.

Madelyn Nardella is crowned Frosh Queen by her predecessor, Dorit Kriss, at the annual Frosh Hop at St. Denis Hall.

Assumption University, circa 1962. The newly built Essex Hall is front and centre, with a Loblaws, which housed the School of Dramatic Arts from 1972 to 2004, at the right. Behind Essex are 'the Huts' (army barracks-cum-classrooms), Cody Hall, University Centre, and Dillon Hall, from left to right.

On October 18, 1963, Assumption University held its 20th and final convocation, after merging with the newly formed, public University of Windsor on July 1st. From left to right, Reverend E.C. LeBel CSB, president and vice chancellor of the University of Windsor, Dr. Clarence Beverly Hillberry, president of Wayne State University, Most Reverend G. Emmett Carter, auxiliary bishop of London and pro-chancellor of the university, and Very Reverend Joseph Wey CSB, superior general of the Basilian Fathers.

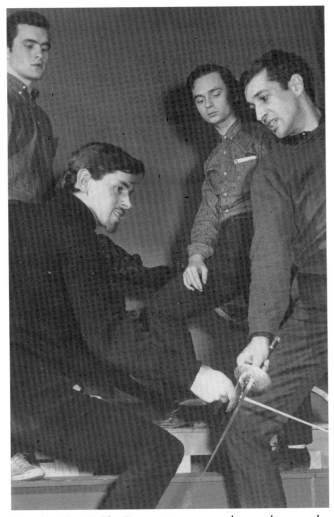

March 14, 1964: Dramatic arts student rehearse the duelling scene for their upcoming performance of Shakespeare's *Hamlet*. From left to right are Edward McAuliffe as Horatio, Michael O'Regan as Hamlet, Bob Seidan as Laertes, and Mike Lyons as Osric.

In the 1963–64 school year, the University of Windsor embarked on an ambitious building program, and appealed to the public for financial support through the Development Fund campaign, which would supplement government grants. Pictured here is the Essex South committee, who would canvass their locale for donations. Holding up the architect's sketches are, from left to right, George Weller, Walter McGregor, Alfred W. Bennie, and Robert A. Patterson in the front row. In the back row are John Baeker, Jack F. Paterson, Gordon Knight, and William Conklin in the back row. The sketches show residences Cody Hall, Electa Hall, and Canterbury College, slated for completion by 1968.

June 1, 1964: The first convocation of the University of Windsor was also the last for one of the most prominent figures in the institution's history: Reverend E.C. LeBel, who would retire at the end of that month. LeBel, seen addressing the crowd, guided the university through a period of great transition, having served as president of Assumption University from 1956 until becoming the first president of the University of Windsor.

Reverend E.C. LeBel stands on the roof of Cody Hall to survey campus on June 30, 1964, the day of his retirement. When he joined the college staff in 1941, only three buildings stood, in contrast to the growing campus he helped develop during his years as president.

LeBel greets the new president, Dr. John Francis Leddy, left, on Leddy's first day as the new president: July 1, 1964. Leddy would oversee the university during a period of explosive growth from 1964 to 1978, as enrollment increased from approximately 1,500 to 8,000 full-time students.

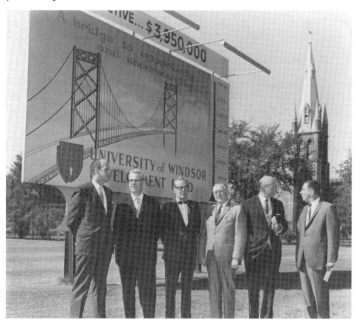

August 13, 1964: "More Money Sought": The University of Windsor's development fund campaign raised its goals to nearly four million dollars. Shown standing in front of the updated objective sign on campus is, from left to right, Walter McGregor, campaign general chairman; Dr. Leddy, president; John J. Stuart, chairman of the board of governors; George Burt, Canadian UAW director; Eli Goldin, campaign vice-chairman; and Robert J. Tebbs, administrative director for the campaign.

August 13, 1965: John Kominar, a graduate chemistry student, is shown behind a cage of test tubes as he works on an experiment for his Ph.D. thesis. Dr. Kominar is now a professor emeritus in chemistry and biochemistry at Wilfrid Laurier University.

September 13, 1965: "Who'll Be Queen?" The six girls in the running for Frosh Queen, chosen out of a record freshman enrollment of 860 students, are, from left to right: Sandy Beauchamp, 18; Carol Cameron, 18; Mary Stapleton, 18; Vicki Wachna, 17; Mary Ann Mulveney, 18; and Liz Kirley, 18. At the week's end, Mary Ann Mulveney was crowned victorious at the Frosh Fantasy Dance at University Centre.

"How low can you go?": Jorge Merino, an exchange student from Peru, demonstrates his skill during an impromptu limbo contest during the University of Windsor's annual International Night festivities on March 10, 1966.

May 28, 1966: More than 4,000 people, including a record 541 graduates, stand for the playing of "God Save the Queen" at the opening of convocation ceremonies in front of Dillon Hall. United Nations Secretary-General U Thant received an honorary Doctor of Laws degree during the ceremonies.

An aerial view of the University of Windsor campus, December 1965. That year, the student population increased by over 20 percent to 2,391 full-time students. Keeping pace with student growth was the building campaign which saw the completion of two major projects: Cody Hall, a men's residence, and the Biology Building. Pictured here is Essex Hall, front and centre, Cody Hall to the left, and Windsor Hall tower to the far right, with the Biology Building immediately in front of it.

The new computer centre at the University of Windsor was up and running in August 1968. Here, graduate student L.C. "Raj" Patil watches over the operation of the Central Processing Unit while J.B. Pollard, director of the computer centre, stands nearby at one of the 'working' units in the system.

Students picketed outside Dillon Hall on November 16, 1967, where Dow Chemical Co. Ltd. was conducting interviews. They were protesting the corporation's production of napalm for use in Vietnam. From left to right are John Kingsmill, Arts III; Tom Gregory, graduate arts; Raman Sood, graduate engineering; and J.A. Blair, a philosophy department lecturer.

September 5, 1968: Florence Roach, director of the school of nursing; Carol Batra; student Mary Ann Renaud; and Anna Gupta, from left to right, look over textbooks for the new nursing course established for the 1968–69 school year. For the first time, the university offered a four-year degree leading to a Bachelor of Science in Nursing as opposed to the three-year diploma courses typical of in-hospital nursing schools.

Fifty-five students occupied the theology department in Windsor Hall on February 11, 1969, starting the sit-in at 3 a.m. They were protesting the dismissal of Dr. William Kelly, a lecturer on comparative religion, who was reportedly dismissed because he "caused tension" within the department. They demanded Kelly's reinstatement, as well as increased student purview over staff appointments. The sit-in ended peacefully after 10 days, with the university administration promising to review Kelly's dismissal and place a student representative on departmental committees. Kelly was ultimately reinstated.

September 25, 1970: Senator Paul Martin declared that he was "overwhelmed" that the library in the new Faculty of Law building had been named after him. Standing in front of the superscription, from left to right, are Walter Tarnopolsky, the dean of law; Paul Martin; and Dr. J.F. Leddy, university president.

Dr. Kathleen McCrone, pictured here in 1971, taught the first women's history course at the University of Windsor, and was instrumental in the establishment of a Women's Studies program.

The relationship between Quebec and the rest of Canada was discussed by a panel of experts at the University of Windsor on February 10, 1969. From left to right are: René Lévesque, leader of the Parti Québécois; Dr. Mark MacGuigan, Liberal MP for Windsor-Walkerville; Walter Tarnopolsky, dean of the law school; Paul Gerin Lajoie, Liberal deputy of the Quebec assembly; and Dr. Laurier LaPierre, head of French Canada Studies at McGill University. Separatism was the major theme of the debate, with the take-away that French Canadians did not "feel at home" in the rest of Canada, according to a *Star* reporter.

October 20, 1971: The University Players began a new season with a classic opener: *Romeo and Juliet*, at Essex Hall Theatre. From left to right are Kathleen Forget as Juliet, Diane Douglass as the nurse, and Robert de Grosbois as Romeo.

In 1971, the School of Dramatic Arts presented the 19th century play *Wozzeck* with a flare of avant-garde offbeat theatre by using modern multimedia techniques. Pictured with her creations is Lauren Miley, at left, standing between the giant heads that some symbolic characters will wear, along with George Neilson, assistant professor and director.

Convocation in front of Dillon Hall, 1972.

Amid cheers and applause, Dean John McLaren happened upon his car in the courtyard of the law faculty, pushed there by his students in a gesture of affection. It took several custodial personnel to remove the car. McLaren was the Dean of Law from 1972–75.

"Judgment Day": More than 400 students crowded into the St. Denis Centre to write their final exams on April 21, 1976. That year, enrollment rose to 6,300 undergraduate and graduate students.

November 13, 1959: Dick Moriarty, Assumption University's athletic director, shows off the Lancers' new uniforms to freshman Diane DeRoller. For the 1959–60 basketball season opener, the team would discard their traditional purple uniforms in favour of the school's new colours: blue, white, and gold.

January 15, 1968: Bob Navetta takes a shot during the game against the University of Guelph Gryphons before 1,750 fans at St. Denis Hall. The Lancers took the game 96–66, and moved into first place in the intercollegiate league; however, their winning streak would come to an end as they lost the OQAA championship to their rivals, the University of Western Ontario Mustangs.

The Royal Military College Pipe Band and Colour Guard gave a half-time performance during the inaugural game at the new University of Windsor Stadium on September 23, 1968. It was the first time since 1955 that local football fans got to see their team in action and the Lancers did not disappoint with a 25–13 victory over the Royal Military College Redmen.

A jubilant Lancer men's basketball team crowds around the Wilson Trophy, having reclaimed the top spot in the OQAA championship on March 3, 1969. In the foreground, from left to right, are head coach Eddie Chittaro, assistant coach Nick Grabowski, and manager Gerry Flynn. Directly behind them are Andy Auch, Sante Salvador, Chris Wydrzynski, Tony Grant, and athletic director Dick Moriarty. In the back row, are Joe Connely, Ed Lanktree, Jack Orange, Mike Crowe (in front of Orange), Gerry Bunce, Bill Tonelli, Tino Lenti, Jack Bolzan, and statistician Abie Shapiro. The team would go on to reclaim their spot as national CIAU champions that year.

The University of Windsor Fencing team proudly display the Walters Trophy after pulling off a major upset over the University of Toronto to win their first Ontario Universities' Athletic Association championship. This was the first time since 1938 that the trophy had been claimed by a member school west of Toronto. Pictured here, from left to right, are: coach Karl Blass, Patrick Brode, Bob Horwood, Tom Strutt, Bruno Ciccotelli, and Bryan Rivers. Patrick Brode went on to be a celebrated author and historian, having published several books.

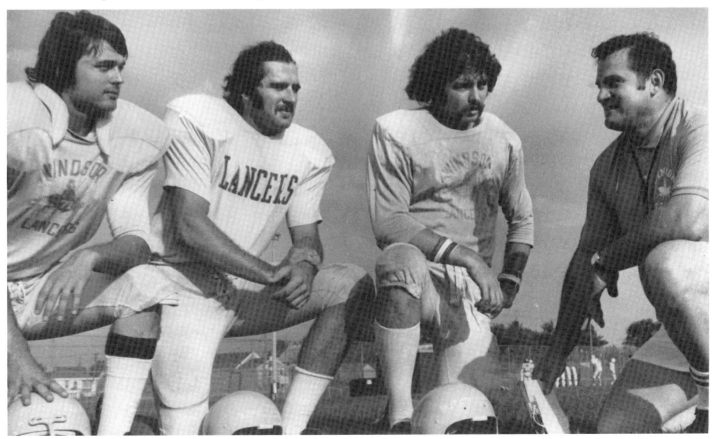

Head coach Gino Fracas, at the far right, takes a knee with players Don Gordon, Wayne Ducharme, and Brian Plenderleith, from left to right, during the kickoff to training camp on August 28, 1973. Fracas coached Lancer football from 1968 to 1986, after his own career in the CFL, where he won two Grey Cups with the Edmonton Eskimos, and a coaching stint for the University of Alberta Golden Bears. A beloved coach and mentor, Fracas was inducted into the Canadian Football Hall of Fame in 2011.

Jennifer Pace demonstrates her skill in javelin throwing on November 7, 1978. Also a shot putter, Jennifer was a decorated track and field athlete, both as a Lancer and on the world stage for her native country Malta, including the 1984 Olympic Games.

November 7, 1978: Andrea Page flies over the hurdle in her signature event, the 400m hurdles. She ran track for the Lancers from 1976 to 1979, winning two Ontario Universities Athletic Association titles in her last years. Page also competed in the 1984 Los Angeles Olympics, reaching the semifinals. After retiring from track and field, she enrolled in medical school and now runs a successful family practice in Windsor.

In February 1979, both the men and women's curling teams won the OUAA championships, sweeping the event for the Windsor Lancers. Standing, from left to right, are the three-time men's champions: Alex Pinchin, Duncan Stauth, Peter DeKoning Jr., and Greg Barlow with coach Doug Bates in the centre. Below, from left to right, Julie Glover, Bev Mainwaring, Sue Barber, and Pat Burt brought home their first women's title.

Cheerleader Sylvia Gava looks up to Stan Korosec, left, and Jim Molyneux during a Lancer basketball practice on March 12, 1980. Her "Windsor Power" t-shirt was donated by the Ford Motor Company, which was sponsoring a broadcast of the Lancers' games at the CIAU national championships in Calgary. Stan Korosec, a Windsor Essex County Sports Hall of Famer, was known as "Chairman of the Boards" as he regularly led the OUAA in rebounding.

March 28, 1963: Several hundred visitors attended the annual open house at the Western Ontario Institute of Technology (WOIT) where the school's 310 students exhibited their training for the public. Among the displays was a Kissometer, designed by the "Ham Club." Pictured testing the calibre of kisses are, from left to right, Michelle Tracy, Bob McLean, Bill Montgomery, and Ross Westfall. WOIT was established in 1958 with an original student body of 104, as a satellite campus of the Ryerson Institute in Toronto.

In 1965, five female students enrolled in WOIT, greatly outnumbered by their 545 male colleagues. However, according to a *Star* reporter, the women hadn't found it a "bachelor-girls paradise" but were strictly interested in their studies. In the back row are, from left to right: Pat Ward, Kathy Caman, and Edith Redden, with Dick Thomas standing behind. In the front row are: Jim Phaneuf, Jane Ruston, Rose Mary Rylett, and Leon Meunier.

November 6, 1964: "Will He Make It?" Gary Waghorn, left, expected to be the first man on the moon, with some assistance from classmate Tony Cianforain. Both students were on the chemistry class float, part of WOIT's second annual parade through downtown Windsor to mark the election of student council.

September 7, 1966: Students attend an orientation day program at Cleary Auditorium, having registered for classes at WOIT for the last time. The institute would be absorbed by the new St. Clair College of Applied Arts and Technology that opened the following year. Over the nine years of its existence, 543 students graduated from WOIT.

September 11, 1967: St. Clair College's first class included around 100 females, which was quite a jump from the previous year's three female students at WOIT. Chatting with the English instructor, Beverly Nykor, are, from left to right: Cathy Tayles, Linda Specht, Lynda Laughton, Karen Chuba, and Cathie MacGregor. About 600 students registered at the college in its first year, in comparison to 1,300 freshmen at the University of Windsor.

Student Council president Brian Seigner and vice-president David Moore promote a freshman blood drive at St. Clair College on September 12, 1967.

September 21, 1967: St. Clair College's first Frosh Queen was chosen out of these thirteen candidates, shown clockwise from bottom middle: Roseanne Bellaire, 19; Marilyn Bridges, 19; Cathy Heinz, 18; Connie Fitzsimmons, 18; Helen Novosad, 19; Marlene Ouellette, 19; Treasure Triolet, 18; Debbie McLennan, 21; Carroll Fraser, 19; Joanne Nadalin, 19; Carole Weepers, 18; Lousie Feldmann, 18; and Linda Bulmer, 18. Helen Novosad was crowned victorious at a dance in Masonic Hall that night.

Dr. R.C. Quittenton, president of St. Clair College, stands in front of the temporary classrooms on the new campus in the outskirts of Windsor on December 12, 1967. In its first academic year, the college's students were housed in both the former WOIT building on Mercer Street and these temporary buildings, awaiting a brand new $13,000,000 facility that would begin construction in the spring.

September 11, 1968: Pat Bedard stands on his head to get his shoes shined during some friendly hazing by seniors Bonnie Buss and Ann Thomas, while fellow freshman Paul Kubenec does the dirty work. More than 400 students marched down Ouellette Avenue for a frosh parade, culminating with the choosing of the Frosh Queen at the Holiday Inn.

September 7, 1971:Work was set to begin on St. Clair College's 7,000-seat outdoor amphitheatre, designed by the college's architectural technology students. Looking over the site plans are, from left to right, Roland Deschamps, president of the alumni association; Andy Fass, student council president; Bill Totten, alumni director; Dr. Richard Quittenton, college president; and Don Yates. Griffin Hollow Ampitheatre opened in Fall 1973 and hosted a variety of acts, from Harry Chapin to The Guess Who. The venue was closed in 1985 and was flattened in 2001 to make way for a student residence.

Pat Ray, left, and Marie Hamelin get some tips on the maintenance of the engine from their instructor, Hanno Barten. This new course, offered at St. Clair in 1971, was designed to introduce women to the "basic upkeep and mechanics of cars."

With placards like "We Love You Mercer" and "WOIT We Miss You" waving in the background, 815 Mercer Street, the birthplace of St. Clair College, was officially closed on November 22, 1971. Charlie Jackson, principle of WOIT from 1960 to 1967, presents the keys to the 81 year-old building to Mayor Frank Wansbrough. The building was demolished as part of the city's redevelopment scheme.

February 11, 1972: 64 St. Clair College students, who just took home a combined total of $6,675 in scholarships and prizes, wave at the camera with vice-president Charlie Jackson, in the foreground.

December 3, 1973: Discarded books litter the library floor at St. Clair College after a two-alarm fire in the new main campus library on November 12. The fire devastated the majority of the reference collection and circulating books, but the cause remained unknown.

December 10, 1974: Kathy Boycott, a first-year student in the landscaping course at St. Clair College, is top of the class when it comes to operating the tractor. She was one of twenty female students in a traditionally male-dominated field.

650 students received their diplomas during St. Clair College's eighth convocation on June 23, 1975, held on the campus' south lawn.

April 26, 1976: Students Greg Bondy and Adrian Maden picket the entrance to the college to show their support for president Dr. Richard Quittenton after talks over his employment with the college's board turned hostile. The board, unhappy with Quittenton's spending on various programs, issued an ultimatum of resignation or firing. 4,500 students, faculty, and staff walked out in solidarity with their president. Community pressure, alluded to in Bob Monks' political cartoon from April 27th, played a large factor in Quittenton's reinstatement. Quittenton left the college of his own volition in 1977, leaving behind a tremendous legacy.

August 20, 1975: This car was built from scratch by a trio of St. Clair College auto mechanic students, including Nick Gisivein, seen at the wheel. They entered the car in a 1,500-mile rally for homemade vehicles, starting at the border of British Columbia and ending in California.

June 28, 1976: St. Clair College president Dr. Richard Quittenton, or Dr. Q as he preferred to be called, had the tradition of kissing the hands of all female graduates after draping their shoulders with the college's green and gold liripipe. Here, he continues the practice with Linda Margaret Koeman, at the college's ninth annual convocation on June 28, 1976.

St. Clair College made its debut in the newly formed Ontario Colleges Athletic Association (OCAA) on November 3, 1967, in two sports: hockey and basketball. Pictured here are the basketball team's starting five, from left to right: Tino Baggio, Al Povoledo, Dwayne Russell, Dave Mardling, and Dave McWhinnie.

February 3, 1968: Dr. R.C. Quittenton, president of St. Clair College, drops a puck at Windsor Arena for Peter Renaud, left, captain of St. Clair Saints, and Thomas Knowlton, captain of University Lancers, at a game between the rivals.

April 7, 1971: In a move to dramatize sport victories and add an air of traditionalism to the relatively new institution, St. Clair College created "battle banners" to commemorate their championships. The standard bearers are, from left to right: Andy Fass, student council president; Keith Kokkola, hockey captain; Roy Confliffe, student athletic association president; and Dan Thomas, basketball captain.

March 15, 1976: Saints' captain Gary Herrington hoists the winning trophy after the men's hockey team handily won the OCAA championship. The team capped off a perfect post-season by defeating Selkirk College for the Canadian Colleges Athletic Association national hockey title.

February 14, 1978: Coach John Martel plans a strategy with team members, Jeannie Brown, Karen Prout, Shelley McFadden, Chris Carson, and Denise Pinsonneault before their exhibition trip overseas. The girls' basketball team went on a fourteen-day tour of Russia and Finland to participate in a tournament in Helsinki.

PEOPLE & POLITICS

The people, not the place, make a community. The post-war period in the Windsor area saw previously explosive population increases slow somewhat, yet nevertheless witnessed a physical expansion of the city and the suburbs. But the people, as always, led the charge.

When 1950 arrived, the city was already being led by popular Mayor Arthur Reaume—who held the city's top spot for a record five terms over 13 years, from 1941 to 1954. He was born in Sandwich, where he became mayor in 1933, before transferring to Windsor city council when that town merged into Windsor in 1935. But the go-getter was not about to stop there. The only blip in his mayoral career came in 1950 when it seemed like Thomas Brophey, a long-time *Windsor Daily Star* journalist, beat him by 38 votes. But a recount proved that Reaume actually won by 16 votes, so he once again claimed the mayor's chair, while Brophey was ousted after just eight days (he did receive a month's pay, though). Reaume also ran

for the Progressive Conservatives in Ontario, but lost in 1943 and ended up switching to the Liberal Party, losing in 1945 and 1948. But there was no quit in Reaume and he ended up winning in 1951 and remained in office until 1967—after helping shepherd Windsor through World War II and a period of serious labour unrest, including the tumultuous 99-day Ford Strike of 1945.

Of course, other Windsor mayors rounded out the busy period from 1950 to 1980. Michael Patrick, who held the city's top job from 1955 to 1964, changed the look of the city by helping spearhead a number of major initiatives such as the new City Hall, the Cleary Auditorium, and additions to Hôtel-Dieu and Metropolitan hospitals. He also did something else special, by envisioning uninterrupted park land on the riverfront, what would become Windsor's jewel. Lawyer John Wheelton held the top position until 1969, when he became an Ontario provincial court judge. He would make headlines again in 1976, though for a tragedy when he, his wife Margaret, and son Robert were killed in a car accident in 1976, returning from their Invercairn Beach summer cottage.

Another strange mayoral twist came in 1969, after Wheelton's resignation. W.C. Riggs, a former Co-operative Commonwealth Federation MPP for the riding of Windsor-Walkerville, served as mayor for a mere five months—after breaking a tie by drawing a queen from a pack of cards. Camera shop owner Frank Wansbrough, a former basketball player who coached the Windsor AKO Juniors to championships in 1948 and 1960, reigned as mayor from 1970 to 1974 until yet another vote flip-flop. It looked like he won the 1974 election by 300 votes, but a recount proved Bert Weeks actually won by 749. Weeks served as mayor until 1982, most notably advocating for the beautification of the riverfront and developing nine parks, including the Ganatchio Trail and Coventry Gardens, as well as Lakeview Park Marina.

Other key political figures from the area abound. Starting it all off for the era was the inimitable Paul Martin Sr., the Liberal MP for Essex East from 1935 to 1968 and a Senator for Windsor-Walkerville from 1968 to 1974. He sometimes used a folksy approach, known for asking audiences around Canada, "Is there anyone here from Windsor?" But he took politics seriously as a particularly left-leaning member of the Liberal Party, serving in the cabinets of Prime Ministers William Lyon Mackenzie King, Louis St. Laurent, Lester B. Pearson, and Pierre Trudeau. As Minister of National Health and Welfare (1946–57), he helped lead the fight against polio and oversaw the establishment of Canadian hospital insurance. Some consider him the father of medicare. He was also the father of Paul Martin Jr., who went on to become Prime Minister of Canada from 2003 to 2006. Senior never saw Junior claim the big office, however, since the elder died at age 89 in 1992.

Another local groundbreaker was workhorse Herb Gray, the longest serving local MP, representing the riding of Essex West/Windsor West from 1962 to 2002, winning an impressive 13 consecutive elections. He became Canada's first Jewish cabinet minister and served as Deputy Prime Minister from 1997 to 2002, one of the few people granted the "Right Honourable" title without serving in the actual position. Known in later years as the Gray Fog, for his monotone fact-filled speeches in response to tough questions in the legislature, Gray never tired of fighting for his beliefs. He passed away at age 82 in 2014.

And when it comes to characters and larger-than-life personalities, Eugene Whelan takes the cake. Or in Whelan's case, an iconic green Stetson. The cowboy hat-clad Whelan served as Liberal MP for Essex-Windsor from 1962 to 1984 (and as Minister of Agriculture from 1972 to 1984). Whelan would even go on to host Mikhail Gorbachev when the future Soviet president was agriculture minister in 1983. "No bull— with him," Jean Chretien told the *Windsor Star* when his friend "Geno" passed away at age 88 in 2013. "He'd call it as it is. And he was very much preoccupied with the average citizen. He was not preoccupied with the big corporations and the big shots in society. That was not his forte."

Mark MacGuigan also made his mark locally and beyond. Born in Charlottetown, PEI, he became the founding dean of the University of Windsor law school and was elected as a federal Liberal representative for Windsor-Walkerville in 1968 until 1984. He was close with then Prime Minister Pierre Trudeau, who appointed him Secretary of State for External Affairs in 1980, then Minister of Justice in 1982. He died of liver cancer in Oklahoma City in 1998.

Of course, highlighting local political stars is only part of the story. Many other politicians, trailblazers, activists, achievers, and characters helped make Windsor's history special, filled with intrigue, drama, and the personalities to match.

February 27, 1963: A tuba player, at far left, leads a parade of Herb Gray, who won the Liberal nomination for Essex-West; Senator and former Windsor mayor David Croll; and Paul Martin, MP for Essex East, into the Cleary Auditorium.

The Windsor Daily Star EXTRA ★★★★

Another Dip
Partly cloudy tonight, Tuesday. Colder tonight.
6 a.m. 18; 9 a.m. 17; 2 p.m. 17
Humidity at 9 a.m. 83 percent
High tomorrow, 27; low, 18
High Sunday, 23; low, 18
Sun sets, 5.17; rises tomorrow 8.01
See forecast, temperatures, page 8

The Canadian Press—Associated Press—United Press—Reuters—Associated Press Wirephoto

VOL. 65, NO. 107 | 28 PAGES | WINDSOR, ONTARIO, CANADA, MONDAY, JANUARY 8, 1951 | Authorized as Second Class Mail Post Office Department, Ottawa | FIVE CENTS

REAUME WINS IN VOTE RECOUNT

December 6, 1950: Arthur J. Reaume, and his wife wink at the camera for good luck as they cast their ballots in the civic election. Reaume was seeking re-election after serving nine years as Windsor's mayor. At far right is Lena Mullin, deputy returning officer.

Mayor Elect Thomas Brophey takes the oath of office from C.V. Waters, city clerk, on December 29, 1950, despite his victory over Arthur J. Reaume being called into question. At the time, Brophey seemed to have won the election by a margin of 38 votes out of the 33,106 cast.

December 11, 1950: Following the closest civic election in Windsor's history, defeated incumbent Arthur J. Reaume called for a recount and requested that the ballot boxes containing the votes be placed under police guard 24 hours a day in the basement of City Hall. Here, Constable Howard Watkins points out one of the seals on the basement cupboard containing the ballots. Following the recount, the headline from January 8, 1951 revealed that Reaume was the winner after all, by a mere 16 votes. Brophey, a former *Star* journalist, served as mayor for only eight days and received a month's pay for his trouble.

Progressive Conservative MPP Myrddyn Cooke Davies casts his vote in hopes of re-election during the 1951 provincial election. From left to right are Jane Davies, Mrs. Davies, Mr. Davies, and Mary Cooper, deputy returning officer. Davies represented the riding of Windsor-Walkerville from 1945 to 1959, following which he returned to his role as rector of St. George's Anglican Church.

Mayor Arthur J. Reaume gives his twelfth inaugural address to City Council on January 3, 1952.

Right Honourable Louis St. Laurent waves goodbye to Windsorites who gathered at the CNR station on June 23, 1953. The Prime Minister made the stop in Windsor as part of his cross-Canada campaign tour. St. Laurent led Canada from 1948 to 1957.

December 19, 1954: LaSalle mayor Herbert Runstedler, at right, presents Lieutenant-Colonel William Griesinger MC, MPP for Windsor-Sandwich, with an ornate ashtray as a token of appreciation. Mrs. Griesinger, left, and their daughter, Rosemary Griesinger, look on. In addition to serving as MPP from 1945 to 1959, Griesinger was a decorated veteran, most notably awarded the Military Cross at the Battle of Vimy Ridge.

Richard Thrasher, candidate for Essex South, talks to one of his stalwart Conservative supporters, Pete Kungel, on the campaign trail. Thrasher served up the region's major upset in the 1957 election and represented the riding until 1962, when he was defeated by Eugene Whelan.

December 11, 1954: Newly elected Michael J. Patrick poses in front of the "ancient" city hall, where he would be the first new mayor to take office in fourteen years, save Thomas Brophey's brief tenure. During Patrick's administration, this building would be demolished and a new City Hall opened in 1958 on the same site.

Mayor Sid Arbour of Tecumseh was confident of his re-election as he cast his ballot in the 1955 mayoral race. Arbour would win over councillor Fred Bistany and served as mayor from 1952 to 1959.

Schoolteacher and longtime CCF (and later NDP) candidate Fred Burr, at right, receives a Valentine from his daughter, Maureen, at the nomination meeting on February 14, 1958. Also pictured, at centre, is Bert Weeks, party candidate for Essex West and eventual mayor of Windsor. Burr would finally be successful in 1967, ousting veteran politician Arthur J. Reaume, and remain in office for 10 years.

March 5, 1958: Prime Minister John Diefenbaker walks by a Progressive Conservative Party billboard in downtown Windsor, bearing his own quote: "Give me the men and I will finish the job."

March 6, 1958: Prime Minister John Diefenbaker buys a *Windsor Star* from newsboy Garnet Taylor at a stop in Essex. The headline tells of the launching of a second United States satellite, Explorer II, and the front page features a photo of Diefenbaker from his visit to Windsor the day previous.

"Mike Greets Mike": Lester B. "Mike" Pearson, leader of the Liberal party, arrived in Windsor for a day-long campaign visit on March 26, 1958. He is greeted by mayor Michael J. Patrick, as both flourish "I like Mike" badges on their lapels.

March 26, 1958: Pearson makes his way through a crowd of supporters with his wife and the Liberal MP for Essex West, Don F. Brown, at the right. Despite Windsor's enthusiasm, Pearson would ultimately lose the election to Diefenbaker's Progressive Conservatives.

December 6, 1960: "The Winnah!" Mayor Michael J. Patrick won his fourth term by a landslide, leading his nearest rival, Hugh Simpson, by nearly 7,000 votes. Holding up Patrick's arm in victory is his campaign manager, Charles Gress, while Mrs. Patrick, at left, celebrates with the rest of the campaign workers. Patrick was Windsor's mayor from 1955 to 1964.

Liberal leader Lester B. Pearson made a campaign stop in Tecumseh on June 8, 1962, for the upcoming federal election. Here, Tecumseh mayor Wallace Baillargeon presentes Mr. Pearson with a tomahawk. Pearson lost the 1962 election but would be successful the following year.

Mayor Gordon Stewart of Riverside relaxes as the vote was counted on December 4, 1962. He returned to office by acclamation and remained the mayor of Riverside until the town was annexed by the City of Windsor in 1966.

"Parade for Gray": Jubilant supporters led by Herb Gray, the successful Liberal candidate in Essex West, staged a traffic-stopping parade on June 19, 1962. Gray, a young lawyer, won a landslide victory in his first attempt at political office. He would represent this riding for a staggering four decades.

April 9, 1963: Eugene Whelan, who was re-elected Liberal MP for Essex South, made his returning office in Room 304 of the maternity ward in Metropolitan Hospital. Whelan joined his wife, Liz, who was expecting their second child. Here, he listens to the election results while Liz writes them down. Whelan represented the riding from 1962 to 1984.

"Solid Liberal": The Liberals swept all four ridings in Essex County in the 1963 provincial election, despite the rest of Ontario returning the Progressive Conservatives to power. The successful candidates are, from left to right: Maurice Bélanger (Windsor-Sandwich), Arthur J. Reaume (Essex North), Donald A. Paterson (Essex South), and Bernard Newman (Windsor-Walkerville).

Ivan Thrasher hired a tugboat to promote his campaign at the Windsor waterfront on September 23, 1963. Unfortunately for Thrasher, his creativity did not pay off with a win in that year's provincial election, as he was defeated by Liberal incumbent Maurice Bélanger. However, after Bélanger retired from politics in 1964, Thrasher went on to win the by-election and represent Windsor-Sandwich from 1964 to 1967.

Windsor, along with the rest of Canada, raised the new Canadian maple leaf flag for the first time on February 15, 1965. Mayor John Wheelton led the ceremony at City Hall, in one of many flag raisings held across the city.

Veteran alderman John Wheelton, at left, defeated incumbent Michael Patrick for the mayorship in December 1964. After serving as mayor from 1965 to 1969, Wheelton resigned to become an Ontario Superior Court judge. He died in a tragic car accident, along with his wife Margaret and son Robert, in 1976.

September 1, 1967: Reeve Lawrence Brunet of Sandwich West Township (LaSalle), divides his working day between the office and a farm in the Ojibway area. Farming supplemented Brunet's income, which was cut after Windsor annexed large parts of the Township in 1966. Brunet served as reeve of Sandwich West Township from 1952 to 1970.

Trudeaumania came to Windsor on June 12, 1968, when Prime Minister Pierre Trudeau held a rally in front of a crowd of 3,000 at Dieppe Gardens. At right, Trudeau is assisted by police as he makes his way through a throng of admirers, many of them teenagers.

November 8, 1965: The entire Martin family, from left to right: Maryanne, Paul, Eleanor, Paul Jr., and his wife Sheila, came out to celebrate another resounding victory for Paul Martin in Essex East. Martin would continue to serve as the Minister of External Affairs under Lester B. Pearson's administration until 1968.

July 29, 1969: William C. Riggs became Windsor's mayor, albeit temporarily, when he drew the highest card, the Queen of Hearts, breaking a four-way tie among the aldermen following Mayor John Wheelton's resignation. At right, Riggs performs his first official act as mayor: welcoming the HMSC Ottawa destroyer and her crew to Windsor. From left to right are Lieutenant-Commander William Jones, Commander Pierre Simard, Samuel Agnew of the Essex-Kent Naval Veterans Association, and Mayor Riggs. Riggs served as mayor until the year's end when a civic election was held.

Frank Wansbrough crosses his fingers for good luck as he casts his ballot on December 3, 1969. Wansbrough would win the hotly contested race and serve as mayor for two terms.

"Tecumseh Changes Hands": Mayor Hector Lacasse kisses the insignia, while deputy reeve Donald Lappan, who would become mayor at the stroke of midnight on December 31, 1970, looks on. Lappan would go on to be a longtime mayor, in office until 1985.

Bernard Newman greets the crowd after winning his fourth consecutive term on October 21, 1971. Newman, former gymnastics coach for Ernestine Russell, was the Liberal MPP for Windsor-Walkerville from 1959 to 1987.

Hugh Peacock, MPP for Windsor-West from 1967 to 1971, congratulates his successor, Ted Bounsall, at right, who retained the seat for the NDP on October 22, 1971. Formerly a chemistry professor, this was Bounsall's first foray into politics. He would represent the riding until 1981.

Liberal MP Herb Gray shares a laugh with Prime Minister Pierre Trudeau on their way to the House of Commons in May 1972. Gray worked closely with several prime ministers, including Pearson, Trudeau, and Chretien.

A political cartoon of Frank Wansbrough featuring his trademark cigar, circa 1972.

February 2, 1974: MPP Bernard Newman is crunched between two defensemen, Dan Sutton, left, and Dwight Duncan, right, during the contest between the Windsor West Young Liberals and the Liberal Allstars. Dwight Duncan would go on to be a Liberal MPP himself, from 1995 to 2003, in Newman's former riding of Windsor-Walkerville until the riding was abolished in 1999.

Essex County more Liberal than ever!

June 19, 1974: Prime Minister Pierre Trudeau and his wife Margaret were greeted in Windsor by city Liberal hopefuls and a crowd of about 3,000 cheering supporters. Candidates Eugene Whelan, Herb Gray (partially hidden), and Mark MacGuigan, surround Trudeau from left to right, as Trudeau forcefully declared that Windsor would remain a Liberal city in the coming election. The headline above from July 9, 1974, reveals that he was right.

A massive snowstorm on election day, December 2, 1974, forced voters to get creative in order to cast their ballots. Here, passenger Gerald Hachey persuaded neighbour Paul Maini to chauffeur him via snowmobile to their polling station at St. Patrick Public School, where roads were virtually impassable.

December 3, 1974: Bert Weeks had a reason to smile after winning the 1974 mayoralty race over Frank Wansbrough. Due to a reporter's error, Weeks left election night believing he'd lost by 300 votes. He was woken at dawn by his supporters, who shared the good news: he'd won by 750 votes!

July 4, 1975: Mayor Bert Weeks took to the mound to throw the first pitch at Tiger Stadium for Windsor night, held in conjunction with the annual Windsor-Detroit Freedom Festival.

June 28, 1974: Agricultural Minister Eugene Whelan dances with his supporters at the Knights of Columbus Hall in McGregor during a campaign stop.

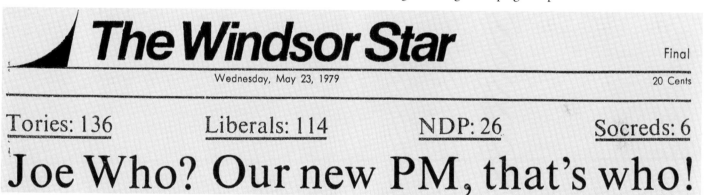

The Windsor Star

Final

Wednesday, May 23, 1979

20 Cents

| Tories: 136 | Liberals: 114 | NDP: 26 | Socreds: 6 |

Joe Who? Our new PM, that's who!

April 9, 1979: Conservative leader, Joe Clark, right, and his wife, Maureen McTeer, join in a singsong at a rally at the Teutonia Club. At far left is Charlie Pingle, the Progressive Conservative candidate in the Windsor-Walkerville riding. Joe Clark would upset Trudeau's Liberals to take power at the election in May.

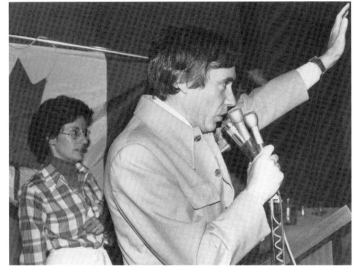

Windsor-Walkerville MP Mark MacGuigan gives a victory speech after narrowly winning his fourth election on May 22, 1979. He represented this riding from 1968 to 1984, including appointments as Canada's Attorney General and Minister of Justice. Before his political career, MacGuigan was the founding dean of law at the University of Windsor.

Herb Gray, Minister of Trade, Industry and Commerce, emphatically defends federal government action for laid-off workers at a meeting on the Canada-US Autopact on June 14, 1980.

November 13, 1979: Paul Martin, and his wife, Eleanor, take a stroll at their home, the Low-Martin House, at the corner of Ontario Street and Devonshire Road in Walkerville. Martin would retire from public service that month, having just completed a five-year tenure as Canada's High Commissioner to London.

September 26, 1980: Sporting his iconic green Stetson, Eugene Whelan, as the Minister of Agriculture, opens the United Co-operatives of Ontario grain terminal elevator at the riverfront in Ojibway.

LAW & ORDER

In 1950, the main police story revolved not around criminals but officers. Calls of police corruption—and turning a blind eye to illegal liquor and gambling—dominated the media. *The Windsor Daily Star* regularly reported on alleged "moral laxity" at the department and unlawful gambling in sin city Windsor. Even though the Police Commission in 1948 deemed the force clean, the trial of local bootlegger Joe Assef in 1950 plunged the department into scandal—and the national spotlight.

Assef received the maximum six months for his illicit liquor operation. And yet, evidence uncovered during the trial proved damning for Windsor Police as an alleged list of Assef's customers included the names of sixteen officers. During sentencing, Magistrate J.A. Hanrahan slammed the force's morality detail for allowing Assef's operations to reach a staggering rate of 5,400 liquor deliveries in 90 days. This time the claims of impropriety could not be ignored, and the rest of Canada took notice. As *Maclean's*

magazine said: "For a $2 ride in and out of the compact blocks of Windsor's business section, any cab driver would point out which of the dingy rooming houses, pool rooms and tobacco stores along Pitt, Sandwich, Assumption, and Pelissier Streets, behind whose false fronts you could get a girl, buy a drink, or place a bet." The provincial government ordered a public inquiry into the Windsor Police Department in March 1950.

The existing police commission was almost completely replaced (only Mayor Arthur J. Reaume escaped the dismissals). Over the next several months, the commission came down hard on the force. It questioned the department's practices, the release of 12 of 22 suspects after a brothel raid, the withdrawal of impaired driving charges, and allegations that convicted persons knew their sentences before court. During an October 17 meeting, the resignation of one sergeant was accepted, one officer was disciplined, and two were fired for theft.

Following the commission's final recommendations, Chief Claude Renaud retired after 36 years of service, and Deputy Chief W.H. Neale followed suit. In 1951—the year cruisers were equipped with sirens—Carl Farrow became chief and a new era began, partly with the creation of the Special Investigations Branch that targeted vice, among other criminality. Training increased and 26 new officers were hired at $2,870 a year.

Police work, of course, never stops. Whether helping with the "coal crisis" of 1950, running the Police Athletic League, or joining various neighbourhood events, Windsor police actively participated in the community. Police headquarters gained space in 1955 when the courts moved to the new Municipal Courts building nearby at City Hall Square. An underground tunnel connected police HQ and the courthouse so officers could easily transport prisoners, though both buildings have since been demolished.

On June 10, 1959, two robbers made off with more than $10,000 from the Bank of Montreal at Wyandotte and Chilver, but not before shooting Constable Brian Pickup, the first to respond to the holdup call. While Pickup wrestled with one suspect, a second shot him in the back. Pickup survived, however, and saw the two crooks sent to prison.

The Windsor Police force increased responsibility on January 1, 1966, when the city amalgamated with portions of Riverside, Ojibway, Sandwich South, Sandwich East, and Sandwich West. The force's jurisdictional area tripled in size and the population it protected rose by 50 percent in one fell swoop. So the department boosted its officers from 216 to 335 and stations from one to three.

Eighteen-year-old spree killer Mathew Charles Lamb discovered a shotgun in his uncle's house and wandered into the East Windsor night on June 25, 1966. Seemingly at random, he shot four people, killing two. Police found the discarded gun in a field and arrested Lamb the following day. At trial, however, he escaped the mandatory death penalty for capital murder when he was found not guilty by reason of insanity. He was committed to the Penetanguishene Mental Health Centre for six years and reportedly made a remarkable turnaround. After his release in 1973 he joined the Rhodesian army. He was killed in action at age 28 in 1976 by friendly fire from a fellow soldier and received a "hero's funeral," according to the Associated Press.

August 23, 1969, remains "one of the darkest days in the history of local law enforcement," according to the Windsor Police. Officers responded to a domestic call on Sprucewood Avenue in what is now LaSalle. A woman rushed out with a four-year-old child. Her husband appeared briefly at the door before retreating inside. Moments later, with the woman and child hiding behind a police cruiser, the man started firing from an upstairs window. According to *The Windsor Star*, "a rain of bullets poured into the doors." Sandwich West Police Department officer Robert Carrick was shot in the head and killed as he scrambled for cover. Fellow Sandwich West officer Robert Ross was shot in the hand and face, and ended up losing an eye. Windsor Constable Al Oakley was shot in the chest, neck, abdomen, both arms and right leg. As officers wielding more firepower arrived, the shooter, William Rosik, surrendered. He was later convicted of murder and sentenced to hang, but had his sentence commuted to life as the noose loomed.

Major crime headlines blared again in 1971. On the evening of May 14 that year, six-year-old Ljubica Topic was playing on Drouillard Road with her brother when a young man offered them money. He sent the boy away with a dime but the girl, who walked off hand in hand with the killer, was never seen alive again. Her body was found in an alley six blocks away. The assailant, however, was never found, despite one of the biggest police manhunts in Windsor's history, following up hundreds of leads. The community felt shock, afraid for their own children. Meanwhile, the cold case continues to haunt the Windsor Police Service, which reopened the case in 2015 with hopes that DNA technology could provide a new lead.

On December 18, 1971, Windsor witnessed the largest cash bank heist in Canadian history—with more than $1.1 million taken from the Royal Bank on Ouellette Avenue. The bank was closed on Saturday at 8 a.m. but 13 employees were counting money from Windsor Raceway when they were interrupted by four gun-toting bandits wearing coveralls and balaclavas, who had disabled the alarm and knew the racetrack money was being counted. They handcuffed bank employees and took off. But they didn't remain free long, and not because of the $25,000 reward the bank offered, a local record. Toronto Police had a hunch about some crooks, tailed them, and eventually swooped in for an arrest. In the end, police only recovered $150,000 of the missing cash, and the culprits' sentences ranged from 15 to 20 years.

The Windsor Police Department continued to innovate their practices as society changed in the late '60s and '70s. In 1968 the department developed an anti-riot plan and trained officers in crowd control. The Community Service branch started in 1974, Detroit River boat patrols returned in 1977 after several decades' absence, the canine patrol began in 1977, a tactical unit was created in 1978, and the underwater search-and-rescue team launched in 1980. The worst year for homicides in Windsor, meanwhile, came in 1977 when 14 people were murdered—though police cleared all cases from that year. Law and order in Windsor often changed between 1950 and 1980, with one main trend: as crime grew in size and scope, so did local policing.

By 1950, Windsor had a reputation as a "wide-open" town, notorious for the trio of "bookies, bootleggers, and bawdy houses." This *Star* editorial cartoon from March 15 refers to the 1950 Police Commission, which would begin a probe into the Windsor Police Department's "moral laxity" the next day.

March 18, 1950: Officers wait to be called in to to testify before the Police Commission. After the trial of bootlegger Joe Assef revealed the collusion of police in his illegal booze business, an inquiry into police corruption in Windsor was ordered by the province. All officers denied involvement with Assef.

Windsor Police Chief Carl Farrow, 1951. Farrow was installed as chief after the Police Commission's report blasted the force's morality detail for allowing vice to "flourish." The resulting shake-up saw long-time Chief Claude Renaud and Deputy Chief W.H. Neale "retire" (with full pension rights). Farrow would usher in an era of discipline and efficiency for the police force.

New safety signs were introduced in 1950 to get motorists to slow down in school zones. Here, Constable Phil Bistany, Wilfred Whitfield of the Civitan Club, and Constable Sidney Stuart set up the first sign near Prince of Wales School on Wyandotte Street West.

May 1, 1950: Constables Don Prosser and Harley Hyland take stock of the liquor supply and bar equipment found after a raid of a blind pig in Sandwich East Township.

December 26, 1951: 502 mink pelts, valued at $12,000, stolen from Martin Birkner, were recovered by Windsor detectives after nearly a month at large. Here, Detective Martin "Bud" Coxon, at left, and Detective Sergeant Chris Pagent take a final tally of the pile of pelts.

All that two bank bandits left behind after a foiled hold-up at the Bank of Commerce, 415 Devonshire Road, was their hats—examined here by Constables Ernie Whicker and Cecil Perry. Wearing Hallowe'en masks and fingers covered by cellulose tape, the two robbers held up the bank staff at gunpoint but fled empty-handed after being surprised by Brinks employees doing a pick-up.

March 12, 1954: Murray D. Cox dismantles the old Walkerville Jail, which was being torn down to make room for an enlarged shipping yard at Hiram Walker & Sons. Built in 1884, the jail sat empty for 50 years before its demolition.

August 15, 1955: A city constable tickets the cruiser of an Ontario Provincial Police officer parked in City Hall Square—with an expired meter!

July 26, 1955: Constable Amos Hennan works the mooring ropes on RCMP boat *Tagish* while their new patrol boat, *Chilcoot II*, follows in her wake. Windsor's RCMP detachment patrolled hundreds of miles from Port Lambton to Long Point on Lake Erie. At the time, *Chilcoot II* was the fastest boat of its size on the Detroit River.

The Riverside Police Association held its second annual Moonlight Cruise on July 22, 1955. Looking over the tickets are Staff Sergeant Paul LaBute, Constable Al Varcoe, and Constable Frank Chauvin, from left to right, with Riverside Chief Constable Bryce Monaghan seated in front. Frank Chauvin became one of Windsor's greatest humanitarians, going on to establish an orphanage in Port-au-Prince, Haiti, in 1988.

Windsor constables run through basic training drills, under the critical eye of Sergeant-Major Lou Denton, on March 13, 1956.

Constable Ralph Sexton stands beside his temporary patrol car, a Volkswagen Beetle, on February 22, 1956. The Windsor Police were testing out the Beetle on behalf of the German manufacturer to see if it had any potential for police work.

"Playing Hooky": Truant officer Inspector Bickford escorts a young boy home, who attempted to turn a school day into a fishing holiday on October 26, 1957.

Five rookie members of Windsor's Police Force were among the first to practise pistol shots in the department's new, "ultra-modern" range. Receiving lessons, from left to right, are Brian Paradise, Charles Williams, Paul Linton, Robert Dwyer, and Peter Bateman. Inspector Arthur Irwin gives pointers behind them, while John Sokal, another rookie, waits his turn.

Constable Robert Mullins checks the smashed storefront window at Shanfields-Meyers Jewellery and China Shop on Ouellette Avenue after a smash-and-grab robbery in January 1957.

September 12, 1957: Sergeant Alec Somerville of Sandwich West prepares police dog Skippy for his first day on the job. Somerville would eventually become deputy police chief in Windsor, but is perhaps most known as a member of the satirical band, the Brothers-in-Law.

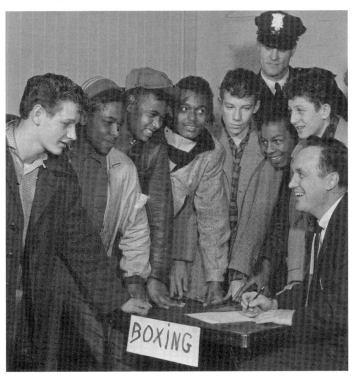

Two masked bandits attempted to escape with over $10,000 from the Bank of Montreal in Walkerville on June 10, 1959. They were captured outside the bank, after chief clerk Norman Wingrover tripped the alarm as the robbers herded him and 14 other employees towards the vault.

Teenagers clamour to sign up for the Police Athletic League's boxing classes on November 29, 1959. Standing, from left to right, are Angelo Delben, Jack Chase, Larry Scott, Leroy Harrison, Bob Johnson, Bill Morgan, and Walt Miller with Constable Norm Hagman behind them as Constable Ted Willis takes names.

Essex County's first paddy wagon hit the road on October 1, 1956, to transport prisoners from lock-up in Essex to Windsor police court. Pictured here are Corporal Harold Lucas, Constable Gordon Smith, and Constable Ron Brown at the wheel.

June 16, 1960: A Windsor "first" was a Willys Jeep for regular police patrol. Inspector Gordon Preston, Crown Attorney Bruce J.S. MacDonald, Police Chief Carl Farrow, Judge Joseph A. Legris, and Mayor Michael J. Patrick, from left to right, inspect the new police Jeep.

Windsor Police Auction, 1964. The annual auction sale, led by auctioneers Stewart McMahon and John McLean, brought hundreds of bargain seekers to buy goods confiscated by the police during the year.

A bold robber made away with cash from Marcel's Pastry Shop, forcing the owner to open the safe and taking nearly $1600. The store was located directly beneath Sandwich East Township's police department headquarters.

August 13, 1963: Mr. Beep, the talking car, and Elmer the Safety Elephant teach 600 Windsor schoolchildren about traffic safety, along with Constable Edward Moreland. Originally created by British Petroleum, Mr. Beep toured in the early '60s with the Ontario and Quebec Safety Leagues.

Windsor detectives captured two men and seized a small arsenal of weapons and a suitcase of cash in a raid on a Drouillard Road apartment on April 27, 1964. From left to right are Gerry Lavergne, John Laforet, John Shuttleworth, and Sidney Stuart.

"Trike Patrol": These cadets, John Edmondson, Noel Ecclestone, Peter Harris, and Dennis Perrault, from left to right, try out the department's new "kiddycar" three-wheelers, used exclusively for parking meter detail, in 1965.

In 1965, Windsor's only police women were the guards for the women's jail—but, they had the power to arrest. From left to right are Ruby O'Brady, Ilah Ridley, Agnes McLester, and Edith Snook.

December 29, 1965: Justice Agnus MacMillan swears in 18 police officers from Sandwich West Township into the Windsor Police Department, in anticipation of annexation which would take effect on January 1, 1966. When the City of Windsor annexed the Town of Riverside, Ojibway, and parts of Sandwich West, South, and East Townships, the Windsor force gained 49 suburban officers to help police the city's new populace, which had doubled in size.

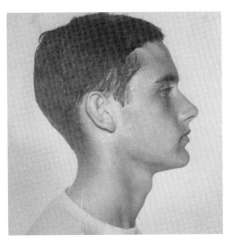

Mathew Charles Lamb's mug shot, June 1966. Lamb went on a shooting spree on Ford Boulevard in East Windsor, killing two strangers and injuring two others. He was charged with capital murder, but was acquitted by reason of insanity. After spending seven years in a mental health institution, Lamb joined the Rhodesian Light Infantry and was given a full military funeral in Salisbury, Rhodesia, after being killed in action.

June 26, 1967: Police officers march past the reviewing stand during the seventh annual Police Inspection and Field Day, held that year at Windsor Raceway.

Constable Allen Reaume was the first Windsor policeman to enter Precinct 2 on Huron Church Road when it opened on December 31, 1965, and he was the last to leave when the movers took everything out (but his favourite chair) on March 30, 1968. The precinct was absorbed by headquarters on Park Street, reducing Windsor to two precinct zones.

Dirty Trick
MILD, DRIZZLE
6 a.m. 32, 9 a.m. 32, 2 p.m. 39
Low tonight 30, high Thurs. 36
(Complete weather page 4)

The Windsor Star

FINAL
★★★★

VOL. 99, NO. 51 · 70 Pages · WINDSOR ONTARIO WEDNESDAY NOVEMBER 1 1967 · TEN CENTS

DEATH LESS THAN INCH AWAY

November 1, 1967: Constable Gerald Janisse shows Detective Sergeant G.G. Lavergne the hole in his cap made by a bullet fired during a drive-by shooting while he was on foot patrol. Only a fraction of an inch spared Janisse from a potentially fatal injury in the random attack.

April 2, 1968: Sergeant Harry Hyland of Argus Protection and Investigation patrols Peche Island from the back of Chief Pontiac. Nicknamed the "Peche Island Mountie," the security guard was hired by Sirrah Ltd., the island's owners, to discourage vandals and would-be thieves.

July 5, 1968: *Star* reporter John Laycock experienced firsthand the effects of the riot-control chemical Mace. Here, Sergeant Major Robert Duncan fires the aerosol spray at Laycock. His verdict? It's no fun, but better than other police methods of physical force.

Riot-helmeted, gas-masked police charge through clouds of tear gas during training on crowd control and civil disturbances on September 19, 1968. Chief Gordon Preston developed a local anti-riot plan in response to the Detroit Riots of 1967 and civil unrest following the assassination of Dr. Martin Luther King.

On August 23, 1969, officers responding to a domestic disturbance on Sprucewood Avenue were met with sniper fire. Sandwich West officer Robert Carrick was killed, while officers Robert Ross and Alfred Oakley were seriously injured. Ross, pictured above with his family, lost his right eye. Shooter William Rosik was charged with capital murder, but his sentence was commuted to life.

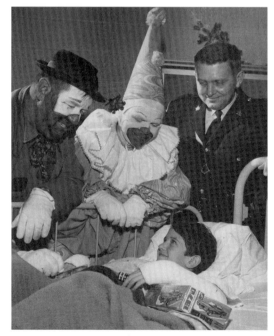

Mario Longo, 8, smiles up at two members of the Windsor Police Clown Troupe as officer Joe Gabala looks on. Mario suffered two broken arms and a broken leg in a car accident in 1969.

June 10, 1969: Chief Gordon Preston, front and centre, stands with his team of detectives from Windsor—and a few from Waterloo—who cracked the brutal murder of Walkerville Lumber Ltd. night watchman, William Snider, and put two killers behind bars. Owner of the lumber company, Cyril Cooper, to the right of Preston, took the involved officers to dinner in appreciation.

More than 50 representatives from various international border agencies took part in a pistol shoot at the Windsor Police Department's Pistol Range near Ojibway Park on July 15, 1969. Taking aim, from left to right, are Don Greer, US Border Patrol; Charlie Rose, RCMP (Windsor); John Holliday, US Immigration; Gene White, US Customs agent; and Ralph DeGroot, RCMP (Windsor).

May 14, 1971: Windsor detectives comb the scene for clues to the murder and sexual assault of Ljubica Topic, age 6. One of Windsor's most infamous cold cases, the investigation was reopened in 2015 because of DNA evidence—an adult male tooth found by the body. The case is still ongoing.

November 6, 1971: Riot police from the Windsor Department block off the Ambassador Bridge during protests against nuclear testing in Amchitka, Alaska. The student-driven protests, which took place over four days and drew up to 2,000 demonstrators, were largely peaceful with only 12 people arrested (and shortly released).

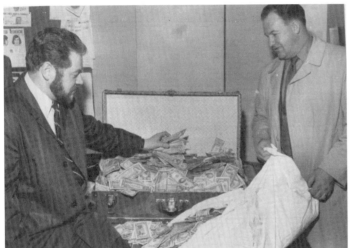

December 18, 1971: Robbers handcuffed 12 employees of the Royal Bank of Canada on Ouellette Avenue and escaped with $1.1 million dollars of unmarked cash, brought in from the Windsor Raceway, in the largest cash bank robbery in Canada up to that point. At top, investigators examine the inside of the bank the night of the heist. At middle left, Detectives James Cole and Richard Beith reveal a trunk full of cash, recovered in a raid on December 21st in Toronto. At middle right, Police Chief Gordon Preston announces at a press conference that six arrests were made and the money recovered—however, a count revealed later that they only had $150,000. The rest of the money was never recovered. At bottom, three of the eight suspects are escorted into the Windsor Jail to make their court appearances on December 24th.

"We Need Our Cops" was the slogan for Police Week in 1974. Here, the kick-off parade passes by Police Headquarters on Goyeau Avenue and Park Street, led by members of the Windsor Police Pipe Band. The Pipe Band was founded in 1967 and chose to wear the Red Gordon tartan in honour of Chief Gordon Preston.

Tim Maitre, at left, and Ryan Camphorst, guards at the Windsor Jail, set up the picket line as part of a province-wide strike on December 3, 1979. The strike was the first-ever by prison guards, and was declared illegal by the province. The guards were looking for wage parity with other law enforcement workers.

Windsor's first female constables, Liz Tuz, at left, and Lisbeth Taylor, were added to the Windsor Police Force in 1975, ending a century-old hiring practice of "men-only."

February 17, 1978: The Windsor Police Department's newest division, the tactical unit, show off some of the heavy-duty weapons they'd have at their disposal in a high-risk situation. The department declined to name the individuals.

June 11, 1979: Children watch as Sergeant Al Oakley and an unidentified constable use their house as cover during a stand-off in the 1000 block of Cadillac Street. Police were staking out a neighbouring home where a suspect barricaded himself for seven hours before surrendering without incident.

Night patrol at the riverfront, 1979.

"ARSON": A house on Elm Avenue exploded in the middle of the night on November 25, 1979, after an arsonist set it on fire while its occupants were away on holiday. Surrounding houses were damaged—including Ted Farron's, where he, his wife, and his six children (plus a child's friend) were sleeping at the time of the blast. During the blaze, firefighter Ron Jones (future City Councillor) was saved from death by two fellow firefighters (see photo on page 350). No one was severely injured or killed in the blast.

THE WINDSOR STAR

The *Windsor Star* has always served one community—but has enjoyed lots of styles, looks, leaders, and even names along the way.

The paper started in 1860 as *The Weekly Record*, and under a new owner became the daily *Evening Record* in 1890, eventually becoming *The Windsor Record*. When W.F. Herman bought the paper in 1918, he immediately changed the name to *The Border Cities Star*. He swapped the name again, in 1935, to *The Windsor Daily Star*, to better reflect the amalgamated Border Cities that all became part of Windsor that year. When Herman died in 1938, his wife Adie Knox Herman took over steering the ship, while Hugh Graybiel became publisher. In true journalistic fashion, in order to avoid redundancy, on November 7, 1959, the paper changed to the name it goes by today: *The Windsor Star*. That was in the day when Knowlton Nash—who would go on to become a household name in Canada as senior anchor for CBC TV's *The National* news program from 1978 to 1988—served as *The Windsor Star*'s Washington correspondent.

Though *The Windsor Star* underwent many changes and reported on everything from world wars to major automotive strikes, it wasn't until the 1950s that some of the paper's biggest upheavals took place. First of all, the paper expanded its footprint downtown. Housed on Ferry Street in a former brick apartment building and a beautiful limestone beaux-arts affair—built by the paper in 1927—*Windsor Star* management decided it needed yet more space to cope with growing readership. In 1953 the paper started construction of an office building and printing press facility on Pitt Street just to the west of its property, a project that would take two years to complete. In 1954 came yet another milestone: the addition of a state-of-the-art, full-colour Crabtree Press from Leeds, England. It ran the length of a city block and, starting in the basement, climbed three stories high at some points. When the big beast started printing, special lights turned on throughout the building to indicate the presses had begun, though astute observers did not really need that confirmation, since the whole place rumbled ever so slightly when newspapers were in motion. Though it would be decades before the paper started printing much colour in the news pages, advertising circulars would often be brightly hued. When it revved up, the new Crabtree could zip 35,000 papers an hour from the press to the mailing room one floor up.

Other accomplishments abound. "It was the first Canadian newspaper to have colour comics, and in 1965 was the first newspaper in Canada to publish a photograph received on the then-revolutionary wire machine," says a February 6, 1993, front-page story celebrating *The Star's* 75th anniversary. "*The Star* was one of the first newspapers in North America to use pagination, allowing editors to compose a full page of the newspaper by computer."

Though they were still heady times for the paper, tragedy struck *The Windsor Star* in 1967. Adie Knox Herman, Hugh Graybiel, and Hugh's son Richard, 47, the heir apparent, all died within six months of each other. As *The Windsor Star* would later recall in its 75th anniversary issue, "Canada's Centennial year, 1967, was a black year at the paper." In 1969, W.L. Lum Clark, who had close ties to the Hermans, retired as president of the paper, setting in motion big changes. No family was left to run things, after all. Mark Farrell, who rolled into town in a flower-power Volkswagen Beetle and served as publisher from 1969 to 1972, brightened things up. During his tenure *The Windsor Star* became the first large daily to endorse the NDP (and call for the legalization of marijuana). Other publishers throughout the era included: J.P. O'Callaghan (1972–76), Bill Wheatley (1976–77), Bob Pearson (1977–79), and Gordon Bullock (1979–84).

Star reporters started to come into their own, making a name for themselves with popular columns and editorial pieces. R.M. "Dick" Harrison led the charge, churning out three regular columns (under separate pen names), in addition to the widely read "Now" daily opinion piece. His prowess holds legendary status at *The Star*, as do his colourful methods—drinking on the job, anyone? John Linblad picked up the torch in 1960, quickly earning himself a reputation as a hound for the facts. In his own words, he was a "high-school dropout, former lumberjack, combat airman, explorer, foreign correspondent, and novelist"—many hats, indeed. From there, Sandra Precop, fresh out of school, became *The Star's* first woman city columnist in 1974. These reporters—and those who followed—earned the paper a reputation for its provocative opinion writers.

In 1968 *The Star* celebrated its 50th anniversary, though it shortchanged itself, since it set its year of birth as 1918, the year W.F. Herman bought the paper, instead of tracing its roots back to 1890 as a daily and 1860 as a weekly. Still, the anniversary provided the opportunity to champion the community and trumpet the paper's many achievements.

In December 1970, meanwhile, employees at *The Star* staged something radical for the newspaper world in Windsor: a two-week sit-in to demand a better contract (a shorter strike would follow later that decade, as well). Members of three craft unions spent their days busying themselves with everything from playing darts to holding church services, but mainly making sure *The Star* did not publish. Their efforts paid off. Strikers received a $43-a-week pay raise over three years, though one *Star* report at the time called the deal "mutually unsatisfactory." But at least the paper returned to porches. "The ink is flowing and the presses are running once again at *The Star* following the end of a two-week sit-in strike," the paper reported on December 18, 1970.

A more momentous event happened the following year, however, when the longtime family-owned paper followed a distinct trend with North American newspapers and was sold to a chain. Southam Press bought the paper in 1971, ushering in a new era of more investigative reportage.

"There was always a lot of local coverage, but the emphasis changed," Jim Bruce, who started as a desk editor in 1964 and went on to become editor and publisher, said in 2016. "Local stories started appearing on the front page more. And the other thing that changed was more emphasis on in-depth reporting and less on chasing fire trucks." But no matter the subject or style, *The Windsor Star* continued one thing: its mission to keep the Windsor and Essex County community informed, entertained, and challenged.

January 10, 1964: Violet Howells, Frances Curry, and Jane Nightingale in *The Star* library, now the photo archives from which the majority of the photos in this book were sourced.

August 30, 1950: A national rail strike posed problems for *The Windsor Daily Star*'s regular delivery of newsprint by train. Here, men load rolls off a transport, carrying 14 tonnes of paper, onto a *Star* delivery truck, ready for the presses.

The composing room, 1950s.

December 16, 1952: The Goodfellows editions of *The Star* roll off the presses onto the conveyor belt and are examined by Preston D. Norton, president of The Old Newsboys; C.J. DeFields, Goodfellows general manager; and Tom Crowley, pressman; from left to right. Crowley, sporting one of his daily newspaper hats, was a fixture at *The Star* for 44 years, from 1926 to 1970.

August 11, 1953: More than 50 members of *The Star*'s editorial staff, plus their friends, gather after a hectic election night spent tabulating the official returns for an anxious audience. Their totals were carried over Radio Station CBE in record time.

Private Clem Jette and Lance Corporal Ron Gagnon keep in touch with home events by reading *The Star* while deployed in Korea in August, 1953.

Passersby examine photographs displayed in *The Star* building's windows in 1953, before the addition. The staff librarians would create collages of unused Associated Press wire photos that *The Star* received daily from Detroit to feature for the public twice a month.

In 1953, *The Star* began a $1.5 million addition onto the back of its Ferry Street building to house the brand new Crabtree presses from England. These shots show the progression of construction over the fall of 1953.

State-of-the-art super colour presses, built by R.W. Crabtree & Sons of Leeds, England, were installed in *The Star*'s new addition in 1954. Three years later, they were fully operational and would serve the paper until 1996.

Delivery truck outside *The Windsor Daily Star* building in the 1950s.

Star staff pose for a funny photo in December, 1955. In the top row, from left to right, is Cecil Southward, Jack Dalgleish, Angus Munro, Rex McInnes, and John Holmes. In front of them are, from left to right, Bill Botwright, Betty Wemsley, Gladys Cada, and Gordon Cunningham.

The classified advertising department in 1956.

December 28, 1957: The big electric sign over *The Star* building dominates Windsor's skyline, in a shot taken from the Veterans' Memorial Building in Detroit. The François Baby house can be seen at the right, while the Security Building, centre, and the Norton Palmer Hotel, far left, rise out of the landscape.

W.C. "Bill" Riggs, at left, collects pledges from fellow employees for the 1957 United Way fundraising campaign. Riggs worked as a linotype operator at *The Star* for 42 years, but is perhaps better remembered as a long-time city alderman who served a short stint as mayor in 1969 following John Wheelton's resignation.

Local columnist R.M. "Dick" Harrison was *The Star*'s first opinion writer from 1925 to 1958. Notorious for his heavy drinking, colourful outbursts, and prolific writing, Harrison was a legendary figure who set the stage for the tenacious opinion writers who followed him.

The Windsor Daily Star quietly changed its masthead for the fifth and final time in 1959, adopting the shortened nameplate, *The Windsor Star*, as it remains to this day.

Hugh A. Graybiel, right, publisher of *The Windsor Star*, and his son, Richard, *The Star*'s general manager and CP director, on April 20, 1961. Both would die eight days apart in 1967. While Richard died from a heart attack at age 47, his father succumbed days later to a broken heart—or so *The Star* staff always claimed.

January 12, 1962: William Hunter, local advertising manager for *The Star*, discusses the award-winning advertisments from Smith's 1961 spring fashion feature with George Robinson, Smith's ad man, at left. The ads, displayed on the wall, were recognized for their design and colour by Retail Advertisements Weekly's annual review—a prestigious award that recognized ads from large companies like J.L. Hudson and Macy's.

The Windsor Star wished its readers a Happy New Year in 1961 from the sign that graced the newspaper building on Ferry Street.

Photographer and photo editor Bill Bishop in the darkroom, circa 1960s. Bishop shot many of the photographs found in this book. This photograph was clearly staged, as the image in the enlarger should be a negative!

The Windsor Star building at Ferry Street and Pitt Street, circa 1963.

"Best in Business": This edition from October 30, 1963, won *The Star* top honours for a second year running in a contest among 91 of Canada's 102 daily newspapers. It was awarded the John A. MacLaren award for typographic excellence on January 20, 1964, for papers over 25,000 circulation.

The familiar yellow *Windsor Star* delivery trucks had a difficult, but successful, day delivering the newspaper after a blizzard on February 25, 1965. Pictured here are the full complement of the dedicated crew, from left to right: Donald O'Neil, Gordon Desjardins, Clare Sawyer, Lyle Widdifield, Cecil Carroll, Wilbur Cudmore, Ted Neilson, Norman Anderson, Larry Fairbrother, and Stan Mason.

September 9, 1965: Department heads look over the early editions of *The Star*. Shown standing are editor W.L. "Lum" Clark, left, composing room foreman Don Bell, engraving foreman Fred Black, general manager Richard Graybiel, press foreman Tom Crowley, publisher Hugh Graybiel, and executive editor Norm Hull. In the foreground is advertising director Bill Viveash.

"Newspaper's Hearth": A close-up of one of the cylinders on *The Star*'s presses in 1968 shows how the metal plates, containing the photos and type, carried the impression to the great rolls of newsprint. Pressman Harold "Smitty" Smith is pictured making an adjustment on one of the plates. The high speed presses could turn out 60,000 newspapers an hour if required, although normal speed was from 35,000 to 40,000.

Don Stewart, a member of *The Star*'s composing room staff, is shown putting together a page for the day's edition on August 21, 1968. As the make-up man, it was Stewart's job to place advertisements and news stories in a balanced arrangement, a feat achieved with close communication with the editorial department.

September 3, 1968: Bob Best, back to the camera, and Bob Mosher, two of the 20-man pressroom crew, look over the day's edition as it rolls from the Crabtree presses. The white streak in the upper right is the fast-moving line of papers travelling at 35,000 an hour to the mailing room one floor up.

Fred Black, art director; Carl Morgan, and Norm Hull, executive editor, from left to right, look over the magazine insert for *The Windsor Star*'s 50th Anniversary special edition, published September 2, 1968. The magazine featured 500 pictures of the most significant stories from the past 50 years. Carl Morgan organized the magazine and would go on to serve as editor from 1977 to 1992.

Truck driver Gord Desjardins looks back at jumper Walter Levergood, aboard the truck, who is handing stacks down to Larry Breen, one of *The Star*'s 1,100 carrier boys in 1968. That year, circulation reached 87,500 and was read by nearly every home in Windsor and Essex County.

The mail room is packed on August 30, 1968, as staff prepare for a massive delivery run of *The Star*'s 50th Anniversary edition at a staggering 232 pages each.

November 20, 1969: Martin Lemieux, age 12, was a grade 6 student at Immaculate Conception Separate School in 1969, but was better known as the kid selling papers at the corner of Ouellette Avenue and Wyandotte Street. As part of youth appreciation week, the Windsor Optimist Club named Martin the newsboy of the year. Martin credited the Radio Tavern and the St. Clair Tavern as his selling hotspots.

The Star experienced the first strike in its history after three of its craft unions walked off the job on December 2, 1970. The mechanical departments—typographers, pressmen, and stereotypers—staged a "sit-in" and no paper was published from December 2–17. Despite the presses grinding to a halt, the other departments still came to work while their striking coworkers occupied a different floor. The labour dispute was largely over wages, but also included issues like severance, apprenticeship regulations, sick leave, and other benefits. With the help of friendly mediator William Riggs, former mayor and retired pressman, a settlement was reached between *The Star* and the three unions who signed new three-year contracts.

May 22, 1973: During a strike by printers, pressmen, stereotypers, mailers, and truck drivers, a shortened edition of *The Star* was produced by management personnel after three days of shutdown. At the top, *Star* publisher J.P. O'Callaghan, with back turned, confronts Sam Bested, chairman of the Council of Unions, in front of cameras in *The Star* parking lot. Below, striking workers attempt to block the delivery trucks from getting to distribution points throughout the city. The primary issue of the strike concerned new technology, namely the use of OCR scanners to turn copy into paper tape, which printers feared would jeopardize their job security. The strike lasted from May 19 to June 1, resulting in a contract with wage increases and lifetime job guarantees, while *The Star* did not concede the procedures for scanning.

June Thomas of the classified ad department was crowned "Miss Want Ad" in 1972 for the second year in a row. The winner was picked based on her ability, accuracy, and ingenuity in receiving and preparing ads for publication.

August 5, 1974: Over three hundred *Windsor Star* carriers were rewarded for the high circulation figures on their routes with a trip to Bob-Lo Island. In 1974, *The Star* had a total of 1,300 carriers through Essex, Kent, and Lambton counties.

This group of writers and photographers were sent to the 1976 Montreal Olympic Games to provide local readers with daily coverage. *The Star*'s "team" are, from left to right, feature writer Paul Vasey, photo editor Bill Bishop, sports editor Jack Dulmage, photographer Bev MacKenzie, sports writer Marty Knack, and photographer Walter Jackson.

August 15, 1978: Star editorial cartoonist Bob Monks touches up cartoon wallpaper for Kelli, Timmi, and Michelle Soulliere. Monks is best known for his time at *The Star* and as a TV personality on the CBC, but also worked as an art teacher at W.D. Lowe. His comics are featured throughout this book.

Harold Boycott, who worked in *The Star*'s composing room since 1923, sets type on a Linotype under machinist foremen Bill Knowler's watchful gaze. By 1974, the newspaper was almost entirely produced with cold type, using the Linotype only for classified ads.

April 16, 1979: Karen Hall with a "New Age" perm that, according to her, made her hair look "like ugly bits of brain." Hall's witty and insightful columns won her a fast and loyal following, making her one of *The Star*'s most familiar faces.

PHOTOJOURNALISM

As the community evolved, so did *The Windsor Star*. Reporters did not always cover simply what happened, but at times dived deeper, with investigation and feature stories using more creative language. Likewise, photography also changed for the better—following a general trend in photojournalism, which tells stories through images—altering the paper's whole look.

At one time, newspaper photographers had to lug large, box-like cameras around, set them on tripods, and arrange photos, often producing rather dull subject matter through posed pictures. But an invention in Germany in 1925 launched a photographic revolution. The Leica camera, designed to use surplus movie film, then shot on 35 mm, let photojournalists truly capture reality—by going mobile. The small, lightweight Leica freed photographers to roam. It would take years, however, before the power of the small camera was widely understood. Not

all photographers used the Leica, either. Still, the 35-mm concept was set, especially since it allowed the use of a variety of lenses, from wide-angle to telephoto. Eventually, by the end of World War II, photojournalists realized that not only could they capture history as it unfolded on the frontlines, but could do so in increasingly creative ways. Only then was modern photojournalism born.

In Windsor, the trend was unmistakable. Before World War II, *The Windsor Star*, like most papers simply did not run many photos. And most were headshots. Part of the issue was that the paper only employed two photographers, pre-war. The other part was technological limitations. *The Windsor Star* did not use 35-mm cameras right away, and Leicas were deemed too pricey. *Star* "photogs" moved to such cameras as the Graflex Speed Graphic, standard press equipment in the 1940s through the 1960s. Photographers used individual film holders that they slid in and out of the camera every snap. Slow and unpractical, the system limited photojournalists to carrying perhaps 48 shots at one time. So photographers could not risk trying fancy fare when they had to get the job done. Nor could they always respond lightning quick. Plus, the motor drive for rapid succession shooting had yet to surface. And before the digital age, photographers had to "soup" their negatives and print pictures at the end of the day—eating a significant portion of their time—before they even knew if they nailed the shot.

Bill Bishop, who started at the paper in 1953, was the youngest of a growing photo staff that included chief photographer Jack Dalgleish, Cecil Southward, Mike Bunt, Walter Jackson, and Gladys Cada. Bishop went on to serve as the *Windsor Star* photo editor from 1972 to 1994. He witnessed not only a lot of stories, but also a lot of journalistic transformation, travelling to such events as the 1968 Liberal convention in Ottawa where Pierre Trudeau beat Windsor's own Paul Martin Sr. for the leadership of the party, and to the 1976 Montreal Olympic Games. Yet, one picture changed things for him—and for the newspaper. Bishop Fulton J. Sheen, famous for his Catholic television show that made him one of the world's first televangelists, visited Detroit for a speaking engagement. Bishop, the photographer on duty, went over to capture the Catholic bishop's event on film.

"Sheen was standing backstage in the shadows with his long robes, and in front of him was the audience, though they couldn't see him yet," Bishop recalled in 2016 about one of his favourite photos. "I thought, that's a hell of a picture. So I took it. I went back to the office and looked at what I had and thought, 'They'll never use this. They'll want the old stand-up shot.' I had the standard, as well. But it turned out they used both."

In the '60s and '70s Windsor news photographers began focusing on details that helped illustrate the story, finding more inspired angles or dramatic lighting, instead of just pointing and shooting. So photography evolved at *The Windsor Star*.

The trend continued with Windsor's own version of conflict reporting, for the 1967 Detroit Riots. In the so-called Summer of Love in 1967, Detroit erupted in rage after police raided a blind pig at 12th Street (now Rosa Parks Boulevard) and Clairmount Avenue overnight on Saturday July 23, 1967. *Windsor Star* staffers did not go over to Detroit, however, until Monday morning, since management deemed the situation too dangerous. Windsorites could see the smoke burning in Detroit from across the river. The mood proved ominous, even in Windsor.

Bishop went over in a car with three *Star* reporters. The National Guard had already moved in, trying to secure the area. "I got pictures of guys hiding behind a tree and shooting," he said. "It was nuts. It was nothing but fires all over the place." When the smoke cleared five days later, 43 people were dead and more than 600 injured—marking one of the deadliest uprisings in US history.

In 1970, racial tension erupted again in Detroit, this time between students at River Rouge High School. The *Star* covered those events, as well. In fact, the *Star* routinely followed Detroit back then, from John F. Kennedy's Labour Day speech on September 5, 1960, before taking the White House, to the 1968 World Series that the Tigers won. Visiting presidents, movie stars, and the Detroit Economic Club—they documented everything.

In Windsor, naturally, reporters and photographers covered everything. But as time went on, younger photographers came along, creating a new breed, a new zest. Yes, they captured the action as news unfolded. But with modern 35-mm equipment, they also had an eye for detail, illustrating the story in inventive, sometimes entertaining ways—providing visual storytelling through still images.

A family swims in the Detroit River at the foot of the Ambassador Bridge, circa 1952.

July 1953 (photo by Jack Dalgleish): Workmen make progress on a road paving project on Sandwich Street (Riverside Drive) from Lincoln to Goyeau.

May 14, 1956: *Star* staff photographer Mike Bunt gestures towards his "whale of an excuse for the editor," when he arrived at the Riverside Sportsmen's Club to cover the annual birdhouse building competition.

August 1962 (photo by Bill Bishop): A collision between a produce truck and car left fifteen tonnes of radishes all over Huron Church Road.

June 6, 1960: A Windsor firefighter grabs a drink while battling a fire at Grace Hospital's Ellis House.

March 1965 (photo by Bill Bishop): A distraught father prays for his son, who was pulled from Little River.

August 14, 1965: Fishing for pickerel in the Detroit River.

May 1966 (photo by Bill Bishop): UN Secretary-General U Thant ties his shoelace during a visit to Windsor.

September 1966 (photo by Bill Bishop): Waiting in the wings is Bishop Fulton J. Sheen, taking a quiet moment before his speech at the opening of the Christian Culture Series.

February 11, 1967 (photo by Mike Bunt): Security guard Peter Munt and his dog protect the $4 million Holiday Inn development on Riverside Drive.

July 1968 (photo by Gladys Cada): Young visitors to Peche Island enjoy navigating the canals in their pedal-operated boats.

September 1970: A janitor prepares the halls of Kennedy Collegiate for the first day of school.

July 1969 (photo by Bill Bishop): A cowboy dodges a bucking bronco during the Freedom Festival rodeo at Jackson Park.

Windsor Star photographer Bill Bishop was among the first to document the violence and racial tensions during the Detroit Riots in 1967 as he toured devastated neighbourhoods on July 25th, with reporters Kevin Doyle and Walt McCall. At top, two men walk beside wrecked homes on 12th Street. A soldier, pictured at bottom left, takes cover from sniper fire behind a tree on the west side of Detroit. Another National Guardsman stationed at Woodward Avenue takes a break, at bottom right.

In April 1970, racial violence broke out after a skirmish between high-school students in River Rouge, an industrial suburb of Detroit. Police used tear gas to disperse crowds and made several arrests. These photographs were captured by *Star* photographer Jack Dalgleish.

September 1970 (photo by Bill Bishop): Windsor boxer Jimmy Meilleur sits in his dressing room, waiting for the call to the ring.

November 1971 (photo by Bill Bishop): Windsor police arrest protesters at the Ambassador Bridge during a demonstration against the Amchitka atomic tests in Alaska.

February 1972 (photo by Cec Southward): With a little help, this driver walks away from his ditched truck after an accident.

April 1973 (photo by Cec Southward): Giant waves from spring storms on Lake Erie flooded Pelee Island and wreaked havoc on shoreline cottages.

July 1976 (photo by Bill Bishop): The parade of athletes at the opening ceremonies of the Montreal Olympic Games.

August 1978 (photo by Stan Andrews): Blackie the dog hitches a ride with his owner, David Little.

September 1978 (photo by Grant Black): A cigar-smoking construction worker is busy on E.C. Row expressway.

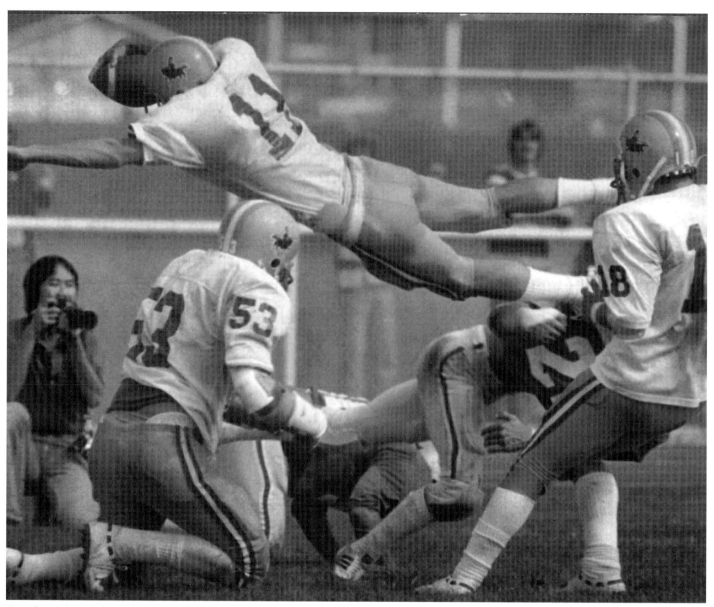

October 1978 (photo by Grant Black): The University of Windsor Lancers' running back Bruce Walker (11) dives across the goal line.

November 1979 (photo by Grant Black): Windsor fireman Ron Jones, just pulled from a burning house on Elm Avenue, embraces his rescuer.

March 1975 (photo by Cec Southward): Behind the scenes, Bozo the Clown gets ready.

August 1980 (photo by Tim McKenna): Riders get some refreshment during the Windsor Star Classic Bicycle Race.

April 1980 (photo by Grant Black): Cindy Crapper hefts the discus in preparation for a WSSA track and field meet.

April 1980 (photo by Tim McKenna): Tricycle owner Doug Clarkson washes the accumulation of winter grime off his pride and joy.

June 1979 (photo by Walter Jackson): The burned-out remains of Most Precious Blood Church, which succumbed to a fire the previous fall.

March 1980 (photo by Cec Southward): This infant, held by a Windsor policeman, was discovered lying on a bed beside her mother who had been shot and killed.

August 1980, (photo by Tim McKenna): Dave McLeod of Windsor Rowing Club is pulled from tangle of steering lines by oarsman Murray Ridley after his shell overturned.

DOWNTOWN

Downtown Windsor has changed so much over the years—with new buildings replacing old ones, and then being replaced in turn—that you could almost believe it's a living, breathing thing. 1950 to 1980 "was a period when a lot of downtown changed," architectural historian Andrew Foot said in 2016. "Many of the buildings on the riverfront went down. A number of Victorian buildings were lost. There was a shift to more modern structures." A working, industrial riverside was transformed over a period of three decades into much more, with an impressive riverfront park offering a great view of the Detroit skyline.

Though it's hard to fathom from this vantage point, when business has largely migrated from city centres to the suburbs, the downtown Windsor of the 1950s remained very much the heart of the city—the place to be for shopping and business alike. But downtown was about more than just commerce. It was the civic arena, the place citizens came to express themselves, to celebrate and debate and protest. And Windsorites came in the thousands and sometimes even in the tens and hundreds of thousands, attending annual Santa Claus Parade, Labour Day Parade, Emancipation Day,

and the Mary Day Parade, well as strikes and protests and rallies.

Though attendance at public gatherings would slowly decline as the '50s gave way to the '60s and then the '70s, and businesses began to leave the downtown core for the new suburban shopping plazas and malls, downtown nevertheless remained central to the community. Some of the popular stores from yesteryear include: the king of downtown meeting spots, S.S. Kresge; Fielding & Campeau on Riverside Drive East, which operated as a family shop for 86 years; the A&P Super Market, which ran from 1940 to 1975; Adelman's Department Store on Pitt Street; Lee's Imperial Tavern, which sat in the same block that once housed the Windsor Castle Hotel (where, legend has it, Windsor's name was chosen); the Heintzman Building, family owned for 40 years; and the CH Smith department store on Ouellette. Neighbouring businesses included Birks Jewellers; Esquire Men's Shop; Steele Optical; and Wilkinson Shoes; Lyttles Bakery, a staple for 52 years, provided java and home cooking; Bartlet, MacDonald & Gow, which grew out of the one-room Donald Cameron's General Store from the 1860s; and Steinberg Miracle Mart, on the corner of Chatham and Goyeau. Of course, the City Market was a mainstay for decades, all the way into the 1990s, when business started to wane. The Windsor Arena, affectionately known as the Barn, remained steadfastly in place; and you could not miss the 'Plywood Palace', only slightly better known as the Holiday Inn, on the north side of Riverside Drive West, the last of the commercial buildings to occupy the riverfront.

During this period, the city's battle against urban blight, both downtown and elsewhere within the city limits, had a big impact on the architectural shape of the core. A pattern of aggressive demolition emerged, beginning with the razing of entire city blocks, that resulted in a loss of architectural diversity. However, Windsor could also count on innovation, which helped to make the core a more modern centre. A new City Hall was completed in 1958. The ambitious Cleary Auditorium, called a "gem on the river" by *The Star*, opened in 1960. The LaBelle Building was replaced with a glass-heavy edifice in 1961, after the building was destroyed in a spectacular fire two years previous. Le Goyeau apartment building rose on Riverside Drive in 1967 for $3.2 million. As the City of Windsor proudly declared in its year-end *Star* advertisement in 1958, "Windsor Tomorrow… is being built today."

But the biggest downtown change—for sheer skyline-altering shock—came in the mid-1970s. Three of Windsor's largest, most prominent hotels were felled, beginning with the granddaddy of all local hostelries: the British-American Hotel, located at the foot of Ouellette Avenue, north of Riverside Drive. It became the centre of debate in 1974 when Mayor Frank Wansbrough approved a proposal to build a Valhalla Inn in its place. In response, a movement gained momentum to replace the commercial riverfront with parkland, and propelled one of its leaders, Bert Weeks, into the mayoralty in 1974 as a direct result of the controversy. From there, the future of the downtown riverfront was set: as buildings were condemned and came down, including the historic British-American

Hotel in 1975, the riverfront was developed into another public space that would come, over the decades, to rival the riverfronts of any other municipality in the country.

Next to face the wrecking ball was the Norton Palmer Hotel, on Park Street just west of Ouellette, which was also demolished in 1975. Victoria Park Place apartment high-rise now stands in its place. The following year saw the destruction of the Prince Edward Hotel, closed since 1967, in the 300 block of Ouellette Avenue, making way for a low-rise Bank of Nova Scotia. These mainstays of downtown commerce and tourism had been outdated by the more fashionable motor hotels of the '60s, including the Viscount Motor Hotel (built in 1963) and the Seaway Inn (built in 1968), though neither proved to have the longevity of their predecessors.

The 1970s also brought another change—that even though it took place far from the core—greatly impacted the fortunes of downtown businesses. Devonshire Mall opened in 1970 on the site of the former horseracing track, Devonshire Raceway. The suburban shopping centre proved popular and convenient, and slowly but surely started draining shoppers and traffic from downtown. Though shops would make a go of it for some time in the city centre, stores such as Bartlet's, Adelman's, and CH Smith closed down in the late 1970s. A poignant example is Steinberg's, which opened as one of Devonshire's anchor department stores. As a result, they closed their downtown location in 1975, after fewer than 10 years in business—leaving behind a large building that would sit vacant until 1992. The city centre endured some tough times but ultimately survived.

Downtown Windsor remained the centre of commerce and culture in the '50s, '60s, and '70s, though it lost ground to suburbanization and to the advent of mall culture. In response, the downtown core began a slow transition from retail to entertainment, largely in the form of bars and restaurants—just part of the ebb and flow of a vibrant city.

F.W. Woolworth Co. at 647 Ouellette Avenue, circa 1980. The Herb Gray Centre for Nonprofit Excellence now occupies this site.

Opening day at the new Metropolitan Store, February 3, 1949. The modern department store at 439 Ouellette Avenue featured two full selling floors, air-conditioning, and a luncheonette with a soda fountain.

Ernest Fielding, the proprietor of one of Windsor's last general stores, Fielding & Campeau Grocery and China Shop, is pictured here in 1949. Merchant stores like this, which operated for 86 years on Riverside Drive near Goyeau Street, were disappearing in favour of modern supermarkets.

November 5, 1949: The old Salvation Army citadel was soon replaced by a new structure at the northwest corner of London Street (University Avenue) and Victoria Avenue, which is now St. Clair College's Mediaplex.

The corner of Park Street and Ouellette Avenue in the 1950s. Birks Jewellers was the successor to McCreery's Diamond Store, and was famous for their blue jewellery boxes and brass "B" double doors. The building now houses The City Grill.

Ouellette Avenue, 1952. Visible storefronts include Waterman's Furs, John Smith clothing store, Fraser's Nut Shop, the Maple Leaf Restaurant, Paris Cleaners, Loblaw's, Pascoe's Clothing, and Lazare's Furs.

Old St. Nick Led Fairyland Parade Through Downtown Windsor

The Santa Claus Parade on November 17, 1951, drew 32,000 people to Ouellette Avenue.

A&P Super Market, pictured at left in 1950, was a stand alone shop at Ouellette Avenue and Elliot Street until Rose Furniture was built next door in 1952. After being vacant for two years, the A&P reopened as Mother's Pizza in 1977.

The interior of Adelman's Department Store on Pitt Street in May 1954. Note the signs advertising their spring lay-away plan.

In the 1950s, Windsor's downtown riverfront was dramatically transformed by the addition of a municipal park and civic auditorium. At left, demolition is underway in 1954 after the city expropriated the Windsor-Detroit Ferry Company's land and the city block behind it. A new retaining seawall was being constructed, with 10,000 yards of clay, to create a riverfront park. At right, the Cleary Auditorium is under construction in 1959, with a completed Dieppe Gardens and Cleary Guest House.

"Man or Mannequin?": Jerry Mackey, window-dresser for CH Smith, places "It" in the storefront window during a week-long contest in November, 1955, for shoppers to guess whether the figure—complete with "mechanical gyrations"—was really a man or just a mannequin.

December 15, 1956: Christmas lights festoon the Ouellette Avenue facade of CH Smith department store. In the 1950s, Smith's was the largest department store in southwestern Ontario with a staff of nearly 300 employees.

City Council proposed a limit on overhanging signs on Ouellette Avenue in 1957. Citing Tecumseh Road, Toronto's Yonge Street, and Detroit's Woodward Avenue as the standard, they considered the signs "ugly" for a business district.

May 3, 1958: This parade of new and used cars, sponsored by the Windsor Automobile Dealers Association and Independent Used Car Dealers, used the slogan: "You Auto Buy Now."

May 23, 1957: The "ultra-modern" Bali-Hi Motor Hotel at 1280 Ouellette Avenue is readied for the first day of business. The Bali-Hi branded itself as "Canada's Most Exotic Hotel" and featured the Balinese Room for dining and dancing. The building was reopened as the IRIS house in 2003.

The 300 block of Ouellette Avenue, 1958. The Wilkinson Shoes building rises at five storeys on the west side, with its famous slogan: "Wilkinson Shoes Wear Like a Pig's Nose." Other visible shops include: Diane Frocks, Jeanne Bruce Ltd. Jewellers, Red Robin Apparel, Calhoun's Hats, Zellers, People's Credit Jewellers, and Pond's Drug Store. On the east side, the Canada Building dominates the foreground with Rexall Drugs and the Canadian National Railway office on its ground floor. Shops behind it are: Trott's Shoes, United Cigars Store, and Palace Cinemas.

LaBelle Blaze Worst Downtown for 13 Years

The LaBelle Building, at the southwest corner of Ouellette Avenue and University Avenue, went up in flames on April 5, 1959. The million-dollar blaze was the worst fire in the downtown core since the S.S. Kresge's blaze in 1945. The building housed Pond's Drug Store, People's Credit Jewellers Ltd., Bell's Coffee Shop, Sportland Sporting Goods store, and 23 offices.

A snowstorm hampers traffic at the intersection of Ouellette Avenue and University Avenue, looking south, circa 1960. Palace Cinemas is playing *The Purple Gang* and *Quantrill's Raiders*, and advertises smoking balconies. Next to it is Belinda Shoes, a tenant of the Heintzman building, which was demolished in 1986 to make way for a expansion of the Palace. The Palace was renovated into new offices for *The Windsor Star* in 2012.

A traffic cop redirects a detour on Park Street in June 1960. The Metropolitan Guaranty Trust, an art deco building from 1928, stands at left. On the right is the Provincial Bank of Canada with Ken H. Baker Insurance and the Capitol Theatre behind it. Today, Provincial Bank is a parking lot while Ken H. Baker is now Phog Lounge.

City Market, July 1960. That summer, outdoor stalls were moved inside to ease the crowded sidewalks on Chatham Street.

Save a three-year hiatus, Lazare's Furs has occupied 439 Ouellette Avenue since 1925. Their iconic sign, which juts out over Maiden Lane, was added in 1942.

These six buildings on Pitt Street West, pictured at left, including the Empire Theatre, were torn down to make way for an expansion to the Federal Building—better known now as the "Paul Martin Building," renamed for Paul Martin Sr. in 1994. The finished addition, pictured at right in 1960, was designed by Johnson & McWhinnie.

By 1960, Bartlet, MacDonald & Gow department store boasted two entrances: the original storefront on Ouellette Avenue (at left) and a new, modern entrance on Riverside Drive (at right). With its beginnings as a general store in 1860, it was one of Windsor's oldest businesses and enduring downtown landmarks. The store closed in 1972 to make way for the CIBC Building.

The southwest corner of Ouellette Avenue and Wyandotte Street, 1961. A syndicate of local businessmen, called Block Two Ltd., purchased this group of buildings—including Dominion Store, Joe's Barber Shop, and White Spots Restaurant—with plans for redevelopment into a shopping centre. The centre, featuring a new Dominion Store, opened in 1965 (see page 365.

Intersection of Ouellette Avenue and University Avenue, 1953 (at left) and 1960 (at right). In 1953, on the southeast corner, is the Heintzman Building with the Palace Cinemas (playing *Ruby Gentry*), the Canada Building, and Prince Edward Hotel behind it. Across the street is the LaBelle Building with Wilkinson Shoes behind it. Eight years later, the Heintzman boasts a new facade—and new tenants Seaboard Loans and People's Credit Jewellers. Palace Cinemas has a new sign while the LaBelle Building was completely rebuilt after a fire.

November 16, 1962: Ouellette Avenue was decorated for Christmas by the Downtown Business Association in an attempt to draw early shoppers. The nighttime store lights include CH Smith department store, Seaway Inn, the Heintzman Music Store, Palace Cinemas, Wilkinson Shoes, S.S. Kresge's, and Fraser Men's and Boys' Wear.

Windsor's main branch of the Bank of Montreal, 200 Ouellette Avenue, was "cleaned out" on April 4, 1964 in preparation for demolition. Designed by local architects Carter and Fraser, the new structure was built on the same spot as the original branch, and had its grand opening in September 1966.

The British-American Hotel at the northeast corner of Riverside Drive and Ouellette Avenue, circa 1964. The original hotel, built in 1832, succumbed to fire and was rebuilt in 1871. There are carvings of lions and seabirds visible above the windows of the west side of the building. In 1974, Valhalla Inns Ltd. of Toronto proposed to build a high-rise hotel on the site. The proposal faced considerable public opposition, spearheaded by future mayor Bert Weeks, who wanted the space converted to a riverfront park. Ultimately, Valhalla's plans were killed and the city demolished the hotel for parkland in 1975.

November 7, 1965: Hundreds were on hand for the rededication of the Essex County War Memorial cenotaph in its new home in City Hall Square. The 106-ton cenotaph was moved piecemeal from its original location at the intersection of Giles Boulevard and Ouellette Avenue.

Windsor's latest Dominion Store opened on December 13, 1965, part of the commercial complex and parking garage on the southwest corner of Ouellette Avenue and Wyandotte Street. The other storefronts, soon to open, would be Reitmans, Beltone Hearing, and Tamblyn Drugs. The Bargain Shop now occupies this storefront.

October 17, 1966: John Gilchrist, owner of Lyttles Bakery, says goodbye after 52 years in business at 507 Ouellette Avenue (at the corner of Maiden Lane).

September 7, 1966: The LaBelle Building, at the corner of Ouellette Avenue and University Avenue, received a modern makeover after a devastating fire in 1959. Its tenants included Bonita Shoes, Tamblyn Drugs, and HFC Shoes. This building now houses a Starbucks.

February 16, 1967: The 15-storey Le Goyeau Apartments was nearing completion on Riverside Drive after many months of delays. The apartment building was part of the city's redevelopment scheme for urban renewal.

The Kent Trust Building, 1968. The office building (foreground) was the first phase, completed in 1966, with the Seaway Inn opening two years later, connected by street-level businesses. The Seaway was the first new hotel opened in the downtown core in 39 years, followed closely by the Holiday Inn.

The Canadian Tire Store on Dougall Avenue at Pitt Street West with a new facade in 1968. The Windsor International Transit Terminal, shared by Greyhound Canada and Transit Windsor, is now located in this spot.

Ouellette Avenue was converted into an experimental street mall for three days in September 1970, closing four blocks from Riverside Drive to Park Street to car traffic.

The Viscount Motor Hotel in the 1970s. The addition of an 18-storey tower in 1967 made it the tallest building in Windsor. The top two floors featured a restaurant and an entertainment venue called "Top of the Town" for its panoramic views. The Viscount closed in 1983 and sat vacant for several years before becoming a parking lot for then-Hôtel-Dieu Grace Hospital.

December 7, 1971: Mayor Frank Wansbrough, second from left, examines an artist's sketch of a new highrise office building for the corner of Riverside Drive and Ouellette Avenue. With the mayor are Norman Phipps of CIBC, John McCool of Oxlea Investments Ltd., and Ted Doyle, CIBC branch manager. The CIBC Building at 100 Ouellette Avenue was completed in 1973.

"Dollhouse View": The demolition of the 112-year-old Bartlet, MacDonald & Gow building was in its final stages on September 9, 1972. The store, and the existing CIBC branch next door, were torn down to make way for the bank's new high-rise.

September 19, 1973: At 14 storeys up, construction worker Mark Giroma stands on his perch, sanding the new CIBC high-rise under construction. Behind him stand many downtown landmarks: a new multi-storey parking garage, All Saints' Anglican Church, City Hall, Municipal Courts Building, Windsor Arena, St. Alphonsus Church, the SW&A bus terminal, Windsor Armouries, and Commodore Club.

The Steinburg department store and supermarket at the corner of Chatham Street and Goyeau Street, 1973. Finished in 1967, it was the signature project of Windsor's Redevelopment Area Two.

The historic Norton Palmer Hotel, at the northwest corner of Park Street and Pelissier Street, was closed in 1974 after 46 years of business. At top right, Norton's last resident, Ted Truesdell, waits for a cab, while at bottom left, Dorothy Viresucker and Cecile Malenfant relax against the mahogany bar in the Wheel Lounge during the hotel's closing auction. The Norton Palmer was demolished in 1975 and Victoria Park Place now stands at that site.

Epps Sportsman Store on Chatham Street, circa 1975. Its famous sign boasts the slogan: "Giant Values... Mini Prices."

CH Smith department store, at the corner of Pitt Street East and Ouellette Avenue, closed its doors on August 14, 1976. The storefront on Riverside Drive was once the Windsor Opera House. Its next door rival, Bartlet's, had closed in 1972, leaving Smith's regular Mrs. Schreier to remark to *The Star*: "The downtown is like a ghost town."

At 22 storeys and a peak of 224 feet, Westcourt Place was Windsor's tallest building in 1976, beating out the Solidarity Tower by one foot, according to *The Star*. Located at 251 Goyeau Street, the building still stands today.

"Last Day": After only 7 years in business, Steinberg's closed its downtown store on June 23, 1975. The building notoriously sat vacant until 1992, when it was torn down to build the Windsor Police Station and Courthouse.

"Reduced to Dust": The remains of the Prince Edward Hotel after its demolition in September 1976. The "Prince Eddy" was opened in 1922, featuring 215 rooms and a large ballroom. After sitting vacant for several years, a low-rise Bank of Nova Scotia building was built in its place.

April 28, 1977: New and old storefronts mix on the Ouellette Avenue strip, including: Business Girl Bazaar, Agnew-Surpass Shoes, Warehouse Records, Le Château, Ronald's Furs, Palace Cinemas, and Trott's Shoes, from left to right.

Adelman's Department Store at 60 Pitt Street East closed in 1979, spelling the end for family clothing stores downtown. The original store opened across the street in 1923. The building was demolished in 1984 and is a parking lot.

The waterfront Holiday Inn on Riverside Drive, just west of Dieppe Gardens, in 1980. Nicknamed the "Plywood Palace," the hotel had a significant public relations problem—plagued by tales of rats, collapsing boardwalks, and poor food. The Holiday Inn burned to the ground in 1999.

The Norwich Block, 1980. Visible storefronts are Fast Eddy's (partially obscured), Monty's Formal Wear, Paradise Chinese Foods, Club Casablanca, Northern Exposure, and Gino's Italian Village & Tavern, from left to right. The Norwich Block was controversially demolished in 2000 to build an office high-rise (Chrysler headquarters) and parking structure.

WINDSOR NEIGHBOURHOODS

Like any city, Windsor succeeded best when individual neighbourhoods did. And there were many, with names like Bridgeview, Little Italy, South Windsor, Remington Park, Malden, and much more. Many of these areas in Windsor were created in the post-war era, as soldiers returned home from World War II and the baby boom began.

After the war, Windsor, like many cities across Canada, quickly faced a housing crisis. In response, the government agency Central Mortgage and Housing Corporation built hundreds of wartime homes in Windsor in the late '40s and early '50s, creating entirely new neighbourhoods in East Windsor (around Seminole Street) and South Windsor. Initially rented out to veterans, these homes were all variations on 1.5 storey structures, creating uniform city blocks. Housing development continued through the next three decades, leading to subdivisions and districts like Bridgeview, Pillette Village, Fontainebleau, and Forest Glade. *The Windsor Daily Star* trumpeted in August 1955: "New records are being set in Windsor for home building." The styles of homes evolved as well, with the traditional ranch dominating suburban architecture. As with the rest of North America, the construction boom of post-war housing changed the nature of Windsor, as people moved out of the core to settle in residential suburban neighbourhoods.

Windsor itself grew, absorbing new communities and changing the cityscape. The big transformations came in 1935, when the city amalgamated with Sandwich, Ford City, and Walkerville, as well as in 1966, when it annexed Ojibway and the Town of Riverside. The '60s change was a long time coming, tracing back to the first tentative proposal to annex Ojibway in 1951. Official annexation hearings began in 1962. Armed with maps, documents, and experts, Windsor planners argued that the county's rural feel would survive if city annexation proceeded. Some county residents felt Windsor would grow too big, too dominant. In the end, the Ontario Municipal Board made the contentious decision to approve Windsor's application, allowing Windsor to annex Ojibway and Riverside, as well as parts of Sandwich East, Sandwich South, and Sandwich West Townships, effective January 1, 1966. Those districts would come to play a part in the local urban fabric, forming their own neighbourhoods.

As essential as it is to urban life, the concept of a "neighbourhood" is hard to define. Generally, a neighbourhood tends to have a school, businesses, stores, main roads at the perimeter, and a specific identity. They have an approximate geographical location, of course, and represent "the personal settings and situations where residents seek to realize common values, socialize youth, and maintain effective social control," according to the Aspen Institute of Humanistic Studies.

In Windsor, Erie Street and the surrounding area, known as Little Italy, represents the quintessential neighbourhood with its distinct personality—proudly Italian-Canadian, with the cafes and festivals to match. But other Windsor neighbourhoods flourished in the 20th century, as well. Certain things had to happen first to create new neighbourhoods, though, to keep up with growth and development. In the early 1950s, a number of Windsor streets still needed paving. In fact, Riverside did not receive new concrete roads between 1929 and 1953. Plus, with a growing population came growing traffic. As a result, Janette, Bruce, Glengarry, and Aylmer all became one-way streets in 1953, causing some confusion at first with motorists. The city also widened main streets and erected more streetlights. However, providing city services to a rapidly growing population also proved difficult. For example, flooding was a nagging problem for Windsor's homeowners. In August of 1955, Mayor Michael Patrick told angry residents worried about unsanitary conditions that "proper sewers" were the answer, though flooded basements continued plaguing the city for decades.

As suburban neighbourhoods continually grew farther and farther from the city core, retail businesses followed their customer base. Strips malls, typically anchored by a grocery store or discount retailer, were all the post-war rage. Dorwin Plaza, one of the city's first suburban shopping centres, opened in 1956 in the 2400 block of Dougall Avenue. Yorktown Plaza on Dominion Road, with its famous sign, also got its start in the early '50s. A thousand-plus people gathered for the opening of Sentry discount department store in Dorwin Plaza on September 13, 1961. *The Windsor Star* said the opening of Gateway Plaza, also on Dougall Avenue, 1962, brought "a new concept in the merchandising field to the Windsor area." Two more strip malls opened on the same street in 1973, though almost 12 kilometres apart: a Kmart plaza (eventually Tecumseh Mall) in the 7600 block of Tecumseh Road East and University Mall in the 2600 block of Tecumseh Road West. As with downtown retailers, the opening of the $15-million Devonshire Mall on August 12, 1970, crippled the suburban strip mall. Other long-standing

shopping areas, like Drouillard Road and Ottawa Street, fell into decline by the end of the 1970s, though Ottawa Street would experience a renaissance years later.

Parks and outdoor recreation spots also played an important part of neighbourhood growth. The Bridge Avenue Bathing Beach and the East Windsor Bathing Beach (with its series of docks for diving and splashing at the foot of George Avenue and Riverside Drive East) still attracted bathers in the early 1950s. The Windsor Yacht Club, formed in 1936, enjoyed growth years in the 1960s. The City of Windsor acquired Ojibway Park on land once known as Yawkey Bush from the Canadian Salt Company in 1957. Councillors declared in September that year that its 100-acre Ojibway property was "intended to be maintained as a natural park." Meanwhile, another city jewel, Jackson Park, had lighting installed in the sunken garden in 1965. The Lancaster Memorial Test Garden in Jackson Park was dedicated in 1967 as part of Canada's Centennial celebrations, with the planting of 12,500 rose bushes—a perfect gift for the Rose City. The sprawling and popular Mic Mac Park, originally called Prince Road Park, opened in 1928 with expansions in 1958 and 1972—the year the 5,000-seat Father Cullen Baseball Stadium opened—and featured everything from a wading pool and picnic area to all manner of sports facilities.

One ambitious city plan that never came about was Peche Island. Over the decades, a number of people, from Hiram Walker to the owners of Bob-Lo Island, proposed turning the 86-acre island into a type of recreational park. The grandest of all the schemes came courtesy of Detroit lawyer E.J. Harris. The American investor envisioned a $30-million resort featuring a hotel, an 18-hole golf course, and a ski hill. The developer, Sirrah Limited, only managed to run the place for one season in 1968 before putting the isle up for sale in 1971. The province eventually acquired it, though it remained undeveloped when transferred to the City of Windsor in 1999.

As streets and parks developed, so did a number of new neighbourhoods where a generation of baby boomers grew up. South Windsor and Pillette Village formed in the 1950s, Fontainebleau in the 1950s and 1960s, Forest Glade in the 1960s and 1970s, and Little River Acres in the 1970s. Various neighbourhoods cultivated their own individuality—adding zest to Windsor's overall character.

January 13, 1950: A delivery wagon makes its way through the mud on Labadie Road. Many residential streets in the Windsor area were unpaved in the early 1950s.

Drouillard Road at Edna Street, April 1951. Looking north, visible businesses include: Ford Plant One, Windsor Cooperative Bakery, and Sigal Brothers Novelties and Toys. The heart of old Ford City, Drouillard Road was a bustling commercial district until the Ford assembly plant left in 1953.

April 29, 1950: This 80 acres of city land, north of Tecumseh Road, would be developed into streets (to facilitate the building of homes). The rough locations of each street—California Avenue, Randolph Street, and Partington Avenue—are indicated by *The Star*.

Wartime houses on Rossini Boulevard, circa 1950. Central Mortgage and Housing Corporation—a government agency created to provide temporary housing to accommodate returning soldiers—built thousands of homes in Windsor after the war, including a project of 500 houses in the east end.

November 22, 1951: One of Windsor's first organized sub-divisions was Bridgeview, where 325 1.5 storey homes were constructed and rented out at $60 per month. Here, the first basement of the new subdivision is dug.

The Star called Riverside the "top residential section of the border area" in 1953. Pictured here are "medium-priced" homes on Eastlawn Boulevard.

March 25, 1952: Nine Riverside cottages were declared unfit for human habitation by Windsor's Board of Health after a flood. These homes, still occupied when this photograph was taken, were demolished and this area became Sandpoint Beach.

Skating at Optimist Park, January 1955. A popular pastime during the winter months, skating cost 10 cents.

East Windsor Bathing Beach, circa 1952. Located at the foot of Riverside Drive and George Avenue, teenagers flocked to the beach in the summer months, despite high levels of pollution in the Detroit River.

Church Street, 1953. According to *The Star*, the "modern growth of the South Windsor development points to the progressive spirit of the community." The majority of the homes in South Windsor were built post-1950, typically in the ranch style.

Howard Avenue in 1953, looking north, at the intersection with Cataraqui Street, Glengarry Avenue, and Aylmer Avenue. Visible storefronts include: Horseshoe Market, Horseshoe Hotel, Horseshoe Battery and Electric Service, and Hamil British-American Service Station, from left to right.

March 17, 1955: Irate homeowners protest the construction of a water tower on residential Benjamin Avenue by the Windsor Utilities Commission.

June 21 1957: Students from King Edward re-enact Jubilee rites in front of the Queen Victoria Jubilee Fountain. The fountain, then located off Devonshire Road at the Pere Marquette Station, was relocated to Willistead Park the following year.

The Henkel Subdivision at George Avenue and Riverside Drive was one of the few new housing developments within city limits in 1955, at a time when Windsor's suburbs were quickly expanding.

Traffic lights were installed at Eugenie Street and Dougall Road on March 12, 1957. The Statler Hotel and Steak House is at centre, with a Cities Service Gas Station at right.

Yawkey Bush on Matchette Road was expropriated by the City of Windsor in 1957. It would become Ojibway Park.

March 22, 1958: The Tivoli Theatre, left, on Wyandotte Street East marked the boundary between Windsor and Walkerville—in fact, the former town line ran right through the centre of the stage! Other businesses include Hudson's Ladies Wear, Imperial Bank of Canada, and Loblaws.

Sandwich Street, circa 1958. Visible storefronts include: Sandwich Furniture, Variety Hardware, Canada Service Stores, Cameo Bar-B-Q, Evelyn Margaret Shoppe, and Sandwich Grill, from left to right.

More than 1,000 persons gathered for the opening of the Sentry discount department store at Dorwin Plaza on September 12, 1961. Located on Dougall Road, Dorwin Plaza opened in 1956 and was Windsor's first attempt at a suburban shopping centre.

An aerial of Metropolitan General Hospital in 1960 reveals the residential streets of South Walkerville that surround it.

Cooler Air
CLOUDY, SHOWERS
7 a.m. 70, 9 a.m. 71, 2 p.m. 77
Low tonight 52, high Tuesday 67
Pollen count 16

VOL. 89, NO. 7   32 Pages

The Windsor Star

WINDSOR ONTARIO MONDAY SEPTEMBER 10 1962

FINAL
★ ★ ★ ★

SEVEN CENTS

ANNEXATION HEARING BEGINS

The City of Windsor began a bid to annex the towns of Riverside and Ojibway, as well as parts of Sandwich South, Sandwich East, and Sandwich West Township in 1962. The city had made an uncompleted proposal to annex Ojibway in 1951, and also had aims to absorb the Town of Tecumseh and St. Clair Beach (which never came to fruition).

Windsor and district officials read over the Ontario Municipal Board's initial findings on Windsor's application to annex its suburbs on November 17, 1962. The proposal was initially denied, as the board only recommended amalgamating services—however, annexation hearings would drag out into 1964.

December 19, 1960: Children play hockey on Little River, despite a warning from the Riverside Police that the ice was precariously thin.

The El Rancho shopping district on Wyandotte Street in Riverside, looking east from Villaire Avenue, in 1963. Storefronts include: Roma Bakery, Frank's Lunch, the Imperial Bank of Canada, Red & White Food Store, Shanfield's, Big V Pharmacy, El Rancho Rambler dealership, and Constantine Confectionary, from left to right.

Remembrance Day, 1963. The Essex County War Memorial Cenotaph was located at Giles Boulevard and Ouellette Avenue, pictured here, before being moved to City Hall Square in 1965.

May 8, 1963: An aerial view of the new Kmart plaza that covered 29 acres and also featured large S.S. Kresge and Dominion stores. Located on Tecumseh Road East and Lauzon Road, this development would turn into the Tecumseh Mall in 1973.

The old Ford City Town Hall, on Riverside Drive at Drouillard Road, met the wrecker's hammer in 1964. Our Lady of the Rosary Church can be seen in the background, at left.

July 20, 1964: American and Canadian boat owners alike found refuge from the heat on Peche Island. Whether or not to develop the island into a recreational theme park was the subject of political debate in the '60s.

August 8, 1964: Children make a wild dash for the nature centre during a day camp at Ojibway Park, which was officially declared in 1961.

Windsor's bid to annex its suburbs was renewed in December 1964. Here, members of the Ontario Municipal Board, J. Al Kennedy and Roy Kennedy, from left to right, review a map of the greater Windsor area before the sessions began. The suburban municipalities, particularly Riverside, were opposed to Windsor's proposal.

February 25, 1965: The 1800 block of Gladstone Avenue is buried under approximately 11 inches of snow during a record-breaking blizzard.

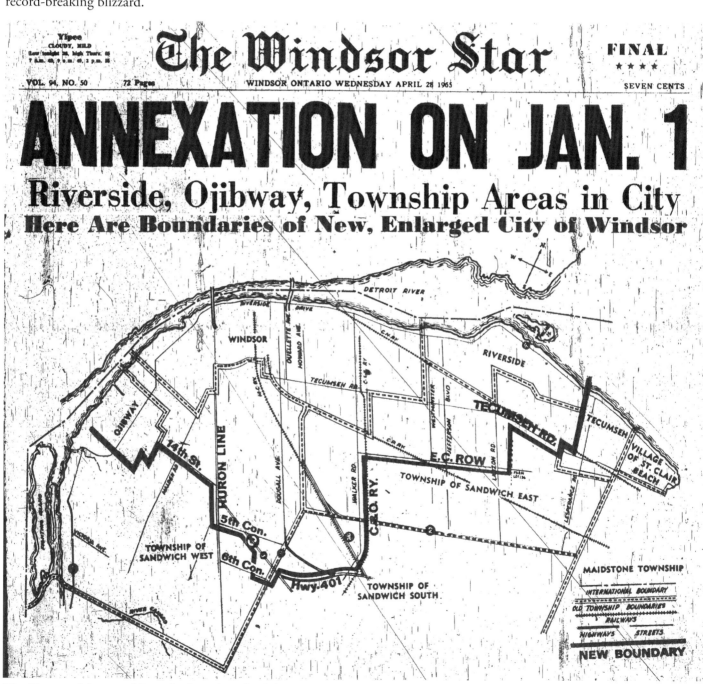

The Ontario Municipal Board released its final decision on April 26, 1965, in favour of annexation. As of January 1, 1966, the City of Windsor would expand to include the Town of Riverside, Ojibway, and parts of Sandwich West, Sandwich East, and Sandwich South townships.

May 13, 1965: Concerned mothers halt rush-hour traffic on Grand Marais Road, protesting speeding on a road where two children had lost their lives since 1948.

The Peabody Bridge, 1966. A damaged guard rail from a fatal collision, circled at right of centre, sparked moves to make the overpass safer. Hiram Walker & Sons Ltd. is located in the background.

June 1, 1965: Looking north from Eugenie Street, work continues on widening Howard Avenue between Highway #2 and Ypres Boulevard. Visible storefronts include Bill's Fina Service, Dominion Glass, Sunco, Border City Tire, and Texaco.

August 13, 1965: Representatives from the city and the surburbs met at City Hall on August 13, 1965, to discuss the mechanics of merging municipalities after the OMB's final decision came down in favour of annexation.

July 16, 1966: "Junior Tarzans" climb up a painted totem pole at Ojibway Park. From top to bottom are Chris Ouellette, Keith Sith, Barry Thibodeau, David Lucier, Richard Seguin, David McNea, and Jim Parent.

Built around 1875 by Hiram Walker's nephew, St. Joseph's Manor on Riverside Drive was used by the Roman Catholic Children's Aid Society until its demolition in 1969. The Windsor-Essex Children's Aid Society building now sits in this location.

July 15, 1967: The Lancaster Memorial Garden, which featured 12,500 rose bushes, was a Canadian Centennial project. The Lancaster Bomber, at centre, was transported to Windsor in 1964.

May 18, 1979: This gatepost, at the entrance to St. Mary's Gate Subdivision in South Windsor, used to mark the entrance to St. Mary's Academy. The school was demolished in 1977 and the grounds became home to the city's newest subdivision.

The wading pool at Mic Mac Park on Prince Road, 1967.

Riverside Drive East, in the area of Little River, was developing into a high-rise residential area in 1971. On the far left is the 26-storey Solidarity Tower (the highest building in Windsor at the time).

Kids play in the fountain at Jackson Park, 1970. The parks and recreation department was not at all pleased with this violation, and planned to beef up its parks' security in response.

Rushton Drive in Forest Glade, 1974. Built in stages starting in the late '60s, Forest Glade is an example of a planned community.

A canoe passes by Maudie the boat (a favourite spot for local kids) in Ojibway Park on May 25, 1977.

March 25, 1978: Boarded up stores were a familiar sight along Drouillard Road, pictured here along the east side of the 1000 block, as the area fell into decline after the '50s.

May 3, 1980: Signs dominate Huron Church Road—a complaint of *The Star*, which declared the roadway a "disjointed mosaic" and an unappealing gateway into Windsor for visitors.

SUBURBIA

Windsor spent much of its early life gobbling up neighbouring towns, though after the First World War, the suburbs starting getting their revenge. The area's first mass merger came in 1935 when Walkerville, Ford City, and Sandwich became part of Windsor, as mandated by the province. Never mind the protests from annexed communities, especially neat and tidy Walkerville—the one town doing fairly well financially, in comparison to the other border cities. Bankruptcy was nigh for Windsor and others if they didn't form a team. So they did, if somewhat reluctantly. Meanwhile, nearby village of Ojibway, incorporated in 1913, and Town of Riverside, incorporated in 1921, were considered suburbs until 1966 when Windsor annexed them, too. Windsor also annexed parts of Sandwich East, Sandwich South, and Sandwich West Townships in one fell swoop. Things were changing fast.

But a couple of suburban towns bucked the trend. LaSalle to Windsor's west and Tecumseh to its east were never absorbed by their bigger neighbour. They might share such things as water supply, geography, and

more, but LaSalle and Tecumseh proudly remain their own towns. The Town of Tecumseh has a more unique old city centre than does LaSalle, though they both brim with residential streets and swaths of bedroom community homes.

"The Windsor way was always, 'Old is bad, new is good,'" local architectural historian Andrew Foot said in 2016. "It's like that in the core, and it's like that in suburbs. Windsor builds new houses and people move farther out."

The Windsor area, of course, was hardly the only place with growing suburbia in the latter half of the 20th century. Most North American communities felt a housing and population boom post-Word War II. The new suburban communities tended to seem more uniform than their urban counterparts—which some people argue applied to their policies as well as their looks.

"The transformation of Canada into a suburban nation eventually led to a suppression of diversity," writes Richard Harris in *Creeping Conformity: How Canada Became Suburban, 1900–1960*. Harris argues that in the early part of the century, urban and suburban development stemmed from a wide range of people and styles. But as the post-war suburbs developed, made affordable for the middle classes, suburban streets and homes grew more uniform and common. In 1900, almost two-thirds of the Canadian population lived in rural areas. By 1960, three-fifths of the nation lived in urban areas, mostly suburbs.

Suburban communities provide affordable housing with lower taxes away from the hustle and bustle of the city, but close enough for work, shopping, and entertainment. The urban and the suburban go hand in hand. LaSalle and Tecumseh provide that type of connectivity to Windsor and the rest of the area. They also did their own thing, with their own festivals—LaSalle and strawberries, Tecumseh and corn—to their own industry. Green Giant was Tecumseh's major company, which helped provide employment, while Windsor Salt, technically in neighbouring Windsor, supplied jobs for many in LaSalle. Both communities benefited from the boats and visitors and activity the surrounding water would bestow upon them. They have long offered their own eateries, roadhouses, and pubs, not to mention parks and trails. Of course, they were also busy doing their own transformations including, yes, amalgamation.

"As the Town of Windsor grew, Tecumseh began to experience new blood when the overflow of immigrants coming to the city began to settle in the peripheral regions as well," reads the Town of Tecumseh's municipal history. Tecumseh began life in 1792 as little more than a postal outlet known as Ryegate with a few families, and was renamed Tecumseh after the famed Shawnee warrior in 1912. The place continued to grow. In 1999, as part of a reorganization of Essex County, the former Village of St. Clair Beach and the former Township of Sandwich South were amalgamated into the new Town of Tecumseh.

On the other side of Windsor, LaSalle was incorporated as a town in 1924. In 1959, however, it temporarily lost its name—but not its identity. The Town of LaSalle dissolved into the Township of Sandwich West. But in 1991 the status of Sandwich West Township changed again and was renamed the Town of LaSalle, what in its heart it always was.

At the end of the day, LaSalle and Tecumseh may be Windsor suburbs, but they extend the city more than just physically; they form an important part of the urban experience.

Sandwich West Township Hall, 1961. The Town of LaSalle was dissolved into the township from 1959 to 1991.

August 22, 1953: St. Paul's School and St. Paul's Church—the first prefabricated church in the greater Windsor district—were among the new buildings recently erected in the growing town of LaSalle. The church and adjoining school are located on Malden Road, across from the Sandwich West Township hall, pictured on the opposite page.

Waterfront homes, 1953. Seasonal floods often threatened these homes, but this did not deter LaSalle homeowners from building on the edge of the Detroit River.

Fishing on the Chappus Canal, one of LaSalle's many inlets to the Detroit River, circa 1953.

August 21, 1954: A landmark for residents of Essex County, the Turkey Creek Bridge carries Highway 18 into LaSalle, the "booming" Windsor suburb which billed itself as "The Friendly Town." According to *The Star*, LaSalle was renowned for the most fertile gardens on the continent.

In 1954, LaSalle was experiencing its biggest building boom since the town was incorporated 30 years previous. Pictured here, at the corner of Front Road and Boismier Avenue, is Alma's Jewellery, in the forefront, and Bart Evon Furniture, with the Sugar Bowl Grill next door. At the far left is the new Dominion Bank.

March 28, 1955: Dr. R.A. St. Denis, at right, hands his $1 contribution to Frank Carlino, president of the LaSalle Chamber of Commerce, to offset the cost of his new address sign. Behind them, Henry Seewald, treasurer, does the actual work of hanging one of the 500 new house signs and street numbers that went up as part of a drive for proper signage.

September 1, 1955: Three of the prize winners from the outboard motor regatta on River Canard receive their silverware. From left to right are Bud Parker of LaSalle; Jim Patterson, Commodore of the River Canard Outboard Racing Association; Johnny Young of Detroit; and Joe Schulte of Belleville, Michigan.

Homes were rapidly being constructed in LaSalle due to a sharp population increase in the 1950s. Here, a group of houses are nearing completion in the Bitwell Subdivision on August 1, 1956. The bell tower of Sacred Heart Church rises in the skyline behind the new homes. LaSalle's population would hit 3,000 by 1960.

December 17, 1955: A frozen-over Turkey Creek provided a perfect skating rink for the children of LaSalle, who could safely skate for miles.

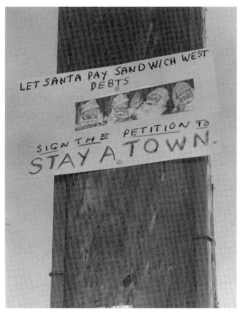

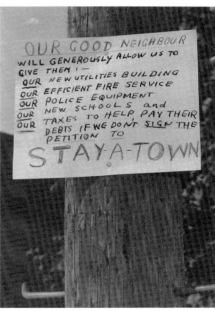

The Town of LaSalle dissolved into Sandwich West Township on January 1, 1959, after a hotly contested debate. In October 1958, the Ontario Municipal Board ordered the merger following a public referendum. However, these anti-amalgamation signs reflect an opposing camp. Their "Stay-a-Town" petition protested what they perceived as Sandwich West debt-loading LaSalle, while expropriating their new infrastructure. Despite officially being part of Sandwich West Township until 1991, residents persisted in referring to the area as LaSalle.

August 8, 1959: Boats line Sunnyside Slip, an inlet adjacent to Wahneta Avenue—a sign of the popularity of recreational boating among LaSalle residents.

"Market Garden of Canada": According to *The Star*, the finest garden vegetables grown in North America were found in LaSalle. Here, workers harvest radishes on July 30, 1960.

 LaSalle's main street, Front Road, expanded commercially in 1960, much-needed in a community where residential growth dramatically outpaced other development. Pictured again at Boismer Avenue, since 1954, Bart Evon Furniture pushed out Alma's Jewellery, and a new shopping development, Brewer's Retail, opened up behind Toronto Dominion Bank.

After 70 years in business, the Palm Beach Hotel on Front Road closed its doors on September 27, 1962, following the suspension of its liquor license.

November 13, 1969: Work was in progress to roof the artificial ice rink in LaSalle, originally constructed in conjunction with Canada's Centennial in 1967.

Malden Village Shopping Centre, 1971. After the City of Windsor annexed parts of Sandwich West Township in 1966, LaSalle suffered the loss of its major commercial and industrial developments, leaving shopping plazas like this few and far between.

Children whoop it up in the LaSalle pool on September 8, 1972. The pool was opened by the LaSalle Youth Centre Committee in 1959 and provided entertainment for up to 200 children a day during the hot summer months.

"Still Sturdy": The Chappus House, on Old Front Road, was nearly 50 years old in 1971, but was in solid condition. It was one of the few houses in Ontario in which concrete was poured from the top down into the frame. The Chappus House saw its glory days during Prohibition as its owners were rumrunners in the illegal whisky business.

Skating on Turkey Creek was an annual tradition for the children of LaSalle, pictured here in January 1978.

Crowds thronged to the Town of Tecumseh in July 1950 for its Mid-Century Celebration. The festival was officially kicked off as Mayor Thomas C. Scott of Tecumseh, Ontario, greeted Mayor J. Floyd Elliot of Tecumseh, Michigan, pictured at top left. Behind them stand two "Indian chiefs" Bob Moore, at left, and Ernie Campeau, at right, who helped lead the parade. At top right, a vanguard of "cowboys and Indians" lead the parade towards Tecumseh Memorial Park (Lacasse Park). At the bottom, representatives from Veterans of Foreign Wars (VFW), the Canadian Legion, and the American Legion salute the cenotaph, while the VFW honour guard presents arms at the wreath-laying ceremony.

The railway crossing at Tecumseh Road, circa 1951. At right is the original train station, where a civic museum is now located, with the steeple of St. Anne's Catholic Church rising in the background. Also visible is the Golden Hotel, a 1920s hot spot, that burned to the ground in 1976.

The Carling Breweries Limited plant, located on the edge of Tecumseh, with its new retail beer store on September 5, 1953. The plant was closed in 1956 and eventually razed, and now is the site of Carling Park.

"It's Booming!": By 1957, the population of Tecumseh reached 4,100, almost double its size in 1940. New subdivisions with modern, low-cost homes, like the one pictured here, were rapidly being built to accommodate the growing population.

"Out with Old": Tecumseh's long-standing Town Hall, which also served as a fire hall and police station, was earmarked for demolition in 1957. A modern multipurpose structure was completed in 1961 on Lesperance Road as a replacement.

"Main Street": Tecumseh Road, the community's business district, kept pace with the growing population. At left, shoppers peruse the selection on May 18, 1957. Storefronts include, from left to right, Robinet Hardware, Rochon's Pharmacy, the Tecumseh Tavern, and the Tecumseh Market. Pictured at right is a street view from 1961, located farther west. Lacasse Printing, E.J. Drouillard & Sons Hardware, the Canadian Hotel, the Post Office, and Paris Tavern are located on the right side of the street, while Tecumseh Utilities, Fred and Nell's Grill, and a Supertest Petroleum station are on the left side.

August 10, 1959: Tecumseh saluted Bert "Mr. Baseball" Lacasse with his own "Day" at Tecumseh Memorial Park to honour his 16 years of service in the Essex County Baseball League. A contour lounge chair and a hand-carved bust were among the gift presentations. Grouped around him, from left to right, are Don Lesperance, a member of the 1959 team; Chuck Renaud, an old-time Tecumseh ball player; Harold Jackson, a former National Hockey League star; and Gerry Craig, a one-time Tecumseh pitcher.

September 8, 1962: Tecumseh boasted three new signs marking the entrance to the municipality, including this one on Highway 39. From left to right are Ben Ormseth of Green Giant of Canada Ltd., Mayor Wallace Baillargeon, and Ken Gurr, who created the sign. Green Giant (then called Fine Foods of Canada) established a factory in Tecumseh in 1931.

October 1, 1964: Mayor Wallace Baillargeon was the first to ride the brand new fire truck, bringing the Tecumseh-St. Clair Beach area's firefighting fleet up to three vehicles. Standing by the new pumper truck are Jake Renaud, fire chief; and Fred Bistany, reeve and fire commissioner, from left to right.

August 3, 1963: A new public library on Lesperance Road was a popular facility among Tecumseh's residents, handing out more than 500 membership cards within weeks of opening.

Plant processing reaches peak
Maize oui! Corn, corn, corn

August 12, 1966: During its 60-day peak season, this conveyor belt gobbled up 62 tonnes of corn per hour, for nine hours a day. That year, the plant handled frozen corn for the first time, in addition to regular canning.

Two jolly Green Giants guard the entrance to the new can manufacturing and frozen food plants opened at the Green Giant of Canada complex in Tecumseh on August 13, 1966. Cutting the ribbon, from left to right, are A.W. Anderson, president of Green Giant of Canada; Ben Ormseth, vice-president; Paul Martin, Minister of External Affairs; Mayor Hector Lacasse; and R.C. Cosgrove, president of the American parent firm, Green Giant.

January 26, 1967: Lucien "Kit" Lacasse, co-editor and publisher, along with the women's page editor, Isabel Deibel, take a look at the final edition of *The Tecumseh Tribune*. The paper ceased publication after eight years, only to be revived months later in September. It remained in print until 2012.

January 19, 1967: Mrs. Tom Dawson officially opened the fundraising campaign for Tecumseh's Centennial project (a swimming pool) with a little help from Earl Langlois, president of the Tecumseh Booster Club; and Mayor Hector Lacasse, at right.

September 23, 1968: Failing to realize the lack of actual ice, eager skaters cluster around a ribbon-cutting ceremony for a new rink in St. Clair Beach. Doing the honours, from left to right, are Robert McWilliams, Reeve Fred Cada with the scissors, and Earl Langlois. The Village of St. Clair Beach was amalgamated with Tecumseh in 1999.

A massive fire at the Green Giant of Canada plant in Tecumseh left the town reeling on October 12, 1973. The fire, estimated at $10 million in damages, destroyed the plant's largest warehouse, a machine shop, and the can manufacturing plant. Pictured at top right, employees and young men passing by pitched in to help the firemen battle the blaze, while a large crowd formed at the gates (seen at bottom left). At bottom right, millions of cans litter the blackened ruins of the warehouse. The plant was rebuilt and remains a key industry in Tecumseh today as Bonduelle Foods.

Tecumseh, "A Most Cordial Town," 1976. The bilingual sign was a nod to the town's heritage, as its original settlers were majority French and dominated the population for generations.

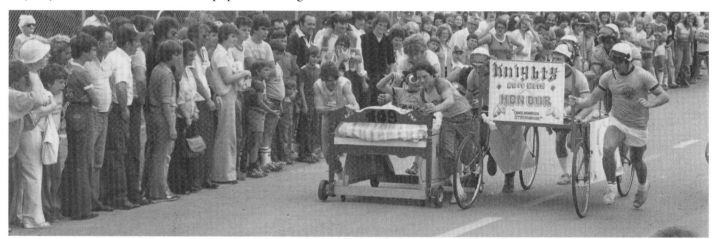

The widely popular Tecumseh Corn festival was first held in 1975 as a way to promote the town's most famous commodity. In 1979, the festival featured its first bed race, pictured above, in addition to events like a parade, concert, and horse show. Mariette Schiller, 18, was crowned "Miss Cornfest" that year—a pageant that continues today as "Miss Tecumseh." At bottom right, Wayne Mayor and Jean Marc Roy hoist a basket of steaming corn at Bert Lacasse park on the opening day of the festival in 1980.

ESSEX COUNTY

Essex County has long fostered its own character, despite an inherent connection to Windsor. While Windsor was growing into an industrial powerhouse, Essex County excelled at another type of production: agriculture. High-quality crops from county farmers were in demand, including tomatoes, corn, sugar beets, soybeans, and more. In 1959, *The Windsor Star* called Essex County the agricultural "Garden of Eden," adding to similar nicknames that have stuck for generations—like the Sun Parlour or the Garden Gateway of Canada. But more than farming drew people to the county. Burgeoning towns like Essex, Kingsville, and Leamington grew in size and nurtured their own business districts and town centres.

The post-war period saw steady population growth in Essex County. According to Statistics Canada, in 1951 Essex County had a population of 97,101, up significantly from the 68,919 identified by the 1941 census. By 1981, the Essex County population had grown to 120,393, a 24 percent increase over three decades. The largest town in Essex County in 1951 was Leamington, with a population of 6,950, followed by Kingsville with 2,631. By 1981, Leamington's population had grown to 12,528 while Kingsville's had doubled to 5,134. The county was slowly closing the population gap with the city.

As the rural neighbour of a bigger city, residents of Essex County faced similar population growth and development pressures, but with a different set of sensibilities. One such case came in the early 1950s when the province started building the Macdonald-Cartier Freeway, better known as Highway 401. The idea was to create a cross-Ontario route that would facilitate ease of travel in a time of mounting vehicle traffic. Great, except for one thing: King's Highway

401 aimed straight through agricultural land, meaning farmers had to accommodate the big plans.

"Farmers were wondering how they were going to be able to work land on both sides of the highway," Jack Morris, the Essex County Warden in 1983 who was first elected to Tilbury West Council in 1972, said in 2016. "Even then people realized that the road was needed. But farmers were concerned about the highway dissecting farms. And that was a legitimate concern."

Morris was still young when the first section of the 401 opened in Essex County in 1955, followed the next year by another stretch closer to the city, with the final leg completed in 1957 heading into Windsor. His father, Charles Clifford Morris (who served as Essex County Warden in 1955), dealt with the fallout from the mega-highway plans by helping constituents navigate the compensation process. In the end, some farmers sold property to neighbours across the highway, while others just worked the land on both sides of the road, and life went on.

Highways weren't the only population-related issue that affected the county. So did waste. Landfills tend to wind up in rural areas, as was the case in Essex County. It might make sense to put landfills near as few people as possible, but still, who wants one next door? So opposition mounted. "There was a lot of controversy as to where it was going to go," said Morris, noting that the province required many candidate sites be considered before a decision could be made. For decades, individual municipalities operated their own dumps. But, around 1970, three large landfills ended up starting in Colchester North, Gosfield South, and Maidstone Townships, taking garbage from the entire area, including Windsor. Of course, since landfills eventually fill up, the sometimes tense discussion on waste continued in Essex County for decades.

Some conversations with the city went smoother. The Essex Region Conservation Authority, established July 18, 1973, to safeguard the area's natural resources, was touted by county leaders as essential to the region's health. Bureaucracy slowed the process somewhat, Morris said, but city leaders generally jumped on board. "We needed something to help get some tree cover back in Essex County," Morris said. "We also needed something to look after the waterways." ERCA began land acquisition, starting in 1974 with the Maidstone Conservation Area, as well as shoreline protection work on Pelee Island and along Turkey Creek. The tree-planting program launched in 1976, going on to add millions of saplings to the area.

The county and city collaborated much more over the years. The Greater Windsor Industrial Commission was launched in 1958, and was renamed the Windsor-Essex County Development Commission in 1974, in order to attract investment and support existing businesses. The thought was the city and the county would thrive better together—a philosophy that seemed suited for economics and tourism alike.

The main industry in Essex County was (and still is) farming—and as a result, food processing—thanks to rich, flat agricultural land. In 1955, Leamington added a long government dock and Kingsville renovated its port, both to accommodate larger ships to better transport produce and other products across North America. In 1961, Leamington created a unique visitor information booth perfect for the Tomato Capital of Canada: a 14-foot-high tomato. Ketchup giant H.J. Heinz, which opened its first plant in Leamington in 1908, added a $9-million expansion in 1964. Harrow was home to the W. Clark Ltd. factory, a canning facility and the town's largest employer until 1969. In the 1970s, farmers found ways to grow even more, as the greenhouse industry started gaining a foothold before going on to become a powerhouse.

The county boasts lots of water, of course, surrounded as it is by Lake St. Clair to the north, the Detroit River to the west, and Lake Erie to the south. Water gives Essex County one of its defining personality traits—as a fun, adventurous host for tourism. In 1955, *The Windsor Daily Star* labelled Point Pelee a "tourist paradise." Pelee Island also attracted vacationers. The island already had a renowned annual pheasant hunt going for years, something that continued through the '50s, '60s, and '70s. Visitors could use their own boats, of course, but most tourists hopped on ferries such as the *Pelee Islander* or the *M.S. Leamington*. By the 1960s, Crystal Bay had a reputation as an ideal place for boating and on-boat partying. And beaches? Absolutely. Seacliff Beach in Leamington was one of the most popular, even before World War II. The Seacliff Hotel also attracted its fair share of diners and dancers. Meanwhile, tourists flocked to Kingsville by the carload and boatload, for recreation and quaint shopping. County shindigs proved popular, too, such as the Harrow and Comber Fairs.

Valentine's Day 1980 conjures bad memories for the Town of Essex. At 2:10 a.m., an entire Essex city block exploded, leveling seven buildings and damaging more than 70 others. Somehow, nobody was killed by the explosion or the ensuing fireball, though six people were injured. The explosion was triggered when a man backed his car into a gas metre at the back of the Home Hardware Store on Talbot Street. But the blast didn't occur until about 20 minutes later, after gas had accumulated in the store and a water heater pilot light ignited it. *The Windsor Star* took a hopeful approach, declaring "The town that calls itself the 'Hub of the County' is down but not out."

Thanks to increased population, agriculture, and tourism, Essex County thrived in the post-war decades. And despite expanded collaboration with Windsor, Essex County offered its own flair, playing out on the farm and waterfront alike.

Three Amherstburg District High School students Claudia Kwasnicki, Carol Gordon, and Carol Salisbury, from left to right, take time out from their final examinations to relax at the local beach, circa 1950.

March 10, 1950: Amherstburg firefighters gather around two new pumper trucks, which had a 500-gallon-per-minute capacity and two hose reels capable of delivering water under 600-pound pressure. Fire Chief Jack Hamilton declared that Amherstburg had "the finest equipment of any town its size in Canada."

Detroit's oldest home, the Park House, found its final resting place in Amherstburg. In the 1790s, its owners floated it, piece-meal, down the Detroit River to Amherstburg. The two-storey house behind it is the Gordon House, built in 1804. Pictured here side by side on Dalhousie Street, both historic homes have been converted into museums. The Park House was moved to Amherstburg's riverfront park in 1972.

June 27, 1953: The corner of Dalhousie and Gore Streets used to be the heart of old Amherstburg, with the home (at left) serving as a customs house and later, the town's first telegraph office.

The Star described Amherstburg as one of "Essex County's beautiful towns," in 1957. Richmond Street, pictured here, was "bustling with activity" at shops like Hamilton Appliances, Reid's Confectionery, Moffat's Drugstore, Falls & Son Insurance, and Hotel Amherst.

Two of Amherstburg's historic homes faced an uncertain future in 1959. At left, the Bellevue Estate was up for sale once again, listed at $50,00—with no interested buyers. The Georgian mansion would become a national historic site that year. Fate was not as kind to the Victorian mansion, Mireille, at right, demolished in 1960.

Jones China Shop, 1975. The designated heritage site is now Lord Amherst Public House.

This housing development, near Amherstburg's Centennial Park, was dubbed "the most modern in the province" by *The Star* in 1969.

July 3, 1962: The Amherstburg Community Band majorettes came out on top over a slew of American teams at a baton twirling contest in Detroit. Standing in the back row, from left to right, are Treasure Triolet, Elaine Ryan, Marianne Ryan, and Brenda White, with Bernadette Brooks and Barbara Bates kneeling in front.

Boating in Crystal Bay, 1969. Crystal Bay is Essex County's worst-kept secret as a spot for camping and parties.

Lyle Dobbyn and Robert Minor, from left to right, set up a new entrance sign to Comber on Highway 98. In 1959, Comber was a police village (a step away from official village status) and its bold claim raised some eyebrows around Essex County.

Emile Lanoue, Gail Froese, John Stacey, and Corinne Lanoue, from left to right, bravely hang on during a ride at the Comber Fair's midway on August 25, 1966.

Side-by-side views of Talbot Street in Essex, 1957. At left, storefronts include Willson's Auto Supply, Semple Optical, Imperial Bank of Canada, Thomas' Grocery Store, Weller's Hardware, and Martin's Drugs (which advertised their location as "Essex by the stoplight"), from left to right. Pictured at right, Rio Theatre and the Stokely Van-Camp of Canada Ltd. factory are visible, including a British American station with gas at 38.9 cents per imperial gallon (that's 8.6 cents per litre!).

Workers wash the accumulation of smoke from locomotives off of the railway station in Essex, June 1976. The station, built in 1887, is now a restored heritage site.

February 14, 1980: This was the scene in downtown Essex in the early hours of Valentine's Day after a massive natural gas explosion nearly levelled an entire city block. Seven buildings were flattened and 70 others damaged. The explosion was caused by an impaired driver backing into a Home Hardware on Talbot Street, hitting the gas metre. No one was killed in the blast.

June 18, 1960: A *Star* reporter surmised that it was "doubtful" if there was another "10,000-gallon can of beans in Ontario." The new water tower doubled as an advertisement for Harrow's largest factory: W. Clark Ltd. After more than 50 years in business, the factory was sold to Sellick Equipment Company in 1969.

June 21, 1961: Langford's Dairy Bar was famous for their candy selection and yearly Christmas catalogue.

An aerial view of the town of Harrow, 1968. The six silos of the Harrow Farmers' Cooperative Association Ltd. were not only a landmark, but served as the area's largest elevator co-op. *The Star* called Harrow, then a town of 2,000, the undisputed farming centre of Essex County.

Riders line up at the horse show during the Harrow Fair in 1965.

"Tourist Mecca": In 1955, *The Star* proclaimed that Kingville's Main Street boasted cars from more states and provinces than any other small town in Ontario. Storefronts include: Sporle's, Greyhound Bus Lines, David's Confectionery, Harry's Meat Market, Hillman's Clothing Store, Super IGA market, The Dutch Kitchen, The Kingsville Hotel, and Peter's Bar-B-Q Inn, from left to right. Pictured at right, in a closer view of the Conklin Block from 1958, new businesses mix with old, including Apex Barber Shop, Ouellette Dry Cleaners & Laundry, The Dutch Kitchen, Carhartt's, and Pickard's.

The Kingsville Harbour docks, 1955. American yachts crowd the docks, which were due for a major expansion to accommodate commercial vessels.

The new water tower, pictured at left, dominated Kingsville's skyline after it was built in 1963. Doomed for demolition, the old water tower (at right)—which stood behind the town hall for more than 50 years—was torn down the following year.

June 28, 1958: New storefronts on Main Street West, Kingsville, gave the town a fresh, modern look according to *The Star*. From left to right are Statham's Pharmacy, Webb & Co., Rivard's Cleaners, Allen's, Mary's Grill, Mcay's Hardware, and G.W. Brown, Jeweller.

November 11, 1972: Kingsville Legionnaires march to the town's Cenotaph for Remembrance Day services.

The weekend crowd at Seacliffe Beach in Leamington on July 6, 1953. The sandy shores of Essex County attracted hundreds of locals, Windsorites, and Americans on holiday.

Talbot Street East, Leamington's main business sector in 1955. The Leamington Hotel, with its 'The Plate Room' dining lounge, is located at left, with Walls' Bargain Shop and Red & White Food Stores behind it. Stores across the street include The Canadian Bank of Commerce, Bowman and Carson Ltd., Kennedy's Tailors, Star Radio, Davidson-Otton Insurance, Lendon Hardware, and Neilson's Shoe Store.

A freighter is tied up at the new dock on Lake Erie to discharge cargo and take on products from Leamington's fields and factories in 1955. Major Canadian, American, and even European shipping companies made the town a regular stop.

Leamington's Carnegie Public Library, 1955. The structure, built in 1912 and designed by John Alexander Maycock, was torn down in 1983 in favour of a modern branch of the Essex County Library.

"Tomato Capital of Canada": Leamington's new visitor information centre was ready to open on May 8, 1961. The tomato, at 18-foot wide, 14-feet high, was an immediate town fixture that would give out ice-cold 6oz cans of Heinz tomato juice to tourists.

The tomato harvest was the busiest season of the year for Leamington. Here, area farmers deliver their goods to the H.J. Heinz processing plant in 1964, which operated 24 hours a day and employed more than a thousand workers at its peak season.

In a ceremony attended by more than 100 dignitaries from across North America, H.J. Heinz officially opened a $9 million addition to its food processing plant on September 15, 1964. The company began in Leamington in 1909, serving as the industrial heart of the community for generations.

Dees Gelderland, standing, and Ralph Will manned their post around the clock at H.J. Heinz on August 4, 1965. The 1,100 employees went on strike for 24 days, seeking better overtime, pensions, and holiday benefits.

October 9, 1965: Russell Snell of Detroit shows off his two hours' catch, as fishermen line both sides of the government dock in Leamington. Catch of the day? Perch!

Leamington served up its own cake for Canada's Centennial in 1967. The candle was officially 'lit' by Miss Canada during the opening Centennial celebrations on New Year's Day.

413

August 18, 1975: Vines, leaves, and rotten tomatoes are picked out of the line at the H.J. Heinz plant.

Centennial queen Cindy Gillett measures the winning beard (4.5 inches) of Alex Hazael, who took top prize in the Beard Growing Contest as part of the town's 100th birthday in 1974.

A view of the H.J. Heinz plant from 1965, featuring the skyway over Erie Street North.

Leamington's fourth annual sidewalk sale on August 11, 1975, left downtown bustling with customers. Storefronts include Royal Bank, Al Law clothing, Wilson's Drug Store, and Diana Restaurant.

Point Pelee was christened a "tourist paradise" by *The Star* in 1955. One of Canada's smallest national parks, it continually drew some of the largest crowds for beaches, camping, and its infamous "smelt runs." Note the cars pulled right up onto the beach.

Cars line up at the entrance to Point Pelee, 1954.

The Pelee Island ferry, circa 1950.

Point Pelee, June 1956. The tip is the southernmost point in Canada, equal in latitude to Northern California.

R.M. Laurie from Ontario Hydro and Mrs. Noah Garno throw the switch, bringing hydro power to Pelee Island and its 500 inhabitants for the first time on July 21, 1955.

Captain Mac Hooper ties up the *M.S. Leamington* to the dock after its first run of the year from Pelee Island to Leamington on March 19, 1975.

"Off to the Hunt": More than 200 hunters crowded the Kingsville dock on October 27, 1977, ready for the two-day Pelee Island pheasant hunt. Here, H.R. Doud and Fred Wigen of Saginaw, Michigan, board the *Pelee Islander* ferry with their dogs.

WINDSOR CENTENNIAL

The best thing about turning 100 is the party. So when Windsor hit the centennial mark in 1954, the city staged a celebration worthy of the next 100 years. In fact, it wasn't just one bash, but a crowded, cheering series of festivities.

The eventual hoopla was set in motion by an earlier party in 1854 when Windsor officially claimed village status (it became a town in 1858 and a city in 1892). A century later, Windsor's 100th birthday party not only showed how much Windsorites cared for their city, but how much civic engagement existed around public events. According to *The Windsor Daily Star*, more than 50,000 people lined the route the afternoon of July 1, 1954, along London Street (now University Avenue) and Ouellette Avenue, to watch elaborate floats and 32 marching bands go by in "the giant" Centennial-Dominion Day Parade—"a highlight of Centennial Year in Windsor." Also, the day included a 600-pound "richly decorated" fruitcake, served in the ornate Prince Edward Hotel Ballroom. Billed as the largest parade in the city's history, the event included a huge, jam-packed reviewing stand, otherwise known as the Jackson Park grandstands. Can you imagine attracting so many people for a parade today?

"The spectacle that Windsor saw yesterday was something that could happen only once in 100 years," reported *The Windsor Daily Star*. "The gigantic Centennial-Dominion Day Parade was the biggest, longest, most colourful, and best that this city has seen in Windsor's 'century of progress.'"

Queen Elizabeth even sent Windsor congratulations from across the ocean. Parade marshal Walter Perry estimated 3,500 people took part in the parade, not counting those watching and cheering. Furthermore, Detroit and Wyandotte provided entries, boosting the international flavour.

The year's festivities included a number of activities, starting with a New Year coach-and-horses procession from the Prince Edward Hotel to city hall for the reading of the official centennial proclamation. As well, a massive "birthday cake" construction on Ouellette Avenue with 100 electrical candles was unveiled April 17, 1954. Not only did hundreds of onlookers watch the candles come alive that Saturday night, so did then Windsor Mayor Arthur Reaume, as well as Sir Cyril Dyson, mayor of Windsor, England, who came in for the event.

Three centennial parties in a row, all featuring participants dressed in period costume from the mid-1800s, attracted more than 1,000 participants in June that year to kick off celebration season. On Sunday, July 11, some 15,000 people watched the All Nations Parade, showcasing everything from Italian to Ukrainian entries, and featured all manner of drum majorettes, at least one of whom, the *Windsor Daily Star* noted, "tramped a sprightly pace."

Old Home Week came in August, where out-of-towners and former Windsorites were invited back to their home city to reminisce and take part in the festivities. As well, the year offered such terribly important cultural activities as a beard-growing competition, won by the decidedly bushy Hank Romanycia. Singing, dancing, skits, a midway: the merriment bubbled over. Plus, in conjunction with Ford of Canada's 50th anniversary, the pioneering car company that started its

Canadian division in Windsor, came the Golden Jubilee Variety Parade on August 15, 1954, with a roster of entertainment. Did anybody attend a private company's shindig? Just an estimated 20,000 people. When Windsor decided to party, especially if it was to fete the city itself on a major milestone birthday, Windsorites went all out.

A poster for the Windsor Centennial Festival, which ran from New Year's Day to Thanksgiving Day in 1954. The festival marked the largest municipal celebration ever organized in Canada up to that point. The poster features a previous City of Windsor crest with the motto "by land, by sea", held aloft by the figure of progress.

A colourful New Year's Day parade kicked off the celebration of Windsor's centennial year. This section of the parade was a historical reenactment of 1854, signifying the day that Windsor incorporated as a village. Above, the costumed actors and horse-drawn carriages with coachmen march down Cartier Place, now Freedom Way, on their way to City Hall. The Windsor Armouries are seen left, while Rowson's Tavern, with its slogan "Good Food You'll Remember," is located at the right.

January 1, 1954: The procession of horse-drawn carriages passes by the Prince Edward Hotel on Ouellette Avenue, en route to City Hall for the opening ceremonies of the Windsor Centennial Festival. D.T. "Red" Hanes drives the lead carriage, while Phil Murphy, a well-known local musician, toots an authentic coach horn.

A large crowd gathered in front of the city hall steps on New Year's Day, 1954, for the official reading of the centennial proclamation. Surrounded by members of City Council and the Windsor Control Board, Alderman Mrs. Cameron H. Montrose, acting for an absent Mayor Reaume, is shown at the microphone reading the declaration which officially opened 10 months of birthday observances.

January 1, 1954: W. Donald McGregor OBE, president of the Windsor Centennial Festival, makes the first cut into a 600-pound fruitcake. From left to right are Michigan Governor G. Mennen Williams, McGregor, Alderman Mrs. Cameron H. Montrose, and Harry Rosenthal, centennial general chairman. Hundreds gathered at the Prince Edward Hotel Ballroom to mark the occasion and receive a slice of Windsor's birthday cake.

April 1, 1954: A crew of eight men raise another prefabricated section of frosting on Windsor's massive birthday cake, which stood 40-feet high upon completion. The centre cake, located on Ouellette Avenue between Park Street and the tunnel entrance, served as the theme centre for the Centennial Festival.

Joe Comuzzi, president of the Student Council of Assumption College, presents Mayor Arthur J. Reaume with the first copy of the Windsor Centennial souvenir program in the mayor's office on April 19, 1954. The program was compiled by the students of the college. Pictured from left to right are Comuzzi, Mayor Reaume, W. Donald McGregor OBE, Harry Rosenthal, and the Very Reverend E.C. LeBel, CSB, president of the university.

Ouellette Avenue served as the Windsor Centennial Festival's biggest advertisement, with its cake centerpiece and display cubicles, shields, and badges extending a full city block. The twenty display cubicles were rented out as advertising space to local businesses as a way to fund the confectionery structure, with the caveat that each display had a historical theme.

April 19, 1954: The 100 candles on Windsor's birthday cake sprang to light as electrical switches were pressed simultaneously by Mayor Arthur J. Reaume and Sir Cyril Dyson, mayor of the royal borough of Windsor, England, in a ceremony attended by hundreds of onlookers.

June 21, 1954: Huge crowds gathered in Reaume Park to watch the fireworks display from Belle Isle that kicked off the summer portion of the Windsor Centennial Festival.

June 24, 1954: One of the biggest crowd pleasers from the Windsor Centennial Historical Pageant was the Charleston number in a scene depicting the Roaring Twenties. From left to right are Pat Pattison, Sandra Mills, and Leda Savchetz.

June 25, 1954: By its fourth showing, the Windsor Centennial Historical Pageant had attracted crowds of more than 1,000 people to Jackson Park three nights in a row. In this scene, Norman Golden, left, in the role of a rumrunner, offers a bribe to police constable Ralph Egypt, which was refused in a sanctimonious fashion by the upright constable.

Photographer Jack Dalgleish captured this shot of the moon slipping off the sun during an 80 percent solar eclipse on June 30, 1954. The hundred candles on Windsor's birthday cake were ready to be lighted in case the sun failed completely, but this precaution was not necessary.

Despite organizers' fears over a lack of civic enthusiasm, more than 50,000 Windsorites defied expectations and lined the streets on July 1, 1954, for the Centennial-Dominion Day "Century of Progress" parade. Here, members of the Detroit School Band head towards Park Street.

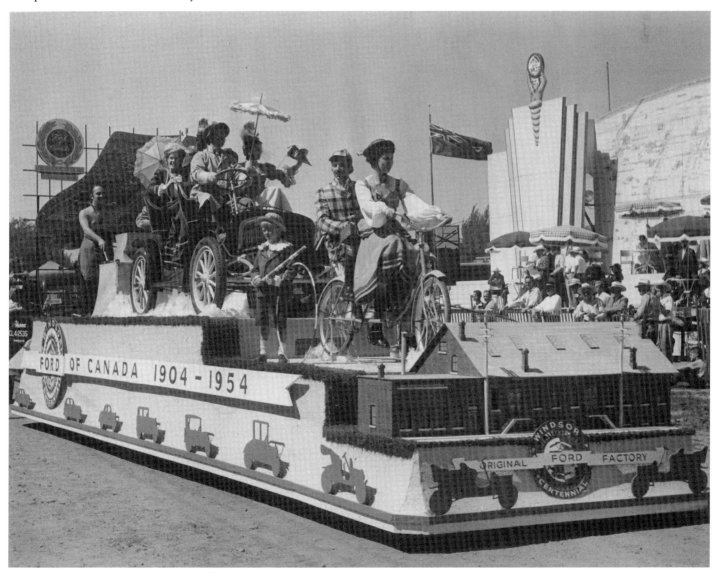

July 1, 1954: The Ford Motor Company of Canada's float passes by the reviewing stand at Jackson Park. Coincidentally, Ford of Canada celebrated its 50th anniversary in 1954, signified on the float by a model of the original 1904 Ford plant and a Model T car.

Huge contingents from Detroit and Wyandotte, Michigan, crossed the river to participate in Windsor's Centennial-Dominion Day parade on July 1, 1954. Motorcycle policemen of the Detroit force were the highlight entry that stretched for nearly seven blocks. Wyandotte also celebrated its centennial in 1954, and Windsor sent its own parade representatives to participate in their festivities on July 4th.

The H.J. Heinz Corporation float passes by the grandstand in Jackson Park during the Centennial-Dominion Day parade.

A crowd favourite, the Scout House band from Preston, Ontario, marches past the Jackson Park grandstand on July 1, 1954.

July 1, 1954: The General Motors Corporation float passes by city officials from Detroit and Windsor seated in the reviewing stand in Jackson Park. Highlighting Windsor's growth over 100 years, lettering on the float showed the city's expansion from a population of 1,050 in 1854 to 127,116 in 1954. The float is being pulled by a 1954 Pontiac Star Chief, the most prestigious car in the company's line-up and the first Pontiac to offer air conditioning.

Miss Pat Jackson and Miss Cassie Nowosielski show off swimwear from the 1890s as part of the Centennial Parade of Fashions on July 7, 1954.

Sally Jane Geier, drum majorette, kicks up her heels as she leads the Italian group during the All Nations Day parade on July 12, 1954.

July 12, 1954: Windsor celebrated its diversity with an All Nations Day event that was kicked off by a parade and float contest. This float, entered by the Ukrainians, was summarized by a reporter as having "ripe grain, pretty flowers, stalwart men, and beautiful girls."

July 12, 1954: Windsor's All Nations Day ended with an outdoor concert held at the band shell in Jackson Park. A crowd of 15,000 attended the evening performance in a show that a *Star* reporter declared had "never been equalled in the history of the city."

The opening night of Old Home Week on August 10, 1954, was a rousing success for the nearly 4,000 who attended. The midway was especially popular with the children as evidenced by Joyce Toy, 9, and Bunny Jean, 4, from left to right, who enjoyed a ride on the miniature train.

Miss Anice Krug, no. 14 in the line-up above, was crowned Miss Windsor at the Firefighters' Field Day in Jackson Park over Labour Day weekend, 1954. As the victor, Krug's height, weight, and measurements were printed in *The Star* as "vital statistics."

An estimated 20,000 people packed Jackson Park on August 16, 1954, for the Ford of Canada "Golden Jubilee Variety Parade," which saluted show business greats from the past half-century. Held in conjunction with Ford of Canada's 50th anniversary, the show covered entertainment from the circus to television, including the four minstrels shown here: Marshall Skinner, Allen Robinson, Michael Geliner, and Aurel Botoson, from left to right.

"His bushy growth of face fur was declared the best of all the 'beavers' grown by men in the Centennial Beard Growing Contest," read *The Windsor Star* on August 16, 1954. The "Brothers of the Brush" Centennial beard growers found their leader in Hank Romanycia, who was crowned before a crowd of 6,000 people at Jackson Park. Romanycia was presented with the Hugh W. Simpson trophy by Controller Hugh Simpson and was rewarded with a kiss by Miss Isobel Chapman, Queen of the Mardi Gras.

Robert M. Fleming, 96, did not win first place in the Centennial Beard Growing contest, and yet he was honoured as the oldest contestant of the near 100 participants. He is presented with a runner-up cup by Controller Robert M. Fuller on August 16, 1954.

THE 1950s

The 1950s were a politically conservative time across North America. The world had basically recovered economically from World War II as the decade came to a close, but the deadliest war in history—and the Cold War tensions that followed—still preyed upon the public consciousness. In contrast to the cautious politics, Elvis Presley broke out in the mid-'50s as the hottest performer in the newly popular genre of rock 'n' roll, considered shocking by the establishment. Marilyn Monroe was the reigning sex symbol, when open sexuality was still largely taboo.

It was an era of social conformity, with cookie-cutter homes managed by suburban housewives. The baby boom was rocking, given people were settling into postwar normalcy again—even though it was still a dangerous time.

Canada participated in the 1950–53 Korean War, sending 26,000 soldiers, 516 of whom were killed,

including six from Windsor-Essex. Canadian Minister of External Affairs, Lester B. Pearson, who went on to become Prime Minister, triggered Canadian pride when he won the Nobel Peace Prize in 1957 for suggesting the creation of a United Nations peacekeeping force to deal with the Suez Crisis. Meanwhile, Windsor made its own headlines.

Mayor Arthur J. Reaume met with US President Harry S. Truman in Detroit in 1950. But as celebrities go, that meeting couldn't match what unfolded in the 1950s in Windsor—a grand place for local royal-watchers. The city enjoyed not one but two royal visits in the '50s. Princess Elizabeth and Prince Philip came to Windsor on October 15, 1951—after King George was diagnosed with lung cancer and could not travel—and were welcomed by sensational crowds. According to *The Windsor Daily Star*, about 300,000 people from Windsor, southwestern Ontario, and the United States lined the

15-mile route the royal couple took under "magnificent autumn sunshine." At Jackson Park, Her Highness promoted camaraderie in a speech that referenced the House of Windsor, the British royal house: "These two Windsors are far apart, but they are close in spirit and understanding."

The royal couple returned July 4, 1959, but this time the monarch visited as Queen Elizabeth II (having ascended to the throne in 1952), along with the Duke of Edinburgh, Prince Philip. And they left in style, sailing aboard the royal yacht *Britannia*, no less. *The Windsor Daily Star* reported that 250,000 people jammed into Windsor for the regal event. Reporters covering the whole Canadian tour called the Windsor stop the "biggest show" up to that point of the royal visit.

In 1953, with polio at its peak across Canada and nobody sure how the disease spread, panic erupted. It was already proven that chlorine in pools helped defend against polio—good news for Windsor's first pool, the Lions Club Pool that opened in Lanspeary Park in 1950. But many citizens started fearing open water. The Detroit River had long been a popular spot for bathing beaches, but it became a source of controversy for many in the 1950s who worried about disease.

On July 12, 1957, a spectacular fire consumed a city asset that had long served as a gathering place for sports, entertainment, and more: the Jackson Park Grandstand and Band Shell. The fire started around 4:30 p.m. after a worker left a pickup truck in the works building at the facility. Faulty wiring ignited the truck—the worker tried in vain to douse the blaze with a fire extinguisher—and it soon spread to the 5,000-seat stadium, built in 1909. Nearby fire hydrants did not work properly, which sealed the fate of the grandstand, bought from the Jockey Club in 1928. As the *Windsor Daily Star* said: "Firemen stood by helplessly with near-empty hoses because of hydrant

difficulties for the first 40 minutes of the blaze." The cost of replacing the stands was estimated at $1 million, and even though the structure was only insured for $84,000, the city financed the rebuilding of both the grandstand (later demolished) and the band shell (still in Jackson Park, but no longer in use) in 1959.

The '50s were the time of the second Red Scare, shortly after World War II when communism rose to the level of bogeyman in the propaganda—with the Soviets leading the charge. As the Cold War raged, the American government created Project Nike that installed nuclear missiles across the country, starting in 1953 and continuing for more than a decade. Anti-aircraft missiles such as the Nike Ajax and later the Nike Hercules were deployed at a number of sites in the Detroit area, including on Belle Isle from 1955 to 1968. These nuclear warheads were less than a mile from Windsor, and yet, it was simply a fact of life in the anxious '50s, where many believed that a nuclear attack on North America was a matter of inevitability.

Windsor reflected the rest of North America at the time, which meant intolerance of political dissent, all while building perfect homes and gardens—at least on paper. The reality was murkier. Windsor was still considered a risqué place to visit. A scandal broke out in 1950 over alleged police corruption and lax attitudes towards vice. According to historian Patrick Brode in his book *Unholy City*, "This was a more vibrant world, in which there was a greater acceptance of sex, and indulgence in alcohol and games of chance; in a word, pleasures." Yet the dichotomy from the seedy side of society and the proper side was immense. On Sundays, for instance, when the second half of the 20th century began, the Blue Laws were in full effect—meaning no drinking or movies or commercial entertainment was allowed. Shopping on Friday nights was even frowned upon. And so Windsor happily went along in the 1950s, officially conservative, unofficially fun.

Queen Elizabeth II and Prince Philip wave to the crowds from the back of their Chrysler Royal Imperial convertible, 1959.

Windsor's annual Soap Box Derby at Jackson Park, circa 1950. Leading this heat is Car 46, with driver Mark Kalbol and pusher William Bozin, both age 12.

Mayor Arthur J. Reaume, at left, and Lyle Bertrand, president of the Lions Club, are surrounded by cheering children at the construction site for the city's first public swimming pool, which was sponsored by the Windsor Lions Club. The opening ceremonies on June 26, 1950, are pictured at right.

November 25, 1952: Stockpiling ammunition after the assault on Hill 355, nicknamed "Little Gibraltar," in Korea are members of "A" Troop, "A" Battery, Royal Canadian Horse Artillery: two local boys, Gunner Gordon Murray of Tilbury and Bill Logan of Windsor, along with Osborne Farnell of Nova Scotia, from left to right. Canada participated in the Korean War from 1950 to 1953, and six soldiers from Windsor lost their lives in the conflict.

February 1, 1950: Ernest Rumpel and David Duncan, from left to right, enjoy pop and Purity ice-cream as a reward for being on their school's safety patrol in 1950.

In the early 1950s, Windsor had a reputation as Sin City, peddling in the vice trades of gambling and betting, prostitution, and after-hours drinking. Here, a police officer shows off a piece of evidence—an illegal slot machine—seized in a raid of a local gambling den.

Children regularly swam in the Detroit River, pictured here near the west end Shore Acres park, in the early '50s. Many Windsorites believed that swimming in the river was the cause of an outbreak of polio, which peaked in Canada in 1953.

In 1951, Princess Elizabeth and her husband, Philip, made their first state visit to Canada. During her stop in Windsor, thousands of people packed into Jackson Park to see the young royal couple.

October 15, 1951: Princess Elizabeth and Prince Philip wave to the crowds as their motorcade travels down Ouellette Avenue, flanked by an escort of RCMP officers. During their visit, the royals watched an assembly line at Ford and listened to the St. Mary's Boys' Choir.

A cold wave in December 1951 saw Lake St. Clair completely frozen over with ice. Here, Eddie Pattison, at left, and Jack Porter ride their bikes on the frozen lake.

December 18, 1951: City snow removal crews were on the job early to clear the streets, here on Ouellette Avenue.

Windsor area Boy Scouts, Girl Guides, and Wolf Cubs practise for a Scout Rally at Jackson Park on June 3, 1954.

"Long Live the Queen": This front-page headline from February 6, 1952, informed Windsorites that, as members of the British Commonwealth, they had a new sovereign. Only months after her visit to Windsor, Princess Elizabeth became Queen following the sudden death of her father, King George VI.

March 20, 1956: Applicants queue up on the street outside of the Gordon Bureau on Devonshire Road. The bureau issued approximately 40,000 plates at $3 apiece that year.

Waiting for the Lions Club pool in Lanspeary Park to open, circa 1950s.

"Swim Caper Foiled": An impromptu swim to Belle Isle on July 19, 1956, by five off-duty Windsor bathing beach lifeguards was called an "unarmed invasion" by Detroit police. Ron Gelinas, Morgan Clark, George Stecko, Bob Miller, and Fred Maxim, from left to right, were let off with just a warning, and swam back to Canada. A proud Mayor Reaume reportedly gave Ron Gelinas a congratulatory phone call the next day.

The 27th Windsor Firefighters' Field Day on September 4, 1956, was called the "greatest fete ever" by *The Star*. A highlight of the yearly event was the Miss Western Ontario pageant, and later, the Battle of the Bands.

Nick Boychuk, in the boat, gets a hitchhiking thumb from Barney Almassy after the 4200 block of Sandwich Street West was flooded from melted snow and ice in 1958.

Norman "Yorky" Haworth climbed 500 feet up the CKLW-TV tower in 1956 on a two-dollar bet, before being talked down by police and arrested. Yorky racked up some 700 arrests for public intoxication, but was a well-known—and loved—Windsor character.

Joan Wins Miss Canada Crown
★★★ ★★★ ★★★ ★★★
Windsor Brunette Tops 28 Beauties at Hamilton Pageant

Windsor's own Joan Fitzpatrick, age 20, was named Miss Canada on July 8, 1957—the first time a local girl achieved the national title.

The Ya-Ya skirt, with its shorter hemline, arrived in Windsor in 1959. This *Star* photograph compared a dress "cut to the conventional length," at left, with the "extra-short" skirt of two women walking in Dieppe Gardens. Reportedly, Windsor girls condemned the trend.

The grandstand and bandshell at Jackson Park were lost to a massive blaze on July 12, 1957. The fire was believed to have been started by faulty wiring in a truck parked in a nearby works garage. At top left, firemen and park employees race for the exit, as the fire grew out of control. A victim receives oxygen treatment, at top right, while firefighters attempt to extinguish the flames on the grandstand, at bottom.

June 22, 1957: Children at the May Court Reception Centre spend their leisure time in front of the television. In the 1950s, the Windsor area was one of the leaders in Canadian television sales, due to the ability to pick up American programming and CKLW-TV. It was rare to find a *Star* photograph with a television in it—that's the competition!

October 27, 1957: Doreen Leslie and Huguette Gervais hold a cake and fruit basket marking the inaugural Trans Canada Airline (Air Canada) transcontinental flight from Windsor Airport.

November 16, 1957: More than 4,000 children crowded Ouellette Avenue, in front of the CH Smith department store, to greet Santa Claus.

January 4, 1958: *Star* photographer Bill Bishop climbed high up on a fire-ladder to take this shot of the city's firemen and their equipment. That year, the department employed 158 firefighters.

Constable Jerry Douglas gives a "warning ticket" to Monica Crooks as the police department cracked down on jaywalking in 1958.

New, modern street lights were installed on Riverside Drive at Devonshire Road, looking east, in December 1958.

A new Nike-Hercules missile base was dedicated on Belle Isle on May 16, 1959. The base was opened to the public and many inspected the new Nike-Hercules, at centre, flanked by two, smaller Nike-Ajax missiles. Visible from Windsor, the missiles were part of a Cold War air defense program and were decommissioned in 1968.

"No More of This!" A city-wide purge of pinball machines was ordered by Police Chief Carl W. Farrow on July 18, 1959. Fuelled by citizen complaints about teenagers, a police task force was created to remove machines—or businesses would be charged as "a common gaming house." Farrow was acting on a 1965 Supreme Court decision that equated pinball machines with illegal slot machines—a ruling that was largely unenforced elsewhere in Canada.

July 2, 1959: 70,000 people crowded into Dieppe Gardens to inspect the Royal Yacht *Britannia*, which arrived at her berth in the Detroit River ahead of Queen Elizabeth and Prince Philip's visit to Windsor. While the curious public was denied entrance onto the yacht, more than 800 sailors on shore leave flooded Windsor's downtown for the evening.

Queen Elizabeth and Prince Philip stopped in Windsor on July 3, 1959, during their Royal Tour of Canada. They were greeted by 250,000 Windsorites and American visitors who lined the streets to catch a glimpse of the royal couple as they travelled from the train station at Ford Plant 6 to Dieppe Gardens. Here, their Chrysler Royal Imperial convertible passes by Windsor's newly minted City Hall, greeted by enthusiastic crowds.

The royal visit in 1959 was capped off with an official farewell at Dieppe Gardens, before Queen Elizabeth and Prince Philip boarded the *Britannia*. Here, Bob Hanes presents Her Majesty with Windsor's gift, an Appaloosa pony named Chief Tecumseh, intended for a child of Windsor, England. Prince Philip was reported to have thought it sporting to ride the pony around the royal yacht's decks.

THE 1960s

The 1960s saw protests and the counterculture age of Flower Power blossom as a reaction to the conservative decade before it—though politics of capitalism versus communism still set the stage. In the throes of the Cold War, Americans often dominated the headlines, even in Windsor. The Cuban Missile Crisis rattled the world in 1962, while popular President John F. Kennedy was shot dead in Dallas on November 22, 1963. The Vietnam War escalated throughout the '60s, in what would become the defining war for a generation. Meanwhile, the United States won the space race on July 20, 1969, when Apollo 11 completed the first manned moon landing with Windsor and the world watching.

In Canada, the '60s were also a time of political upheaval and cultural change. The Canadian Bill of Rights became law in 1960—the same year that the Quiet Revolution started in Quebec, secularizing the province and setting the stage for a growing separatist movement. The maple leaf started adorning the new Canadian flag on February 15, 1965, after the Great Canadian Flag Debate. Canada celebrated its 100th birthday on July 1, 1967, when Windsor witnessed its biggest parade in

history up to that point, thanks to some 3,500-plus marchers and 32 bands heading from the riverfront up Ouellette Avenue to Jackson Park. In 1967, the World's Fair came to Montreal as Expo 67, which put Canada on the map and instilled a sense of pride across the country. Trudeaumania erupted in 1968 when Pierre Trudeau became Prime Minister.

The Beatles and the Rolling Stones dominated the charts as rock 'n' roll took over. But it was not all fun times. American racial unrest in 1967, the Summer of Love, affected Canada when riots left 43 dead and the City of Detroit smoking, sending an ominous signal to Windsorites across the river. Moreover, because Windsor sat next door to Detroit, during the Vietnam War when some 30,000 Canadians voluntarily enlisted in the US and perhaps even more American draft dodgers came north, Windsor was a popular exit and entry point. As a result, Windsor erected the North Wall monument on the riverfront in 1995 to honour Canadians killed in the Vietnam War.

Windsor witnessed some big stories of its own, of course.

One of the area's most shocking tales of the 1960s was the case of the Dickerson children. The *Windsor Star* banner headline on July 29, 1960, said it all: "Confined to home 11 years, three children hospitalized." Neighbours did not know. That is, until Gordon Dickerson, 15, walked out one day while his mother was at the dentist and told a neighbour something that seemed hard to believe: he and his sisters, aged 17 and 13, had not been allowed outside in more than a decade. His mother, Shirley Dickerson Leach, later told reporters that she and her husband kept three of her six children from a previous marriage inside because they didn't want landlords to know how big their family was. Police took the children (who were underdeveloped and likely malnourished) to Grace Hospital where a nurse asked the oldest girl whether she liked her new friends. She reportedly replied: "Very much, but I will miss my mother."

Later that same year came one of the deadliest tragedies in Windsor history. Shortly after 2 p.m. on October 25, 1960, the Metropolitan chain variety store at 439 Ouellette Avenue exploded—killing 10 and injuring 100. *Star* reporter Walter McCall, driving north on Ouellette only a few hundred feet from the blast when it rattled the entire downtown, recounted the horror in the next day's *Windsor Star*.

"I was in hell," wrote McCall, who had pulled over before dashing back to the catastrophe. "For close to two hours I scratched and dug through a macabre world of living and dead." He saw wounded people lying in the smoke and debris, or milling around in shock, such as one bleeding man staggering from the wreckage. "A young woman, also bleeding badly, slowly pulled herself up, dumping piles of bright sweaters and clothing from her back," McCall wrote. "There were others, too, unconscious or unable to move, scattered about the pavement. Debris and merchandise was ankle-deep." The explosion, caused by a broken gas line in the basement—the furnace was being swapped from coal to gas—knocked out the building's rear wall. The first and second floors collapsed into the basement, trapping employees and customers, many of them seniors who had earlier sat at the lunch counter. Hundreds of rescuers helped search for survivors and the dead. The building was demolished years later, though the nightmare was not soon forgotten.

Tragedy struck again on December 21, 1966, on Walker Road just north of Highway 3. Kids were heading home on their schoolbus when, the *Windsor Star* said in a 2014 retrospective piece, a "barreling truck overturned onto them and dumped its load of death." Eight children were killed and 16 injured on that slippery winter day when they were buried under a 20-ton truckload of sand. It marked the worst traffic accident in the history of Essex County at the time. The trucker was charged with dangerous driving, while the community grieved en masse. One story began this way: "Eight Christmas trees have lost their glow and many presents lie meaningless this morning after an accident which killed eight children." A park with a commemorative plaque to the eight lost children was built near the accident site in 2014.

Other signs of the times in Windsor included the Emergency Measures Organization, a government agency that helped communities prepare in case of nuclear attack. As a result, some Windsor model homes included underground fallout shelters—a crazy concept decades later, but one that seemed sane at the time. In 1960, voters approved Sunday movies for the first time. A Windsor institution was born in 1964, when Brentwood Recovery Home opened as Charity House, thanks to tough-love Father Paul Charbonneau as well as Jim and Kay Ryan, in a former restaurant at Wyandotte and Chilver. The 1965 Auto Pact boosted Windsor's auto industry and development in Windsor chugged along full steam, as the downtown skyline transformed and the city physically expanded in size and amenities.

As Bob Dylan said: the times they were a-changin'. Like much of North America, Windsor shed its conservative style in favour of a more carefree approach, with fashion and politics. Despite political turmoil and tragedy, Windsor enjoyed some great times in the 1960s when, no matter the politics, development continued unabated.

August 11, 1960: Henry Bird, civil defense coordinator, examines the entrance to a fallout shelter built in a model home on Randolph Avenue at Cabana Road. The Canadian government urged private citizens to build fallout shelters in case of a nuclear attack.

In the early '60s, the City of Windsor monitored air quality to detect radiation pollution. Here, Patrick Costello, at left, and L.R. Keddy change the filter on the machine, on the roof of City Hall.

Crowds gather by the Cleary Guest House in Dieppe Gardens, 1960. The Recreation Department showed films outdoors on Sunday nights throughout the summer months.

CONFINED TO HOME 11 YEARS, THREE CHILDREN HOSPITALIZED

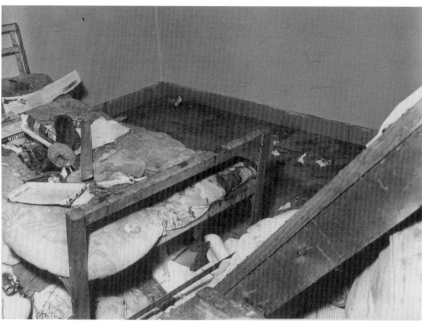

July 29, 1960: Three children were confined for 11 years in their family home in Tecumseh, pictured at left. The mother, Shirley Dickerson Leach, claimed that she hid three of her six children (the others were raised in the open) because landlords frowned upon renting to large families. The children lived in the upstairs room, pictured at right, with boarded up windows.

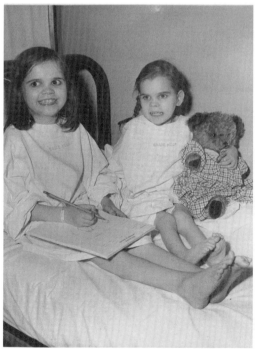
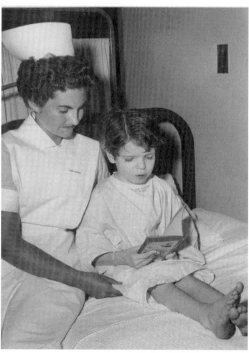

The Dickerson children were immediately hospitalized due to their visible underdevelopment. After weeks of investigation, doctors determined that their condition was a combination of a glandular deficiency and their confinement. The Children's Aid Society eventually dropped their case and returned the Dickerson children to their mother, as the children did not want to be separated from her. This story inspired V.C. Andrew's novel, *Flowers in the Attic*. Left: Connie, 17, and Glenda, 13. Centre: Gordon, 15. Right: Connie blows out the candles on her 18th birthday cake, helped by Gordon, while their mother looks on.

Square Dance Party, 1961. Square dancing was all the rage in Windsor in the '60s, with events held weekly at local ballrooms.

Artificial Christmas trees made of aluminum were flying off the shelves in 1961. Here, fire inspector Phil Murphy shows the recommended type of direct lighting equipment.

'Fallout' Honeymoon
★ ★ ★   ★ ★ ★
Couple's 9 Days in Shelter

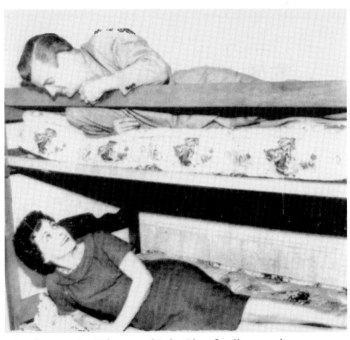

March 3, 1962: Edwin and Lila Glen finally got a honeymoon after 14 years of marriage after being selected as the "lucky couple" to spend nine days in a model fallout shelter during the Junior Chamber of Commerce's annual Home Show.

October 25, 1960: A gas leak caused an explosion at the Metropolitan Store on Ouellette Avenue. The rear of the store collapsed, leading to 10 fatalities and 100 injuries. At top left, a crowd forms outside the storefront, moments after the explosion, while a kitchen worker is escorted to safety at top right. Pictured below, civilians help firefighters and police dig through the rubble to recover victims of the explosion.

Windsor . . . City of 1,000 Heroes in Disaster

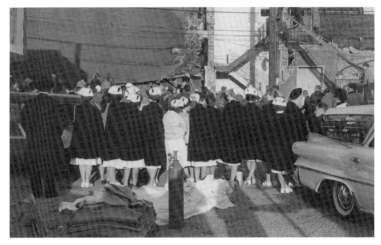

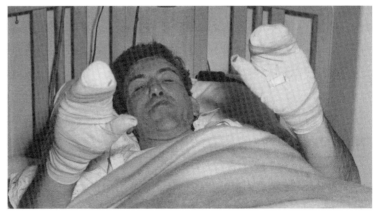

Hospital-bound victims are carried out of the destroyed front entrance, at top left, while an injured man is comforted after being rescued, at top right. The interior of the store, post-explosion, with collapsing infrastructure, flooding, and damaged merchandise, is pictured at bottom left. Nurses wait for victims to be pulled from the rubble, at middle right, while store manager, Joe Halford, is shown in the hospital after managing to claw his way out of the basement. The rescue efforts lasted for days after, and an inquest was ordered into the explosion.

July 30, 1962: British freighter *M.V. Montrose* began to sink into the Detroit River after colliding with a tug-propelled barge upon leaving the Detroit Harbour Terminal beneath the Ambassador Bridge. Pictured at right, large pumps drain the *Montrose*; it took two months of salvage operations for the ship to be fully afloat.

By the mid '60s, larger families were the norm due to the post-war baby boom. Mrs. Stanley Cecile is pictured here, as part of a *Star* feature on Mother's Day, surrounded by her seven children: Wayne, 9; Mickey, 8; Mary Ann, 7; Brian, 5; and Janine, 4, from left to right, with Dianne, 3; and Teddy, 1.5 on her lap.

"Beatlemania, the strange new disease, was detected on Ouellette Avenue" on August 14, 1964, in the words of *The Star*. At right, teenagers camped out in front of Vanity Theatre to wait for the first Windsor showing of "A Hard Day's Night," the Beatles' first full-length film. Mary Kalosis, Teresa Dulzniewski, Linda Stanyer, and Theresa Kujat, imitate their idols, at right.

"Up She Goes!" Astonished drivers along Riverside Drive stopped to gape at a number of new, shiny cars which were hoisted into the Cleary Auditorium through a second floor window. The cars were part of the Chrysler Canada Ltd. car show on September 13, 1963.

August 29, 1964: A Lancaster Bomber arrives in the Detroit River, en route to Dieppe Gardens where it would become a memorial to World War II veterans. It was moved to Jackson Park in 1967.

Windsor held a full military funeral for Rear Admiral Walter Hose, known as the Father of the Canadian Navy, in 1965. Here, naval officers give three volleys of gunfire as a final tribute.

December 21, 1966: A truck collided with a school bus at Walker Road and Highway 3. The truck overturned and spilled tonnes of sand into the bus. Despite the efforts of rescue workers, eight children died.

Popular columnist Eppie Lenders, aka Ann Landers, of the "Dear Ann" advice column visited Windsor in 1967, and planted a kiss on Mayor John Wheelton when he presented her with a key to the City of Windsor.

An estimated 7,500 Miles for Millions marchers headed out from Windsor Stadium on December 2, 1967, for a 32-mile walk-a-thon. The goal of the march, sponsored by the federal Centennial International Development Program, was to raise $50,000 to build a mobile farm school in Uganda.

July 29, 1968: Six teenagers picketed the Capitol Theatre during its showing of the Vietnam War movie, *The Green Berets*, arguing that the film was American pro-war propaganda.

June 19, 1967: People lined up for a quarter mile to visit the Confederation train during its stop in Windsor as part of its cross-Canada trip to celebrate Canada's Centennial.

May 8, 1968: The Windsor Dragway's "official" car was a 1968 Chevrolet Camaro, presented by Webster Motors. On the construction site of the soon-to-be dragway off Manning Road are Sandwich South Reeve Bob Pulleyblank, Mike Wheatley, and Bryan C. Wheatley, from left to right. The dragway was operational from 1968 to 1971.

February 2, 1969: Robert and Douglas Gale, draped in flags, argue in the Cleary Auditorium lobby with John McArthur, one of the Windsor residents who arranged for a Viet Cong visit. Members of the National Liberation Front (the opposing side to the Americans in the Vietnam War) gave a lecture before a crowd of 450 people.

Dan Gobbo and Rita Nasarkiewicz pose before a fashion show at Herman High School, featuring the latest "party-going" outfits for 1969. The mini-skirt represents one of the largest fashion trends of the '60s.

Pur-r-r
SUNNY, MILD
6 a.m. 37, 9 a.m. 36
Low tonight 44, high Sat. 68
(Complete weather page 2)

The Windsor Star

ONTARIO
★ ★ ★

VOL. 101, NO. 34   50 Pages   WINDSOR ONTARIO FRIDAY OCTOBER 11 1968   SEVEN CENTS

TIGER TOWN GOES 'PIE-EYED'

After the Detroit Tigers won the World Series in 1968, fans in Windsor waited hopefully at Windsor Airport, in hopes that the plane carrying the victorious team back from St. Louis would land there instead of Detroit's Metropolitan Airport (where thousands of fans jammed the runways). To these fans' disappointment, the Tiger plane finally landed at Willow Run Airport instead.

And How!
SUNNY
6 a.m 68, 1 p.m. 80
Low tonight 60, high Tuesday 80
(Complete weather page 6)

The Windsor Star

FINAL
★ ★ ★ ★

VOL. 102, NO. 119   40 Pages   WINDSOR ONTARIO MONDAY JULY 21 1969   TEN CENTS

EAGLE MOON EPIC ENDS WITH LUNAR BLASTOFF

Windsorites joined in the space race, along with hundreds of millions of people across the world, to watch Neil Armstrong take man's first steps on the moon on July 20, 1969. Another *Star* headline read: "Windsor Joins in Moon Acclaim" and reported that there were few people out on the streets that night, and lights were on in every home, watching their televisions.

October 2, 1969: Students from the University of Windsor and St. Clair College joined in protests across Canada against the Aleutian A-blast, American nuclear testing in the Aleutian Islands in Alaska. At top, more than 200 St. Clair College students block Detroit traffic at the tunnel, while 400 university students did the same at the bridge, pictured at bottom.

THE 1970s

The 1970s were a pivotal time for social change, the natural fallout from the countercultural 1960s. With the backdrop of Vietnam and Watergate in the US, the '70s saw a lot of economic upheaval. A global oil crisis, sparked by the 1973 oil embargo by the Organization of Arab Petroleum Exporting Countries, led to higher gas prices for years. By the end of the decade, disco kept the beat pumping on pop charts and in discotheques across the continent. Women's Liberation was in vogue, increasing the push for equality in wages and much more.

The October Crisis hit Quebec and the rest of Canada in 1970 when radical nationalist group Front de Libération du Québec kidnapped British diplomat James Cross and killed provincial cabinet minister Pierre Laporte—prompting Prime Minister Pierre Trudeau to invoke the War Measures Act, which imposed martial law. By the end of the year, all the kidnappers were arrested. However, the violence, and ongoing issues of Quebec separatism, triggered anxiety across Canada—especially after René Lévesque's Parti Québécois was elected in 1976. The 1980 Quebec referendum on independence, however, was defeated 60-40.

The politically charged decade produced newsworthy events in Windsor, as youth activism only increased from the late '60s. On November 3, 1971, some 4,000 university, college, and high-school students showed the power of youthful protest when they shut down the Ambassador Bridge to demonstrate against the planned American nuclear test on Amchitka, one of the Aleutian Islands off the coast of Alaska. Two local protesters were arrested at a smaller rally at the Windsor-Detroit Tunnel. Similar demonstrations were held at a number of Canada-US border crossings that day, decrying the pending blast code-named Cannikin. Critics feared an explosion of that magnitude could trigger a tsunami that would hit the BC coast. It was a time when US President Richard Nixon barely hid his dislike of Canadian Prime Minister Pierre Trudeau, leaders on different sides of the political spectrum. Trudeau did not try to sway his American counterpart. The blast went off anyway, becoming the largest underground nuclear test ever conducted by the United States.

The atmosphere of protesting against injustice brought a new movement to Windsor in the '70s: Women's Liberation. Feminism, then considered politically radical, fought for women's rights and equality. In 1970—the same year that the Commission on the Status of Women released its report—Windsor had its first meeting of the local branch of Women's Liberation, but it did not draw a crowd: only four people showed up. However, the movement only grew from there. By 1972, the group was picketing a local Supertest Service Station for bringing in "Miss UniRoyal," a 25-foot bikini-clad statue, to advertise a tire sale. Though perhaps hesitant at first, local women—galvanized by an era of change—seized the opportunity to transform their status in society.

Tragedy struck at home a few years later. A powerful tornado ripped through the Windsor Curling Club on April 3, 1974, crumbling the back wall and ripping off most of the roof, killing eight people and injuring 30. Another victim succumbed to their injuries months later. The storm left a path of destruction 22 kilometres long and up to 200 metres wide. It came howling across the Detroit River from Michigan as part of the 1974 Super Outbreak, one of the most violent tornado events ever recorded, when 148 twisters touched down in 13 States over 24 hours. The Windsor tornado flipped over a crane at Devonshire Mall before inflicting horror at the curling club and causing $1.8 million in damage in 1974.

The snowstorm of 1978, which clobbered Windsor on January 26 and 27, also left a deadly wake. As the worst winter storm to hit the area in two decades, its force proved immense. It killed 13 people in Ontario, including four in Essex County. The Great Blizzard of 1978, also known as the White Hurricane, was a giant northeaster that battered the central United States and Ontario. The two-day blizzard closed all Essex County schools—some for several days—and caused a series of blackouts across the area. Local snow removal budgets skyrocketed while people continued digging out for days.

Tragedy struck again high above Windsor on July 10, 1979, when two Cessnas collided, killing all five people—three Americans and two Canadians—on board both aircraft. The planes crashed in the Riverside Drive East and Riverdale Avenue area, spreading flaming debris over 10 city blocks. Miraculously, nobody was hurt on the ground, even though a wing landed on a home, a plane crashed into a field across from the Windsor Yacht Club, and other wreckage rained down on the wider Riverside neighbourhood. The crash came after Detroit air-traffic controllers failed to notify their Windsor counterparts that a US plane was using Canadian airspace for an approach. Windsor Mayor Bert Weeks later told a federal air safety inquiry that the accident could have been avoided if Windsor had a radar tower.

As the '70s drew to a close, Windsor's once-booming automotive industry was feeling the effects of high oil prices and increased competition. By 1980, fuel-efficient Japanese imports from Toyota and Honda were starting to cut into Canadian and American market share. The Big Three were negotiating tougher. Workers' gains slowed somewhat, but still kept coming. The low Canadian dollar and high productivity allowed Windsor to continue manufacturing vehicles, even as global competition heated up.

Windsor in the 1970s endured its share of tragedy and economic upheaval, though it also proved a liberating time. The protest counterculture dovetailed naturally with the city's union movement, which never surrendered a fight on behalf of workers. Through all the adversity, Windsor's tough character remained intact.

A pedestrian wonders what it's all about—gas prices, that is.

June 29, 1970: Hundreds of teenagers crowded into Windsor Arena for a marathon 12-hour rock festival, featuring bands like Frijid Pink and the MC-5.

Trevor Lewis demonstrates proper tie-dying technique for *The Star* on July 24, 1970.

"Double Decker Parking": The parking spaces doubled between the Kent Trust Building and Seaway Inn with the introduction of the "Space-O-Matic" on June 26, 1970.

"Just Groovin": 400 people filled Ambassador Park on July 12, 1970, for an outdoor rock concert by the Glass Candle from Amherstburg and Windsor's Rockets.

Mercury contamination in Lake St. Clair and Lake Erie meant that all fish caught were seized and disposed of by the government. Here, Gordon Drouillard hauls a 60-pound sturgeon destined for the landfill.

December 26, 1970: Youngsters put their toboggans through their paces on the downhill runs at AKO Park.

October 8, 1970: Roland Renaud works on the computer console at Centennial Secondary School. The $120,000 machine was used for computer science and data processing classes.

November 17, 1970: A caravan of 25 buses from San Francisco, carrying 200 members of a "hippie family," were denied entry into Canada at the Detroit-Windsor Tunnel. Here, two members of the commune push their van back to the United States. An immigration officer reportedly gave this reason: "they aren't our kind of people."

February 8, 1917: Six hundred teenagers competed in a 12-hour dance marathon at the Windsor Armouries. Called "Moccasin Marathon," the event raised money for the Ontario Native Development Fund.

April 24, 1971: Kindergarten teacher Evelyn McLean, and her assistant Shelley Fairthorne, explain how Daylight Savings Time works. Until 1972, Detroit remained on Standard Time, leaving them one hour behind Windsor.

Students took to the streets on July 13, 1971, with a unique demand: jobs. Here, 15-year-old Geraldine Menzies hands out an information leaflet to Doris Brown.

July 28, 1971: Paul Kale and Debbie Henderson, both age 20, take their first legal drink at the Dominion House, after the province of Ontario lowered the drinking age from 21 to 18. It was raised up to 19 in 1979.

November 3, 1971: Thousands of university, college, and high-school students marched across the Ambassador Bridge to Detroit to protest the US nuclear weapon test planned at Amchitka Island off the coast of Alaska. The demonstration halted bridge traffic for three hours.

November 6, 1971: Students meet for an anti-war rally—a last-ditch attempt to stop the Amchitka nuclear testing planned for that day. The bomb went off as scheduled.

Students at W.D. Lowe Secondary School pitched in with a city-wide clean-up in 1971, after Mayor Frank Wansbrough declared war on litter.

July 15, 1972: Members of Windsor Women's Liberation staged a protest in front of Harry Myers' Supertest Service Station on Wyandotte Street West, expressing their displeasure with the 25-foot statue called "Miss Uniroyal," which made an appearance in Windsor to advertise a tire sale. At right, "Miss Uniroyal" receives a more "appropriate" outfit from the activists.

November 10, 1972: Three members of Women's Liberation do a layout for the next issue of their monthly tabloid, *Windsor Woman*. From left to right are Beverly Walker, Jean Dearing, and Selma McGorman.

November 29, 1973: Colleen Paquette (at right) stands with Canadian poet and short story writer Bronwen Wallace in front of the Women's Place at 1309 University Avenue. The centre was a community space for women to meet or participate in workshops and consciousness-raising sessions.

A severe storm on St. Patrick's Day in 1973 plunged Essex County into a state of emergency, with 3,000 people evacuated and damages in excess of $5 million. At left, debris washes up against the CNR tracks near Stoney Point after extensive flooding, while Mrs. Dess Soulliere gets neighbourhood youngsters to give her a boat ride home to 533 Jarvis Avenue, at right.

Smelt fishermen scoop up a bountiful harvest at Point Pelee. The annual smelt runs drew large crowds of amateur anglers in the 1970s, which were declared safe despite mercury contamination in nearby Great Lakes.

'MILLION TO 1'--8 DIE

April 3, 1974: A tornado ripped through the Windsor Curling Club on Central Avenue, tearing off the roof and knocking down the west wall (pictured above). Eight people were killed and one other succumbed to injuries months later. At bottom left, firefighter Joseph Kato stands amid the wreckage, while damaged cars outside the club are shown at bottom right.

October 19, 1976: John Breault, 17, and Terry Fysh, 18, model T-shirts, created by a group of 20 Kingsville teenagers after the police commission told Kingsville Police Chief Jake Boldt to crack down on "young punks."

"Off and Rolling": Windsor's annual soapbox derby was taken to new heights in 1975. Pictured here is the starting line at the derby held at St. Clair College.

November 17, 1977: Windsor OHIP employees demonstrate in City Hall Square against the health ministry transferring OHIP operations to London.

The OPEC embargo of 1973 and resulting gas crisis throughout the '70s left Canadians facing shortages and higher prices at the pump. Here, lines of motorists fill up before a scheduled price increase in 1977 to 83.9 cents per gallon.

This photograph of cars lined up at Suny's Gas Bar at the University Mall prompted *The Star* to declare: "GAS. It's enough to give you indigestion..." as prices continued to climb over a dollar per gallon.

The Windsor Star

| 56 Pages | Thursday, January 26, 1978 | 15 Cents |

Area at mercy of raging blizzard

The historic blizzard of January 1978—remembered as the White Hurricane—wreaked havoc in Windsor and across the northern United States. The storm claimed the lives of four people locally and left thousands without power for hours. At top, a woman tries to hitch a ride on Ouellette Avenue, while motorists dig out their cars at bottom left. Corporal Dave Bishop guides an army truck out providing aid, through the storm, at bottom right.

July 10, 1979: Two light airplanes crashed over Windsor's east side, killing all five passengers in both planes and scattering wreckage over a wide residential area around Riverside Drive East and Riverdale Avenue. At top, plane wreckage burns across from Solidarity Towers apartment building. At bottom left, an officer stands by debris on Dormar Street (which a resident extinguished with a garden hose), while a firefighter works on a wing that landed on a garage at bottom right. No civilians on the ground were hurt.

May 14, 1979: Clarence Langlois, Larry Langlois, and Dean Percy practise yo-yo acrobatics at Assumption Park. The yo-yo was the hottest new toy in the late 1970s.

BIBLIOGRAPHY

"40 Years of Conservation," Essex Region Conservation Authority, Erca.org.

"70 Years: 1936–2006," CAW Local 195, 2006.

"85 Years of Freeds: Still Standing, Never Standing Still," Freeds, Freeds.com.

"A Golden Age: Some Assembly Required: A History of Auto Work and Workers in Windsor," The Windsor Public Library, Projects.windsorpubliclibrary.com.

"A hero's funeral for Lamb," The Associated Press, *The Windsor Star*, Pg. 1, November 15, 1976.

"A History and Profile," Windsor Regional Hospital, wrh.on.ca.

"A Walk Through Our History 1941–2001," CAW Local Workers, 2001.

"About Us: Heritage," Assumption University, Assumptionu.ca.

African Canadian Roads to Freedom, Greater Essex County District School Board, Windsor, February 2011.

Anastakis, Dimitry, "From Independence to Integration: The Corporate Evolution of the Ford Motor Company of Canada, 1904–2004," *The Business History Review*, 2004.

Anglin, Gerald, "He Blew the Whistle on Windsor Vice," *Maclean's Magazine*, Pg. 7, May 1, 1950.

"Annexation Hearing Begins: Claim County Would Survive Changes: Admission of Briefs Launches Deliberation," *The Windsor Star*, Pg. 1, September 10, 1962.

Battagello, Dave, "Tayfour site to host Dieu artifacts," *The Windsor Star*, Pg. A1, September 28, 2013.

Battagello, Dave, "Violent death stalks family of Brooks' killer," *The Windsor Star*, Pg. A2, January 24, 2012.

Bell, Spike, *Memoirs of a Border City: Windsor and Essex County*, Spike Bell, Tecumseh, ON, 2009.

Bell, Spike, *Windsor: Photographic Art by Spike Bell*, Spike Bell, Woodstock, ON, 1998.

Billingsley, Lloyd, *Our Time After a While: Reflections of a Borderline Baby Boomer*, iUniverse Inc., Bloomington, Indiana, 2010.

"Black History," Tourism Windsor Essex Pelee Island, Visitwindsoressex.com.

Blackadar, Bruce, and Gord McNulty, Al Strachan and Gord Henderson, "Police suspect local brains, outside help: Bankers offer $25,000 for 'iron-clad' information," *The Windsor Star*, Pg. 1, December 20, 1971.

Briggs, Dave, "Hotel was pivotal to downtown trade," *The Windsor Star*, Coming of Age ed., Pg. D17, May 8, 1992.

Brode, Patrick, *The River and the Land: A History of Windsor to 1900*, Biblioasis, Windsor, ON, 2014.

Brode, Patrick, *Unholy City: Vice in Windsor Ontario, 1950*, Essex County Historical Society, Windsor, ON, 2012.

Brownell, Claire, "Infamous bank heist remembered: Great Canadian robbery turns 40," *The Windsor Star*, Pg. A1, December 17, 2011.

"Call Public Hearing, 10 Dead: Workmen Seek Last of Victims," *The Windsor Star*, Pg. 1, October 26, 1960.

Cameron, Elspeth, *Multiculturalism and Immigration in Canada: An Introductory Reader*, Canadian Scholars' Press, Toronto, ON, 2004.

"Canadian Multiculturalism: An Inclusive Citizenship," Citizenship and Immigration Canada, Government of Canada, cic.gc.ca.

Canty, Rebecca, Sarah M.J. Jarvis and Dean Corriveau, "Cultural Engines: Celebrating Windsor Public Library, Windsor Symphony Orchestra and Art Gallery of Windsor," Windsor Public Library Cultural Engines Imprint. Windsor, ON, 2013.

"Chinese Canadians in Windsor," chineseinwindsor.com.

Colling, Herb, *Turning Points: The Detroit Riot of 1967, A Canadian Perspective*, Natural Heritage, Toronto, ON, 2003.

"Council to Rush Action on West Side Flooding: 'Unsanitary' Conditions Stir Anger: Mayor Declares 'Proper Sewers' Answer to Troubles," *The Windsor Daily Star*, Pg. 3, August 3, 1955.

Crawford, Blair, "Fire destroys Ramada: Arson suspected as blaze levels controversial riverfront hotel," *The Windsor Star*, Pg. A1, April 9, 1999.

Cross, Brian, "1945 Ford Strike: The Players: union: Roy England," *The Windsor Star*, Pg. B2, September 2, 1995.

Cross, Brian, "Bigger, better and busier; When The Star spoke, the community listened," *The Windsor Star*, Pg. H2, December 1, 2012.

Cross, Brian, "Many in Big V 'family' to profit from sale: The drug store chain that started in Windsor has always concentrated on neighbourhood service," *The Windsor Star*, Pg. D5, October 24, 1995.

De Bono, Spiros, "Police tangle with pickets," *The Windsor Star*, Pg. A1, September 5, 1968.

"Detroit Slaying Tied to Windsor Bookie Circles: Gambler Tells Vengeance Tale," *The Windsor Daily Star*, Pg. 3, March 11, 1945.

Edwards, Chris, *A Forgotten City*, edited by Elaine Weeks, Walkerville Publishing, Windsor, ON, 2013.

Edwards, Chris, *Windsor Then: A Pictorial Essay of Windsor Ontario's Glorious Past*, Walkerville Publishing, Windsor, ON, 2011.

"Emancipation Day," Windsor Mosaic, Windsor-communities.com.

"Essex reels: Town is down, but not out," *The Windsor Star*, Pg. 1, February 14, 1980.

"Explosion Rips Variety Store: Hunt Victims as Rear Wall Falls in Rubble: Metropolitan Store Scene of Big Blast," *The Windsor Star*, Pg. 1, October 25, 1960.

"FCA Canada celebrates 90th anniversary," FCA Canada, June 2015.

Francis, Azra D., *A Datebook of the City of Windsor (1748–1992)*, Studio High Techniques, Toronto, ON, 1992.

Gavrilovich, Peter, and Bill McGraw, eds., *The Detroit Almanac: 300 years of life in the Motor City*, Detroit Free Press, Detroit, MI, 2000.

"General Motors' Parade of Progress," General Motors Corporation, Detroit, MI, June 22, 1955.

Gervais, Marty, *Ghost Road: and Other Forgotten Stories of Windsor*, Biblioasis, Windsor, ON, 2012.

Gervais, Marty, "A 'miracle' keeps them here," *The Windsor Star*, Pg. E6, March 21, 1987.

Gervais, Marty, *People of Faith: The Story of Hotel-Dieu Grace Hospital 1888 to 2013*, Black Moss Press, Windsor, ON, 2013.

Gervais, Marty, "Urban myths surround E.C. Row Expressway," *The Windsor Star*, Pg. A3, September 26, 2005.

Gindin, Sam, *The Canadian Auto Workers: The Birth and Transformation of a Union*, James Lorimer & Company, Toronto, ON, 1995.

"*GM: 90 Years of Windsor History*," CAW Union Local 1973, Windsor, ON, 2010.

Golden, Reuel, *Photojournalism 1855 to the Present: Editor's Choice*, Abbeville Press, 2009.

Haldane, Sue, "Assumption Parish was the beginning," *The Windsor Star*, Coming of Age ed., Pg. D4, May 8, 1992.

Harris, Richard, *Creeping Conformity: How Canada Became Suburban, 1900–1960*, University of Toronto Press, Toronto, ON, 2004.

Henderson, Gord, "Chrysler 0 answered: Windsor gets a billion reasons to be hopeful," *The Windsor Star*, Pg. 1, May 12, 1980.

Henry, Natasha L., *Emancipation Day: Celebrating Freedom in Canada*, Natural Heritage Books, Dundurn Group, Toronto, ON, 2010.

Hill, Sharon, "Final pin has fallen at Bowlero," *The Windsor Star*, Pg. A2, June 30, 2015.

Hill, Sharon, "Tried, true trailblazer; C.E. Jamieson celebrates 90 years of taking care of you," *The Windsor Star*, Pg. C3, May 10, 2012.

Hill, Sharon, "'You could hear somebody screaming:' 35 years since Essex inferno," *The Windsor Star*, Pg. 1, February 19, 2015.

"Historical Highlights," FCA Canada Inc. Archives.

"History of GM Canada," Detailed GM History, GM Canada, GM.ca.

"History of LaSalle Police Service," LaSalle Police Service, Police.lasalle.on.ca.

"History of Ojibway Prairie," Ojibway Nature Centre, Ojibway.ca.

"History of the Capitol," The Capitol Theatre, Capitoltheatrewindsor.ca.

"History of the Multicultural Council of Windsor and Essex County," Multicultural Council of Windsor and Essex County, Themcc.com.

"History of the WSO," Windsor Symphony Orchestra, Windsorsymphony.com.

"History of Windsor," Citywindsor.ca.

"History," Town of Tecumseh, Tecumseh.ca.

"History," Windsor Police Service, Police.windsor.on.ca.

"How It All Started," Windsor Light Music Theatre, Windsorlight.com.

"Immigrant Laws Liberalized: Family, Skills Stressed," *The Windsor Star*, Pg. 1, September 12, 1967.

"Insurance Only $84,000 on Historic Landmark: Grandstand Built Here in 1909: Old Structure Originally Owned by Michigan Group," *The Windsor Daily Star*, Pg. 3, July 13, 1957.

"Introduction: Windsor's Scottish Heritage," windsorscottish.com.

International Metropolis, internationalmetropolis.com.

Jarvis, Anne, "Old Vanity Theatre a symbol of downtown's long, sad slide," *The Windsor Star*, Pg. A1, March 24, 2016.

Jarvis, Anne, "Time for the civic square," *The Windsor Star*, Pg. A3, April 21, 2014.

Kappler, Brian and Gord Henderson, Mike McAteer and Lorne Gannon, "The U.S.-Canada rift… A border closed… and a continuing trade row," *The Windsor Star*, Pg. 1, November 4, 1971.

Karibo, Holly M., *Sin City North: Sex, Drugs and Citizenship in the Detroit-Windsor Borderland*, The University of North Carolina Press, 2015.

Kennedy, Terry, "Confined to Home 11 Years, Three Children Hospitalized," *The Windsor Star*, Pg. 1, July 29, 1960.

Kennedy, Terry, "Mother, 41, Sobs Out Tale of Hideaways," *The Windsor Star*, Pg. 1, July 30, 1960.

Kent, Fraser, "1,000,000 New Stand Cost: Faulty Jackson Park Hydrant Hampers Firemen: Truck's Wiring Believed Cause: Bandshell, Covered Seats Reduced to Ashes by Blaze," *The Windsor Daily Star*, Pg. 1, July 13, 1957.

Laycock, John, "The good ol' days: Former Elmwood Casino employees reminisce about the glory days," *The Windsor Star*, Pg. E1, February 7, 1998.

Laycock, John, "Vivid anecdotes punctuate Elmwood history," *The Windsor Star*, Pg. E1, February 7, 1998.

Lindblad, John, "Windsor Stages 'Biggest Show:' Tour Group Impressed," *The Windsor Daily Star*, Pg. 2, July 4, 1959.

"Local 1973 — 25th Anniversary," CAW Union Local 1973, Windsor, 1998.

"Lounge Lizard? Walkerville's Metropole Was the 'In' Spot," *The Windsor Star*, September 10, 2011.

Lyons, Linda, "Tracking U.S. Preferences Over the Decades," Gallup.com, 2005.

Maga, Timothy P., *Eyewitness History: The 1960s*, Facts on File, New York, 2003.

Mason, Philip Parker, *The Ambassador Bridge: A Monument to Progress*, Wayne State University Press, Detroit, 1987.

Mays, James, *Chrysler Canada's Glory Years,* Allpar.com, 2001.

Mays, James, *The Chrysler Canada Story*, Allpar.com, 2001.

McCall, Walter, "I was in Hell—by Walter McCall," *The Windsor Star*, Pg. 1, October 26, 1960.

McLachlan, Lloyd, "Area at mercy of raging blizzard," *The Windsor Star*, Pg. 1, January 26, 1976.

Meyer, Bob, and Bill Petrusiak, "Murder Charged in Shootout: Sniper fells three policemen," *The Windsor Star*, Pg. 1, August 25, 1969.

Morgan, Carl and Herb Colling, *Pioneering the Auto Age*, TraveLife Publishing Enterprises, Tecumseh, ON, 1993.

Morgan, Carl, *Birth of a City: Commemorating Windsor's Centennial, 1992*, TraveLife, Tecumseh, ON, 1991.

Mumford, Lewis, "The Neighborhood and the Neighborhood Unit," *Town Planning Review 24*, Liverpool University Press, 1954.

Nash, C. Knowlton, "Canadian Firm Gets $25 Million Order from U.S.," *The Windsor Star*, Pg. 1, November 13, 1959.

Newman, David, *Postcards from Essex County*, Biblioasis, Windsor, ON, 2012.

North Star Cultural Community Centre, *End of the Journey: A Brief History of Windsor's African Canadian Community*, North Star Cultural Community Centre, Windsor, ON, 2007.

"Our History," Giovanni Caboto Club, Cabotoclub.com.

"Our History," University of Windsor, Uwindsor.ca.

"Our History: Celebrating Over Fifty Years of Fighting for Progress for Our Members and Their Families," Uni444.ca.

Pearson, Craig and Daniel Wells, *From the Vault: A Photo History of Windsor*, Biblioasis, Windsor, ON, 2014.

Pearson, Craig, "'Greatest freedom show on earth'; Windsor's Emancipation Day has attracted thousands since 1932," *The Windsor Star*, Pg. B1, July 30, 2011.

Pearson, Craig, "'No bull' Whelan stood up for the little guy, ex-PM says," *The Windsor Star*, Pg. A5, February 21, 2013.

Pearson, Craig, "A sign of the times? Century-old United Church becomes mosque as population dwindles," *The Windsor Star,* Pg. A1, August 21, 2015.

Pearson, Craig, "Detroit Riot scars linger; Forty years after conflict, Motor City moves on," *The Windsor Star*, Pg. A1, July 21, 2007.

Pearson, Craig, "Diocese to put historic St. George's Church up for sale: officials asking $250,000 for Walkerville property, buildings," *The Windsor Star*, Pg. A4, November 25, 2016.

Pearson, Craig, "Forgotten no longer: Memorial to honour eight school bus crash victims," *The Windsor Star*, Pg. A1, November 1, 2014.

Pearson, Craig, "Pearson to Person: Can a friendly block retain its charm?" *The Windsor Star*, Pg. E4, April 16, 1998.

Pearson, Craig, "The last pastrami: Bittersweet day at deli; Tears, laughter as Elias marks end of tasty 45-year run," *The Windsor Star*, Pg. A3, July 27, 2013.

Perry, Walter, *Progress*, 1935.

Plaut, Jonathan, *The Jews of Windsor 1790–1990: A Historical Chronicle*, Dundurn Press, Toronto, ON, 2007.

"Police Seek Assef House 'Secret Room:' Come Away Empty Handed But Rumours of Cache Persist," *The Windsor Daily Star*, Pg. 3, March 11, 1950.

Power, Michael, *Assumption College: Years of Uncertainty 1855–1870*, Assumption University, Windsor, ON, 1987.

Rennie, Gary, "Waste on top of waste," *The Windsor Star*, Pg. E1, April 20, 1991.

"Rising Dragon: Chinese Canadians in Windsor," Chineseinwindsor.com.

Sacheli, Sarah, "Colourful publisher dies at 93: Mike Farrell slew the sacred cows," *The Windsor Star*, Pg. A2, April 11, 2006.

Schmidt, Doug, "GM plant sold, trash recycling planned; Jones group paying $12.5M, says sales rep," *The Windsor Star*, Pg. A1, August 4, 2012.

Shaw, Ted, "U of W buys landmark eatery; TBQ to close doors in Sept," *The Windsor Star*, Pg. SR6, May 9, 2014.

Shields, Bill, "Queen, Philip Taking it Easy: Cruise on Georgian Bay Follows Sarnia Stop," *The Windsor Daily Star*, Pg. 1, July 4, 1959.

Shiels, Bob, "50,000 See Big Centennial-Dominion Day Parade: 3,500 Participate in Giant Spectacle," *The Windsor Daily Star*, Pg. A3, July 2, 1954.

Spalding, Derek, "Colourful Star columnists carry tremendous responsibility," *The Windsor Star*, Pg. SR6, June 4, 2015.

"Star celebrates 75th anniversary," *The Windsor Star*, Pg. A1, February 6, 1993.

Statistics Canada, statscan.gc.ca.

Stewart, Robert Earl, "Portrait of a Scandal," *Walkerville Times Magazine*, Walkervilletimes.com.

Sutton, Bob, "8 Die, Charge Driver," *The Windsor Star*, Pg. 1, December 22, 1966.

Techko, Tony, and Carl Morgan, *The Olympians Among Us: Celebrating a Century of Excellence*, TraveLife Publishing, Tecumseh, ON, 1995.

The Auto Pact: Investment, Labour, and the WTO, edited by Maureen Irish, Kluwer Law International, The Netherlands, 2004.

The Greatest Freedom Show on Earth, DVD, Directed by R.J. Huggins, Ottawa, ON, Orphan Boy Films, 2015.

Thompson, Chris, "Fast Eddy's auction a memorable bonanza," *The Windsor Star*, Pg. A5, February 5, 2015.

Thomson, Carolyn, and Beatrice Fantoni, "Iconic United Grill up for sale; Plans for building not yet decided," *The Windsor Star*, Pg. SR2, August 7, 2015.

"Two planes collide, five dead: Miracle saves all on ground," *The Windsor Star*, Pg. 1, July 10, 1979.

"Unions replacing church is claim," the Canadian Press, the *Windsor Daily Star*, March 11, 1949.

Vallee, Brian, "Three Star unions sign new contract," *The Windsor Star*, Pg. 1, December 18, 1970.

Van Wageningen, Ellen, "Ottawa Street merchants balk at Sunday shopping," *The Windsor Star*, Pg. A3, October 9, 1990.

Vasey, Paul, Bill Hickey and Dick Spicer, "Tears and a lost glow," *The Windsor Star*, Pg. 1, December 22, 1966.

Vasey, Paul, *The River*, Biblioasis, Windsor, ON, 2013.

Veres, Louis Joseph, "History of the United Automobile Workers in Windsor 1936–1955," Master of Arts Thesis, University of Western Ontario, 1956.

"Volcano Restaurant and Pizzeria," Italian Canadian Community, Windsor Mosaic, Windsor-communities.com.

Weeks, Elaine, "Well Hung! A Brief History of the Art Gallery of Windsor," *The Walkerville Times*, Walkervilletimes.com.

Wells, Don, "The Impact of the Postwar Compromise on Canadian Unionism: The Formation of an Auto Worker Local in the 1950s," Litjournal.ca.

"What Started As a Dream Turned into the Largest Independent Home Furnishings Store in Canada," About Us, Tepperman's, Teppermans.com.

"Where Did Our Rights Come From? The Rand Formula and the struggle for union security," Unifor, Unifor.org.

White, Michael Gladstone, *Reflections of Windsor*, J-K Printing, Windsor, ON, 1989.

White, Michael Gladstone, *Windsor: A Moment in Time*, Windsor Jaycees, Windsor, ON, 1988.

Wilhelm, Trevor, "Survivors still haunted by deadly tornado 40 years later; April 3, 1974 curling club tragedy," *Windsor Star*, Pg. A1, April 3, 2014.

Wilhelm, Trevor, "Time running out on cold case: Four decades later, a broken tooth could help solve six-year-old girl's murder," *The Windsor Star*, Pg. A1, April 18, 2015.

Willick, Frances, "'Sad' auction draws ex-workers; Transmission plant contents on block," *The Windsor Star*, Pg. A3, September 23, 2010.

"Windsor Stages 'Mary Day' Parade," the Canadian Press, *The Quebec Chronicle-Telegraph*, Pg. 12, May 2, 1958.

"Windsor stands 10 deep for Centennial: 32 bands in 3-hour parade," *The Windsor Star*, Pg. 3, July 3, 1967.

Interviews:

Bishop, Bill. Interviewed by Craig Pearson. Windsor, ON, June 2016.

Brown, John Lloyd. Interviewed by Craig Pearson. Windsor, ON, August 2016.

Bruce, Jim. Interviewed by Craig Pearson. Windsor, ON, April 2016.

Calhoun, John. Interviewed by Craig Pearson. Windsor, ON, July 2016.

Davison, Carl. Interviewed by Craig Pearson. Windsor, ON, June 2016.

Foot, Andrew. Interviewed by Craig Pearson. Windsor, ON, May 2016.

Harding-Davis, Elise. Interviewed by Craig Pearson. Windsor, ON, May 2016.

Laycock, John. Interviewed by Craig Pearson. Windsor, ON, July 2016.

Morris, Jack. Interviewed by Craig Pearson. Windsor, ON, June 2016.

Musyj, David. Interviewed by Craig Pearson. Windsor, ON, April 2016.

Wagenberg, Ron. Interviewed by Craig Pearson. Windsor, ON, August 2016.

INDEX

ACKNOWLEDGEMENTS

Sharon Hanna:

I have to begin by thanking Dan Wells, publisher at Biblioasis and co-author of the first volume of *From the Vault*, for allowing me to take part in this extraordinary project that he envisioned and created. His guidance and belief in the importance of local history are the unseen hands behind this volume. My thanks, of course, also belong with Craig Pearson for his professionalism, journalistic instinct, and enthusiasm throughout this entire process. Thank you for showing me the ropes.

To my coworkers at Biblioasis: Chris Andrechek, Ellie Hastings, Grant Munroe, Meghan Desjardins, and Natalie Hamilton—you each played a part in making this book, and I couldn't ask for a more dedicated and generous group of people to work with. Chris Andrechek, our production manager, deserves special mention for the many, many hours he spent typesetting and laying out this book. It is an incredibly daunting task to transform a stack of photographs and captions into a book like *From the Vault*, but Chris has found just the right balance between story-telling and visual aesthetics. And he has done so with tremendous patience for the constant tweaking and photo-swapping of editors like me, for which I am very grateful.

So many people have helped shape this book, whether by lending their expertise or simply sharing a photograph or a memory. Many thanks to archivist Michael Fish at the Windsor Public Library and Heather Colautti of Museum Windsor for helping me track down elusive *Star* photographs and fill in other gaps. I must also thank Ron Foster at Windsor Regional Hospital and Gord Gray at Unifor 444 for graciously allowing me to access their organizations' archives. To Marion MacLeod, for the many hours spent with me in the archive—and the insight into Windsor's music scene. I also had the pleasure of talking with many former *Star* staffers, including Bob Sullivan, Dick Spicer, John Laycock, Karen Hall, Michael Frezell, Paul Vasey, Tom McMahon, and Walt McCall. The memories of their career days have made this a richer book, by far. I've saved one *Star* member for last, photographer and photo-editor Bill Bishop. Bill has contributed so much to this book, beyond the fact that its pages are filled with his photographs. Thanks to his razor-sharp memory, many details have not been missed. It has been an honour to get to know him.

Lastly, to my family and friends. I am grateful for your love and support—and offer a half-hearted apology for my endless 'did-you-know' anecdotes or unsolicited tours of downtown, though I can't promise that they'll stop. Windsor has always been a part of me, but now I feel that I understand it better. And I'm proud to be from here.

Craig Pearson:

You might think I would know how hard it is to write a book like *From the Vault, Volume II*, since I also wrote the first one. But I must have some sort of literary amnesia. I forgot what a gargantuan task it is to research and tell the rich story of Windsor and Essex County. Certainly, producing a book this big and detailed is a team effort. First off, I'd like to thank the hard-working, always-positive Sharon Hanna, for compiling such fabulous pictures, writing informative cutlines, and politely pushing me to provide my best—and a little bit more. I'd also like to thank Biblioasis publisher Dan Wells, who co-wrote the first volume with me and who conceived the whole idea: a history of the area based on *Windsor Star* photos. He's an idea man and a stickler for quality work and it shows. I'd like to also thank the Biblioasis team for their professionalism. As well, I'd like to thank *Windsor Star* Editor-in-Chief Marty Beneteau for backing the project from the beginning and for once again opening up the paper's tremendous archives for the book and the community. Thanks, as well, to the talented *Star* journalists who came before me. And thanks to the following people who provided their invaluable insight for the book: Bill Bishop, John Laycock, Owen Jones, Elise Harding-Davis, Andrew Foot, David Musyj, Lloyd Brown-John, Ron Wagenberg, Jack Morris, and John Calhoun. Love to my mother Ann for her unyielding encouragement. Of course, love to my wife Bev and son Spencer for their ongoing support and for understanding that I was on a mission. Finally, thank you once more, Windsor, for your storied history. You're an inspiration.